THE BATAAN DEATH MARCH

THE BATAAN DEATH MARCH

A SOLDIER'S PERSONAL STORY OF SURVIVAL AND CAPTIVITY UNDER THE JAPANESE

LIEUTENANT COLONEL PATRICK RAFFERTY
WITH CHAD GODFREY

FRONTLINE
BOOKS

Praise for *The Bataan Death March:*

'Lieutenant Colonel Rafferty's story reminds us again how the Greatest Generation earned its reputation with millions of "average" Americans displaying uncommon courage and sacrifice in unimaginable circumstances. These Americans answered the call in the Nation's hour of greatest need, and in doing so, literally saved the world.'
General David D. Thompson, US Air Force and US Space Force (Ret.)

'*The Bataan Death March* is a gripping first-person account of brutal imprisonment under the Empire of Japan—a must read and a true gift from Patrick Rafferty and his grandson, Chad Godfrey. It is a sad, powerful, and timely reminder of the consequences of defeat and subjugation by a misled and delusional race of people who are led to believe they are naturally superior to other human beings. We should never again become so weak in military strength and resolve as to invite these horrors on current and future generations of Americans.'
General Kevin P. Chilton, US Air Force and NASA Astronaut (Ret.)

'The horrors experienced by the men on that most infamous of journeys, the Bataan Death March, and their subsequent treatment in the camps, are difficult for us to comprehend today. Possibly equally as astounding, is how so many of the POWs found the inner resilience to carry on, to somehow survive in circumstances that would break the toughest of men. Lieutenant Colonel Rafferty, with Chad Godfrey, gives us a unique insight into this world of pain, humiliation, death and disease – and, most importantly, on each man's determination to fight on against what seemed to be an endless, unremitting, ordeal.'
John Grehan, author of Corregidor: Siege and Liberation, 1941–1945

First published in Great Britain in 2024
by Frontline Books
An imprint of
Pen & Sword Books Ltd
Yorkshire - Philadelphia

ISBN 978 1 03611 343 8

A CIP catalogue record for this book is available from the British Library

Typeset by Lapiz Digital
Printed and bound in the UK by CPI Group (UK) Ltd, Croydon, CR0 4YY.

Printed on paper from a sustainable source by
CPI Group (UK) Ltd, Croydon, CR0 4YY

Pen & Sword Books Limited incorporates the imprints of Archaeology, Atlas, Aviation, Battleground, Digital, Discovery, Family History, Fiction, History, Local, Local History, Maritime, Military, Military Classics, Politics, Select, Transport, True Crime, Air World, Claymore Press, Frontline Publishing, Leo Cooper, Remember When, Seaforth Publishing, The Praetorian Press, Wharncliffe Books, Wharncliffe Local History, Wharncliffe Transport, Wharncliffe True Crime and White Owl.

For a complete list of Pen & Sword titles please contact
PEN & SWORD BOOKS LTD
47 Church Street, Barnsley, South Yorkshire, S70 2AS, England
E-mail: enquiries@pen-and-sword.co.uk
Website: www.pen-and-sword.co.uk
or
PEN & SWORD BOOKS
1950 Lawrence Rd, Havertown, PA 19083, USA
E-mail: uspen-and-sword@casematepublishers.com

CONTENTS

This book is dedicated to the soldiers who did not survive The Bataan Death March or the Japanese prison camps of WWII, particularly the young men who were murdered in undignified and cruel ways far away from home and loved ones. Their sacrifice lit a path to survival for many others.

This book is also dedicated to the wife and children of Lieutenant Colonel Patrick Rafferty: Dorothy, Bud, Gina, Helen, Patsy, Joan, and Brian. The world has benefitted from your world-class humor and kindness.

Lastly, I dedicate this book to Dapper himself, who will always be a giant to a grandson looking up to a hero.

PRAYER FOR A PRISONER

By Unknown

O God, who didst deliver from his chains
The blessed apostle Peter and restore him to liberty
Loose the bounds of the servant now in captivity
And through the merits of that same apostle grant to him too
Mother of God, our Mother, remember thy sons in military service
Protect them against all dangers of body, mind, and soul
Grant them a deep love for thee and an enduring loyalty to His son, Christ our Lord

AUTHOR'S NOTE

Sometime around late 2002, I was living in Los Angeles, California. "Living" meant I was waiting tables, waiting to be discovered, that kind of thing that aspiring writers and actors do as time passes by quickly. I remember sitting down to a couple beers on my couch one night, finally having a moment to listen to the "prison tapes" my cousin, Mike Greene, had sent me from his new home in his new country, Ireland, where he still resides. These were, of course, the audio tapes that my aunt Regina (Mike's mother) had saved from the late 1970s after essentially forcing my grandfather, Patrick Rafferty (who my sister, Jacey, and I called Dapper), to finally tell his story of imprisonment during World War II in the Pacific. Knowing I was dabbling in different writing projects at the time and trying to make it a career somehow, Mike sent me the tapes with a note "if you're looking for a good story, this will knock your socks off." I had always held our Dapper in the highest regard, in a way that a grandson might immortalize a grandfather who died when the grandson was only 4 years old. He was a hero to me. I used to see the old pictures of him standing with planes that he flew, or I would hear his surviving family tell stories about "The Colonel" as some called him. Almost every story I was fortunate to hear would usually mention his handsome looks, his sense of humor, or his toughness. As with most heroes, he was out of reach to me but I always kept him close to my heart as a kid, even after he had passed. After listening to these tapes that night and for the next 24 hours straight, I felt a cauldron of emotions take over me that would resurface in coming years on occasion when I thought of Dapper. The emotions would also come whenever I'd see footage on television, or read a news story, about prisoners of war being treated unfairly, or being executed by their captors. I remember being stunned by the execution of American journalist James Foley by terrorists who had abducted him in Syria—James being the same age as me with a similar background, just a young kid with an adventuresome spirit looking to do his work as a journalist. Upon the birth of my sons, Grant and Charlie, I decided to turn these feelings and emotions into action, to do my level best to help tell the story of their great-grandfather in a way that paid proper homage to his life and legacy. In those moments of contemplation, I had begun to share with family that I would try to turn my grandfather's story into a book. In my estimation that holds to this today, I wondered if it could possibly be the last first-hand account we would hear from a prisoner of war and Death March survivor from World War II, and with that came a responsibility and opportunity that the storyteller in me could not ignore. I have always had a deep sense of love for this country and I've always had appreciation for what it could be, and has been many, many times, in its best form and in its many great moments. Like so many others, having a grandfather who paid a steep price engrained an especially deep pride in me about the red, white, and blue. Many Americans of all backgrounds still hail from families that have flags waving above their front doors for good reason, even when it is not the 4th of July, and mine is one of those families. So it is with great respect and admiration for my grandfather and the millions of other American men and women who have died, or have been wounded as a result of their service to our country, that I am now fulfilling a personal promise to bring those old tapes to life. Rest in Peace, Dapper.

Chad Godfrey
Norwell, Massachusetts
2024

FOREWORD

From the moving voice recordings left behind by Patrick "Dapper" Rafferty, an airman from my hometown of Boston, one comes to understand the remarkable experiences of a young pilot sent abroad to World War II's Pacific Theater. It is a remarkable story that keeps alive the incredible life and death experiences of the Greatest Generation. Moreover, it is a distinct possibility that this will be one of the final first-hand accounts of World War II, one of few ever from an American prisoner.

The story of Patrick Rafferty and his mates takes us back to a different time in our history as it is told against the backdrop of post-Depression America, a much simpler America that looked inward. It was an America convinced that the oceans around us would keep us out of foreign wars as we focused on healing and building at home. Hitler and Japan were "over there," perhaps a similar misjudgment that America had made with the First World War, the type of miscalculation for which many young men like Patrick Rafferty and their loving families would soon pay. It was at this time and in this context, before anyone could conceive of an attack upon our nation, that Dapper was recruited into the Army Air Corps as a young officer and learned to fly. What was to come for him, of course, was entirely unexpected.

Within months of completing his pilot training, Rafferty deployed to the Philippines, arriving months before the attack on Pearl Harbor. Still, the war raging in Europe and in parts of Asia seemed plenty far enough away and, therefore, unlikely to reach the United States. In simple language, we were wrong.

December 7th put an end to our flawed thinking before the smoke had even cleared in Hawaii. A horrific period in the lives of millions of Americans had begun in the instant the ships were hit at Pearl Harbor. The most victimized, we must remember, would be young warriors like Dapper who did not, would not, think twice about offering their service to their country. Braveness defined.

Still scrambling to process what had just happened at Pearl Harbor, the U.S. forces and our Filipino friends, all under the command of General MacArthur, were left overmatched in the Philippines when they were swiftly invaded and overcome by the Japanese. Defenses quickly collapsed and the invaders captured the American defenders of Bataan, and when they did, they deliberately subjected them to the most barbaric and inhumane treatment imaginable. This, of course, started perhaps one of the worst war crimes in modern history, the infamous Bataan Death March, a devilish but accurate name for what ensued.

The 65-mile forced march in unbearable conditions, with men already depleted from weeks of fighting while undernourished, was just the beginning. Our brave Allied soldiers were soon moved to jungle camps where they would remain for most of the war—if they stayed alive somehow—starving and battling tropical diseases as they assumed new lives in these hard labor prisons. Later, most were shipped to Korea to serve as slaves in the Japanese economy, until liberated by U.S. forces at the end of World War II. In between the Death March and liberation were years of physical and mental torture that we should all remember and seek to understand. Men like Patrick Rafferty deserve as much.

After enduring this ruthless and inhumane treatment for nearly four years, Rafferty still held onto hope for a return home to America and, God willing, to start a family and career. Regardless of where fate might take him, he would never be allowed to forget his time as a prisoner, the inescapable distress of having lived that experience. For this and many other reasons, we can all hope he was intensely proud of his service and what he and his fellow prisoners endured for their country.

Patrick "Dapper" Rafferty was the real deal, a young warrior in our Greatest Generation. *The Bataan Death March* takes its place amongst our best military stories. This story, passed from Rafferty to his grandson, Chad Godfrey, is the tale of our Battling Bastards of Bataan, the never-quit brothers in arms we will forever hold in the highest regard.

Semper Fidelis,
General John F. Kelly, US Marine Corps (Ret.)

INTRODUCTION

What follows is an account, more or less chronological and entirely factual as I remember it, from my time before, during, and immediately after being a POW in the Pacific Theatre of World War II.

I am recounting this period of my life some thirty-four years after the fact in 1979 and, memory being what it is (particularly memories of such an experience, during which I occasionally was not what most people would think of as "of sound mind," for reasons that will be obvious), I cannot say that every last recollection is 100% accurate. But I can say that I have made every effort to be forthright, honest, and error-free in my account, and where I know that my memory has failed me to any degree, I indicate as much.

One thing I will not do is speculate as to why I survived when many thousands of others died, and I refuse to engage is such speculations for the simple reason that there is no answer. Death came at many times and in many forms, but one thing about it that never changed was its utter randomness. I could easily have been shot, succumbed to hunger or thirst, drowned, been eaten by sharks, or died from malaria or other diseases, as so very many others did alongside me, at times within arm's reach. I can say that my *desire* to live never wavered, and perhaps that, along with a massive amount of good luck and spiritual belief, was enough for me to still be here when others are not. It's as good an explanation as any.

Now, in order to really understand a war story, you have to first have a basic understanding of war: how it's planned, and how it's fought. In this case, my own war story is best understood, at least at times, against the historical backdrop of what was happening in the larger conflict, which is to say from just before the Japanese attack on Pearl Harbor, in late 1941, until the Japanese surrender in August 1945, when I was freed from captivity after more than three years as a POW. But in order to understand that backdrop, there are certain terms and concepts with which you should be at least glancingly familiar. Otherwise the whole thing is likely to seem like a big unruly mess without proper context.

Having said that, it's my feeling that most military history is far too jargony, written as to be almost obscure to the layman, so wherever possible I will avoid military speak and opt for plain English.

At its simplest, there are two concepts that encompass everything that happens in a war: strategy and tactics. Strategy is the planning, and tactics is the execution. Strategy is long-term and can be almost philosophical, whereas tactics are shorter-term, day to day, week to week, often if not always dictated by the specific situation and circumstance.

The American strategy in the Pacific was, most broadly, that of island-hopping. By the time we entered the war, the Japanese had established a series of island fortresses from the Alaskan Territory to the Solomons, and hoped we would make the mistake of trying to fight for every last one of them. That was the Japanese strategy—to ensnare America into a fight so long and costly that we would eventually agree to a peace favorable to Japan, out of weariness for war. But American commanders had no intention of playing into that strategy. Instead, they chose key territories held by Japan and concentrated on those, leaving other, heavily-guarded and fortified islands to simply wither in the rear as the bulk of American power hopped ever closer to the main island of Japan. In this way, we avoided having to confront a good portion of the forces allayed against us, effectively neutralizing those forces, while on the other hand using almost all our *own* forces at the point of attack each time.

Japan made two big mistakes in their strategy. The first was failing to anticipate the galvanizing effect that Pearl Harbor would have on the American public. Japan imagined it would make us wilt; instead, it made us furious, single-minded in our determination to avenge such a cowardly act. The other Japanese mistake was to overestimate their own warmaking capacity while simultaneously underestimating ours. The single greatest factor in the outcome of all of World War II was the United States' vast resources and industrial output. Over time, we just overwhelmed both the Japanese and the Germans with the amount of materiel we were able to put on the battlefield, in the air, and on the water.

Speaking of the Germans, it might be helpful in understanding the principles of strategy and tactics to illustrate them further using the German example. Hitler's strategy was based entirely on speed. At the outset of the war, many military minds hadn't updated their strategic thinking from the dreadful, man-consuming trench warfare of World War I. Consider the French, for example, with their Maginot Line, a massive network of bunkers, gun emplacements, and other fortifications. It was formidable, but it was also fixed—almost completely useless against the German strategy of the *blitzkrieg*, which simply moved around and past the fortifications. Hitler followed Napoleon's principles of strategy—to commit massive amounts of men and equipment to a fight and move so quickly that the enemy was overwhelmed. And that's exactly what happened. It took only six weeks for German mechanized and armor divisions, along with the Luftwaffe, to subdue Belgium, the Netherlands, Luxembourg, and France.

With that, the only European country still fighting against Germany was Great Britain. Hitler's strategy here ended up proving flawed. He didn't have the air power to attempt a full-scale invasion of England, so he resorted to bombing campaigns to demoralize and terrorize the British public. But he also got impatient, and in his impatience, he made a huge mistake—turning around and attacking Russia. Had he paid attention to Napoleon's example in this instance, he would have known to invade Russia is to court ruin. As it was for Napoleon, so it would be for Hitler. He left himself open in the west, and Great Britain, along with American air power, took advantage, bombing strategic targets all over Europe and, eventually of course, landing at Normandy for the big counteroffensive. In the meantime, Germany got bogged down in Russia, weakened by the frightful winters, and it wasn't too long before the U.S. and British closed in from the west, the Russians from the east—and Hitler, we're told, cowered and committed suicide in a Berlin bunker. There are other, mostly conspiratorial theories about an escape for Hitler under the cover of darkness with powerful allies ushering him to a safer location, perhaps South America, but I do not buy into those theories. Regardless, the Germans were unequivocally beaten by superior strategic minds, and we thank our Gods for that.

Now let's turn our attention to tactics for a moment. Consider the Korean War—in which one of the greatest tactical moves ever made by any army anywhere took place. This was Douglas MacArthur, who you may recall from your history books. The war wasn't going well for UN forces, led by the Americans. They'd been pushed all the way down to Pusan, just about shoved right into the sea, in fact. But MacArthur had two things to his advantage: uncommon boldness, and knowledge of a little-known fact regarding the tides in Inchon, on the west coast of Korea. Twice a year an extraordinary tide occurs, fifteen to twenty feet higher than usual. The North Koreans never worried about a landing at Inchon because normally the water wasn't deep enough for it to be done. But MacArthur waited for that extraordinary tide, and when it came he floated two divisions of infantry right smack into the North

Korean supply lines. The North Koreans were so completely taken by surprise that they never recovered—the forces fighting in Pusan turned and ran for home, and the pursuing UN forces crushed them against the landing force at Inchon, like a hammer against an anvil. By this single, daring, brilliant stroke, MacArthur effectively ended the war, though it would continue for some time after the Chinese became involved and, after clashing with Truman, MacArthur was ordered home and retired after a fifty-year career.

So that's your primer on tactics. Now let's turn to defining a handful of terms that fall under the category of Principles of War. The two big items in this category are Offense and Defense, but it also includes Isolation of the Battlefield, Air Superiority, Conservation of Forces and Surprise.

Think for a moment about any kind of contest—sports probably is the easiest analogy. Imagine a hockey game in which one team spends the entire time crowded around their goal, doing everything to keep from being scored on but never going up the ice to attempt to score themselves. That's defense, of course, and to play nothing *but* defense would obviously not work well in a hockey game. A team has to score goals—be offensive—in order to secure a victory in the game. Same with war, generally speaking. But there was a time, in warfare, when just playing defense was not only successful at winning conflicts, but was actually the dominant principle of war.

Picture a city-state in mid-Europe in the 8th, 9th, 10th century where vandals coming off the steppes of Russia decided to loot some town, the inhabitants pulled in behind the walls of the town, mounted their spearmen with bows and arrows on top of parapets and the opponent comes rushing across the plains with massive numbers of horsemen, pounding at the gate and throwing rocks over the walls. The aggressor, the force on the offensive, merely spend themselves against this fortified town and eventually find out that they cannot successfully assault and then withdraw. So in that sense, the defense won a victory.

But in modern warfare, you can't just pull up the drawbridge and wait for your enemy to tire himself out (refer, once more, to the fate of the Maginot Line). You have to incorporate both defense and offense into your strategy and tactics. In 1942, the Japanese were on the offensive all across the Pacific—Taiwan, the Philippines, Singapore, New Guinea, New Britain, Guadalcanal, etc. The Japanese intelligence services saw where the Allies were weak, and attacked those weaknesses with great success. Offense and defense, of course, are hand-in-glove. A general has to take stock of his resources, figure in what he knows about his enemy's resources and positions, and make a decision about whether to attack or defend, and when, and where, and for what reason. Any mistake in these hugely complex decisions can lead, eventually, to defeat.

Once a general has made a decision to attack, the next principle of war that comes into play is Isolation of the Battlefield. He must be very sure as to the strength of the enemy's ground forces, naval power, if any, and—above all in modern combat, as demonstrated time and again in World War II—air capability. He has to look at both of his flanks so that once he commits troops to the attack, he's not going to be attacked on the flank by the enemy who can take reserves out of some area and cut in behind him. Preventing a successful flanking maneuver is maybe more important than anything else. An army is no better than its supply line—Hitler, and Napoleon before him, both learned that the hard way in Russia. To get behind the enemy's frontline forces and cut off their ammunition and food and rescue squads and communications renders even the most powerful and massive army useless. The frontline troops can't stay up there very long unless the supplies are constantly coming through. I don't know of any soldier who can fight much longer than 24 or 48 hours on an empty belly. Hence, having ensured that he cannot be outflanked, and having estimated the strength of the enemy and decided that he has a force superior to that of the enemy for that particular engagement, our general launches his attack.

Which brings us to Air Superiority. I mentioned earlier that Hitler wasn't able to launch an invasion of Great Britain because he couldn't subdue the Royal Air Force, and without air superiority, any attempt at invasion was doomed before it began. This is an absolute certainty, by the way—any knowledgeable observer, if the Germans had attempted to invade England under the conditions following the surrender of France, would have thought them mad. This was one of the biggest ways in which warfare changed in the short period between World War I and World War II. Airplanes existed in WWI, of course, but they were largely ineffectual from a tactical standpoint. By 1940, however, as evidenced by both the attack on Pearl Harbor (which, remember, was executed entirely with air power) and the German *blitzkrieg*, which relied on air superiority, the airplane had not only come into its own, but also made obsolete some previously cornerstone technologies and tactics—the battleship, for example. It's helpful, maybe, to think of an airplane as a kind of long-range artillery. Whereas the biggest guns can fire effectively at a range of maybe fifteen miles, planes can carry an equivalent amount of explosives for hundreds or even thousands of miles. The whole game had changed because of air power, and any commander who ignored or neglected it did so at his and his men's peril.

Next is Conservation of Forces. This is an older principle of war, as it's always been important to conserve men and materiel no matter the time or place where you're fighting. In fact, the phrase "pyrrhic victory" is a reference to a failure to conserve forces that dates back to 279 BC. King Pyrrhus, having just defeated the Romans in the Battle of Asculum, was congratulated on the victory, and he replied, "One more victory like that and we shall lose the war." What he meant, of course, was the victory had cost so much of his own forces that he wouldn't be able to continue to fight, and sure enough he was not. But everyone needs refresher courses, and the world's military minds got a refresher in the importance of Conservation of Forces during WWI. Again, the Germans made the mistake of thinking they could just throw unit after unit into the fight, no real strategy or tactics, just trying to win through a huge expenditure of manpower. It didn't work, and it cost many, many lives in a futile effort. So a general must carefully consider how many men he can commit to an engagement, how many he must keep in reserve to prevent things like flanking or envelopment maneuvers by the enemy, and how to conserve his troops, that is, minimize losses in the engagement he's planning. He also has to conserve things like ammunition, food, fuel, medicine and medical capability. He has to conserve *everything*, be as efficient as possible with every resource, and when he judges that he has a gathering of men and materiel superior to the enemy, he can engage upon the offense and hope for a victory.

The last principle of war is Surprise. You'll recall my telling you about MacArthur landing at Inchon two hundred fifty miles behind the North Korean forces, who were attacking the UN forces at Pusan perimeter. Well, the last thing in the world that the North Koreans expected was for someone to come in on their flank at Inchon. It should have been not just unlikely but impossible, except for that twice-a-year tide. What a surprise. It so shocked the North Koreans that they knew they had to get out of Pusan as fast as possible. That was the end of the North Korean army, right then and there. Also I referred previously to Pearl Harbor, I mentioned it because I wanted to bring out the idea of the blunder it turned out to be on the part of the Japanese. But at first it looked like an absolute victory, crippling to the American Pacific fleet, and this was due in part to the fact that the attack was a complete surprise. These days there are some who would tell you that Roosevelt and his top commanders knew the attack was coming, but I don't think that's the case. Surely Pearl Harbor was an outpost, several thousand miles off the west coast of the United States, but an attack like that?

Never. Hence, the surprise. And surprise, although it is considered as an independent principle to watch, really dovetails with tactics, that is, surprise tells you to strike the enemy where he least expects you. To do it in a startling way, such that the opponent is overwhelmed by your move.

So there they are—the principles of war, and so as I may use those terms in the text to come—offense, defense, isolation of the battlefield, conservation of forces, air superiority, surprise—you'll have a general idea of what I'm talking about. Any general who willfully, or out of ignorance, violates any principle of war is courting disaster, and any general that violates *two* principles of war may be sure he's heading for defeat.

Finally, some really dry but necessary terminology.

In his memoirs, Winston Churchill tells of having suggested to Stalin that the Pope be invited to one of their wartime conferences. Stalin—what a cynical character he was—said in response to Churchill's suggestion, "How many divisions does the Pope have?" Aside from being a funny anecdote, and illustrative of Stalin's cynicism (he didn't care a whit about moral strength, only raw material power), it raises the question of how armies are organized and why. I'll attempt to give a brief primer on both.

A squad is the smallest group of soldiers, 12-14 men led by a sergeant, a three-stripe non-commissioned officer. Several squads together make up a platoon, 40-60 men, commanded by a second lieutenant, which is the lowest commissioned officer rank. Three or four platoons make up a company, commanded by a captain. Five or six companies, 800 to 1,000 men, form a battalion, which is led by a lieutenant colonel. Two to three battalions, 2,000 to 3,000 men, make up a regiment, commanded by a colonel. Five or six regiments comprise a division, usually commanded by a major general. Different kinds of divisions vary somewhat in size; for example, an airborne division, which by definition is lighter and more mobile than many other types of units, may be less than 14,000 men. Whereas a heavy unit like artillery or armor, with all the tanks, trucks, and troop transports, can be upwards of 16,000-17,000 men. The largest of all is the Marine amphibious division, which depending on its assignment can be outfitted as its own small, independent army. Thus when the First Marine Division landed at the Pacific island of Penilou in 1944, it carried its troop replacement with it and numbered a whopping 27,000 men.

Obviously, these units of organization—squadron, battalion, etc.—are parts of the whole. They are the various subordinate parts into which an army, navy, or an air force must be divided in order to solve the problem of command. It should be evident that no single commander can exercise direct control over any sizable force. General Eisenhower certainly should not have taken every soldier and sailor in his massive D-Day force and placed each one of them in a particular spot and told each what to do. Having made his general plans and preparations, he issued his general orders to the commanders of his army groups, who then issued their orders to the commanders of all of their armies who issue theirs to their corps who finally gave orders to their division commanders. And really, the chain of command goes even deeper than this. Ultimately ending with the sergeant who leads a twelve-man squad. Naturally, each relay of a Senior or Supreme Commander's orders to a lower level has the potential to diminish or to twist or distort the original, in the same way that rumor changes character as it goes from mouth to mouth. However, formal or written orders usually go no lower than the division. This is probably because the division is the smallest unit in modern warfare combining all arms, that is—infantry soldiers, artillery, armor, and engineers to build bridges or to destroy bridges, to build piers, to build anything required by the field commander. The division also has service and supply units such as transport and quartermaster (the officer in charge of supplies). A division also has a medical unit and intelligence.

Among all these designations and fighting formations, the battalion remains the basic fighting unit. Remember I said it has 800 to 1,000 men. It is the battalion which ultimately closes on and then destroys the enemy. While capable of fighting within the framework of a regiment or division, the battalion may also operate independently, because the battalion is the smallest unit with the optimal combination of fighting power and mobility. It will most often have a company of light and heavy machine guns and a platoon of artillery, as well as mechanized units for speed. It's a very flexible unit, capable of completing, on its own, many of the tasks that need doing on a battlefield. And invariably it has a seasoned officer in command. As a result, the Division Commander entering battle thinks chiefly of how many battalions he has to deploy.

It is also worth noting that the ratio of combat battalions to non-combat units is quite small. In fact, it is amazingly small as compared to other armies. There is—at least there was in the Philippines—an expression called "Division Slice." What this refers to is the actual number of soldiers required to keep a battalion or regiment or division in the field, and that number is roughly 51,000 men. Recall that a division has about 15,000 men. You can see that the ratio is about one to five. That is, it takes five men in the rear area to support one G.I. up in the foxhole. But I think in actuality the ratio is a little higher than that. It's probably more like six or seven in the rear area to support one frontline soldier. In fact, the truth is even with a combat division, when the commander has committed his battalions, there are very few men actually under fire at any one time. This is because of the customary two-up-one-back deployment by which commanders fight their battalions—that is, two fighting and one in reserve at any given time. Of his three companies, he commits two and keeps one in reserve.

So now you see that when a division is on the line, proper support troops to the rear, you're talking about 60,000-75,000 bodies, and relatively few of those are in combat at any one time. So when the rear brigade commander hears that such-and-such a division lost 227 men in this particular engagement, that's a very fierce loss, relative to the number of men who are actually fighting.

I hope that these explanations will help make sense of the text to follow. But I also know that it's difficult to grasp these concepts, and the way they play out on an actual battlefield, upon hearing them for the first time. In fact, you might well be placed in the position of not being able find the black-eyed peas because they are in a coffee tin marked "Buttons." Nevertheless, I hope the forgoing will at least help a little as I get into things like unit strengths during my time in the Philippines, or later, when I discuss MacArthur and his campaign to retake the Philippines back from the Japanese.

For now, I'll leave it at that and proceed to tell my own story of what happened in the Pacific between 1941 and 1945.

Chapter 1

I'D BE AN OFFICER

In September of 1937, when I entered Boston College in Chestnut Hill as a freshman, war was the furthest thing from my, or really anyone else's, mind. There were rumblings in Europe, of course, and the Japanese had invaded China a few years earlier, but those conflicts seemed too distant to ever ensnare the United States, let alone me personally. I was a college kid, a "strap-hanger" we were called on the public transportation system, a janitor's kid with eight brothers and sisters trying to improve my lot little by little, and that was all I intended to do, or imagined I would do, for the next four years.

But of course, life has a way of altering our perfectly-laid plans, and for me that began in the summer of 1938. I was working at the Wentworth Hotel in New Hampshire, a big Victorian resort by the sea, where people had been vacationing since 1874 (and where, in an interesting coincidence, the Russian and Japanese delegations came together in 1905 to end the Russo-Japanese War). The late thirties were not a great time for the country financially, though, and I was unable to make enough money that summer to return to school. Tuition at Boston College was only $300, but I couldn't scrape that together, so instead of returning to school in the fall of 1938 I went south, to Pinehurst, North Carolina, to work and save money so I could return to BC in 1939.

This delay might seem like no big deal, but it ended up making a huge difference in the trajectory of my life.

Because by 1939, tensions in Europe had become actual armed conflict, when the Germans invaded Poland and started World War II. And even though talk of the war in the U.S. still mostly centered around how it had nothing to do with us and we could avoid getting involved if we chose, preparations were still being made, quietly, for the possibility that we might not be able to sit it out.

One example of these preparations was the fact that a month after the Germans invaded Poland, Boston College became the only school in New England designated as a site for a CAA—Civilian Aviation Administration—flight training program. This was military money being spent on civilian training, mind you. The government said they wanted to bolster the number of young pilots available for commercial aviation, but, really, they wanted as many pilots trained in the basics as possible in the event we got pulled into the war. I hadn't ever really thought about being a pilot, but with the program so close at hand, and so easy to enroll in, I decided, *why not?* It consisted of 180 hours of classroom instruction and 35 flight hours in a Piper Cub, a little single-engine monoplane used mostly as a trainer. The classes met Wednesdays and Fridays in an amphitheater on the BC campus, and flight training happened down in a seaside town called Plymouth closer to Cape Cod. There were thirty of us fellas in the class, and 215 hours of high-quality instruction cost us only $35 apiece. It was a good deal, we all agreed. Similar training, unsubsidized, probably would have cost a thousand dollars or more.

But there's always a catch, and wouldn't you know it, right after we completed the program in the spring of 1940, who should suddenly appear on campus but a couple of handsome officers from the Army Air Corps. And they weren't there randomly—they wanted to talk with those of us who had just graduated from the CAA program. I ended up chatting with a fella who turned out to be a second lieutenant, though that didn't mean anything to me at the time. He had a briefcase with a bunch of pictures of the planes I could fly if I joined the Air Corps—B-17s, a four-engine bomber, and the DC-2, a twin-engine passenger aircraft that carried 14 people in addition to the crew. Beautiful machines if I'd ever seen one. Their complexity and power grabbed me by the hand and started to pull. These were a long way from the little Piper Cub I'd been trained on, and that was supposed to be enticing. But honestly, these beasts were so far from what I knew it seemed impossible I could ever actually fly one. I looked at the cockpit of the B-17, with all its hundreds of toggles and switches and handles and instruments, and I said, "Nah, that'd be too much for me." I declined the offer to apply to the Air Corps. It was a matter of confidence, or lack thereof. And two weeks later, when I received a letter from the recruiting office with an application enclosed, I ignored it.

By then, I was back at BC and the spring semester of 1940 was over, so I went back to work at the Wentworth for the summer. Or so I thought. Because even though in my mind I was done with the Army Air Corps, they certainly weren't done with me, and not two more weeks had gone by before they sent yet another application directly to the Wentworth and informed me the flight training would begin in July.

Now why, when they'd asked twice before and I'd said no twice before, did I then change my mind? It's hard to say. Curiosity, probably, more than anything else, which is a way of saying I don't think I took it very seriously or really thought anything would come of it. I think I just had this idea that I'd go down for a day, check out what they were doing, and come right back. I was young and I hadn't seen a whole lot of the world—nothing much outside my neighborhoods yet—that's one of the big things they promise you. In retrospect, a military likely worked off a formula, complete with a number of reach-outs required to secure a commitment from an apprehensive young man like myself.

Whatever the reason, I went to the head waiter at the Wentworth, a guy named George Thornton. I told him what was going on and asked if I could take a day to go down to Boston and get squared away with these people, find out what they wanted. And this was no small request, mind you. The summer season for the hotels in New England ran from June 10th until September 15th, and there was no such thing as a day off for anyone that entire time. At this time in American history, there were no days off for the worker, and none of us wanted one, frankly. A day off did nothing but remind us of when it was even worse in the Depression a handful of years earlier. Still, George agreed, and I caught a ride down to the Army recruiting office in Boston, opposite South Station. There, on the second floor, they offered to make me a second lieutenant if I agreed to the training. One year of school, and at the end I'd be able to fly anything and—here's the big thing—I'd be making $230 a month. Quick math told me that was more than $55 a week, which most doctors and lawyers didn't even make at that time. It was a lot of money, certainly more than I could make at the Wentworth.

Now I started to think a lot more seriously about what this guy was proposing. I asked if I could give it some thought, and I went out and found a little restaurant where I considered, over coffee and a Camel, what my prospects would be if I didn't take the offer the Army was making. Things were still tough—the end of the Great Depression—and guys my age were still having a very hard time of it, even with a college degree. It was hard to make a living at all, let alone one good enough to get married and raise a family, things I wanted to do.

So I went back up to the second floor and signed the papers. I was informed that in no time at all I'd receive railroad tickets and travel allowance to Tuscaloosa, Alabama and to bear in mind that the letter that came with the tickets would be orders—now that I'd signed,

I belonged to the Army, and failure to follow orders would mean real trouble.

After that, I wasn't sure what to do. Eventually I took the subway out to Brookline, and walked to my parents' house on Upland Road, just above Brookline Village on the hill. My mother was, of course, surprised to see me.

"You didn't get fired from the Wentworth, did you?" she asked.

"No," I said.

"Oh, thank goodness," she said.

"Actually, I'm thinking about joining the Army," I told her.

She thought this was a perfectly awful idea; for a second it seemed she might drop dead of apoplexy. "The Army!" she said. "Of all the places to work! The enlisted men don't seem to have much to do. If you drive past a military post, you see all these men just picking up leaves and trash and cigarette butts."

"I'd be an officer," I assured her. "A second lieutenant."

"Well the officers look nice in their uniforms, I suppose," she said, "but I think they just do a lot of drinking and swapping wives. Please don't have anything to do with the Army, Bud!"

Of course, I already *had* plenty to do with the Army, given that I'd signed the papers. There was no way around telling her, so I just came out with it. "I've already signed up," I said. "I'll be off to Army pilot training sometime in the next few weeks."

Before she could blow a gasket, I assured her I hadn't gotten secretly married, I wasn't a deviant, and I didn't see much of a difference between being in the Army and being anywhere else. If you wanted to live a halfway decent life, you could do that anywhere, if that was your general attitude. Mother wasn't entirely convinced, but of course that didn't really matter—I'd signed, and that was that. The Army didn't care how my mother felt about it, and I would not be relieved of my obligation because she thought I'd made a mistake.

So then I returned to the Wentworth and told old George the news. He wasn't pleased, in part because I was, if I may say so, a good worker, responsible, reliable. And I was leaving George in the lurch, departing suddenly just as the summer got going. But he said, "Well, good luck. Things are getting pretty bad in Europe, and who knows, we might all be in this before too long anyway."

Which turned out to be a pretty astute observation on George's part. Even now, in June of 1940, as Hitler was taking Belgium, the Netherlands, and France in just six weeks, there was still very little talk of the United States entering the war. But George seemed to know—and I think I knew it, too, and a lot of other people who weren't talking about it nevertheless knew it—that we couldn't stay out of such a big fight forever. If we tried to wait it out, it would come looking for us. But anyway, at that point, no one really knew for certain. It was just news reports and talk.

Within a few weeks I received the brown envelope from the Army Recruiting Service, and in no time at all I found myself in Brookline bidding adieu to my family, boarding a train for Tuscaloosa, and points unknown thereafter.

Chapter 2

CLARK FIELD

We arrived on 29 July, 1940, thirty of us, all from New England. We had a distinct look, we were told, and I wasn't sure if that was a compliment or otherwise. My mother would often say my friends and I had hard heads and bright smiles, speaking about the large litter of friends I had in the neighborhood as a kid. And I thought *that* was a compliment. But I wasn't sure what to make of our receivers immediately identifying us as Boston and Maine fellas. So here arrived the New England boys to Tuscaloosa, Alabama. It was a Sunday and our orders told us we didn't have to report until Monday morning, but once Monday came things began to move quickly. Tuscaloosa had a small airfield, just a hanger about 150 feet square, a few auxiliary buildings, and a bigger building that served as a barracks and mess hall. We weren't there for long, only three and a half months of primary training. We did get a bit of exposure to a limited number of mostly outdated aircraft while in Tuscaloosa, but we came to believe this was a pre-requisite training of sorts, the kind of basic overviews and not-too-difficult physical training that perhaps new officer recruits would get as to not turn them off or away prematurely. After we had wrapped up the primary training in Tuscaloosa it was onto Montgomery for more advanced flight instruction with newer aircraft. And we welcomed this as it felt like a graduation onto the next phase if not just a needed change of pace.

In Montgomery we flew the BT-14, an updated version of the BT-9, which itself had only been in service for a few years. The BTs were trainers only—no armament, two seats, one for the student and one for the instructor. In the BT-14 we learned more intensive, dangerous work—flying by instruments (that is, using only instruments to navigate, as one would have to in bad weather or on a moonless night), flying in different formations, and lots of takeoffs and landings, which were the most technically challenging and dangerous parts of a flight, assuming you aren't being shot at. Eventually, we started doing cross-country flights. Once we were finished in Montgomery we were supposed to go to Texas for further advanced training, but it turned out to be a lot easier to bring the planes to us than to bring us to the planes. So we stayed put in Montgomery after all, doing our last round of training in the T-6 Texan, a more advanced plane than either of the BTs. My fascination with flying military planes had reached new levels and I was very pleased with my decision to have joined the Army Air Corp. Most of the fellas were as far as they told me.

It was during this time that one of my instructors mentioned that he'd served a tour in the Philippines and liked it quite a lot. I wouldn't know the Philippines from the Grenadines, of course. At that time, before the war, the Army was an all-volunteer outfit, which meant among other things that often, particularly as an officer, you could request a particular assignment and stand a fairly good chance of getting it. And so as my graduation from flight school approached I needed to start thinking about where I wanted to be stationed and what I wanted to fly. You could request fighters or bombers or transport or reconnaissance. If you wanted to go overseas, at the time there were just four options for Army Air Corps: Panama Canal, Hawaii, Alaska, or the Philippines.

Of course, I was young, unmarried, and had never really been anywhere. Before flight training I'd never flown in an airplane in my life. When I was a kid we took a trip in dad's car to Moosehead Lake in Maine, went a couple of times to New York City, and once to Newport, Rhode Island. I went as far south as Annapolis once, to recover a car that my sister Mary had abandoned on one of her trips from Miami back to Boston. But that was it. So everything lined up for me to go overseas, really, and I went to the administrative office and filled out the paperwork for assignment to a bomber outfit in the Philippines. By the time I graduated, on March 15th, orders had been issued sending me to the Pacific, and I was to await Army transport upon an addition to my orders.

I had a couple of weeks to wait, and in the meantime I was assigned to test-fly trainer aircraft that had been recently repaired. A heck of a job, really, especially for someone as green as I was. But the Army doesn't like letting men just sit around, and anyway, I was eager to fly, regardless of whether it was in a plane that may or may not have been airworthy. Someone had to test them out, I suppose. And I never really thought about it as something hazardous, though certainly it was. We just went and did it—that's all. That would remain true throughout the time in the service when I was actually flying aircraft rather than rotting in a prison camp. A lot of the flying we did in the Philippines was not under ideal conditions, with perfect equipment, or even sometimes with proper airfields. But we had orders, and we carried them out without thinking about it much one way or the other.

Before too long, on April Fool's Day in fact, I was ordered to Sumter, South Carolina east of Columbia. There I boarded a decrepit old steamer called the *Chateau Tierry*, which took three days to make the voyage from South Carolina to New York City. I had a week's leave of absence before setting sail for Manila, so I took the opportunity to go back and visit family. My mother, despite her misgivings about the Army, was very impressed with my uniform, as were my sisters and brothers. They forced me to do a couple photographs outside the family home that they would put in a picture frame, and who wouldn't like that? I was honored. They kept asking me what the gold bar on my shoulder was for, and I explained what a second lieutenant was, a commissioned officer, with authority over enlisted personnel. It was pleasant to be home, always nice to be in Massachusetts as it's waking up from winter and to share what my life was like down in Alabama, a place no one in my family had ever visited or heard much about. But I was itching now for the next stage to begin—to see the world—and when my leave was up I was happy to return to New York to start the next journey as an Army Air Corpsman.

In New York harbor I boarded the S.S. *Washington*, then the largest ship in the Merchant Marine, and met up with fellas soon to be thicker than thieves, Jay Mercer, Billy Rowe, Billy Post, and several other new second lieutenants. They were mostly heading either to the Panama Canal Zone or Alaska, whereas me and Mercer were in for a much longer trip—when we dropped the Alaska men off in San Francisco, we would continue onto Hawaii, and then, of course, the Philippines. Mercer, a Duke University graduate, was smarter than me and I enjoyed his company and the conversation. He also had an understated toughness about him that I gravitated towards. And that toughness would be on full display in the coming years.

The *Washington* was, at the time, under the control of United States Lines. She was a glorious, beautiful ocean liner, 800 feet long, A through E decks. At the time, one of the most luxurious ships in the world, with terrific service for almost a thousand passengers, most of whom, aside from us, were embarking on a worldwide cruise—or at least they thought that's what they were doing. About that change of plans for these fine people in a minute.

We set sail on April 22nd or 23rd, and arrived at the Panama Canal six days later. At the canal you have to wait, sometimes for hours, to enter the locks, which are massive concrete pools that fill and drain to raise and lower ships so they can pass through the canal. It took only ten minutes to fill a lock with enough water to raise a ship the size of the *Washington,* and the only thing used to move the water was gravity. A true marvel of engineering. And the most miraculous thing about it, you can move a boat from the Caribbean to the Pacific in only six hours. I was a long way from Brookline and loving it. My eyes had never been so wide, the breeze hitting my face carried a freshness, a vigor I had never felt in the air. There sure is something to say about getting about, traveling to new places with a few comrades to enjoy the experience.

We stayed in Panama for four days, during which time the *Washington* took on a noticeably more military configuration. Five hundred American troops came aboard, along with a good number of military dependents, and then we sailed up the west coast, arriving in San Francisco five or six days later.

When we arrived in San Francisco, everything aboard the ship—other than the sudden embarkation of 500 soldiers—was still normal. As was everything in the city—there was no sign of war preparations, just a beautiful, lively city that beckoned to us. Given that we were traveling as civilians and had no responsibilities on board, we could come and go as we pleased while in port. Jay Mercer, our new friends, and I took full advantage, eating and drinking and hitting the usual tourist spots. We took day trips outside the city, Napa and environs, which that time of year is so green it almost hurts your eyes. After four more days of enjoying the time on land, We returned to find and boarded the *Washington* for transport across the Pacific to Hawaii. And that was when things really changed.

We returned to find both the fore and aft decks of the ship suddenly loaded with very large crates, maybe twelve by twelve by forty, each lashed down with heavy chains and stenciled with the words "OPERATION PLUM." It would turn out Operation Plum was the code name for the U.S. Army troop and equipment buildup in the Philippines prior to World War II—of which I, of course, was a part. But I had no idea what it meant then. That information was way above my pay grade. I just knew that with those big crates aboard, we couldn't use the ship's pool (as much) or badminton areas any longer.

On the passage to Hawaii, the talk aboard the ship was all about those boxes and what they were, what they meant. Here you had all these people who had paid a lot of money to cruise around the world, and all of a sudden the military took over the ship and put these crates everywhere. They could talk and complain about it all they wanted, but they couldn't actually do a thing about it.

And once we got to Hawaii, it got worse—at least for the civilian travelers. Because while Mercer and I went out and had a grand time, nearly killed ourselves trying to surf (after which I decided to limit myself to swimming), went out in Oahu at night, toured banana and pineapple plantations during the day, the remaining civilian passengers on the *Washington* were told, in no uncertain terms, that their journey had come to a premature and abrupt end. In retrospect, of course, they'd be damn happy to not be going where the *Washington* and its men were heading into next.

That's right—everyone was summarily thrown off the ship, including the crew, in Hawaii. Now the Army took complete control of the *Washington* for the last leg of her journey to the Philippines. In place of the tourists, another 1,500 soldiers boarded the ship—organized units, officers and their men—and we set out once more. Pretty much the moment we left port, quartermaster units began retrofitting the entire ship, with lumber taken on in Hawaii, to maximize the number of soldiers who could be berthed. Bunk beds everywhere, stacked as many as six high, in the dining rooms and ballrooms on A deck. The ship was being fully converted to a troop transport as it sailed, and accordingly, for the first time on the trip, I was expected to be in uniform.

Still, it was a great passage across the Pacific, taking some twelve days, and even though life had taken on something of a military feel, in general it was still very casual. We played volleyball and swam in the pool below deck when we could. The food was terrific and we even had a little movie house on board. The weather grew warmer as we went, and we spent a good part of each day sunning ourselves. Because despite the Army takeover of the ship, it still did not feel like war, and we were, in fact, not at war, though by now a good part of the rest of the world was. Little indications that this was changing would continue to accumulate, though. For one example, on the *Washington* two massive American flags were painted on either side of the ship, and lights rigged up over the sides so the flags were fully visible at night. For another, beginning in flight school I'd had $6.30 taken out of my paycheck every month for government life and disability insurance. Suddenly, on arriving in Manila, that $6.30 started appearing again in my paycheck without explanation. But we figured out the explanation: the government thought we were going to be fighting sooner rather than later, and didn't want to have to pay out on tens or hundreds of thousands of dead and disabled troops. We could keep our $6.30 a month, and take our chances.

The only real gesture we made toward discipline in our passage to the Philippines was to lay off the cocktails and exercise every day in the sun, so that Mercer and I were in fine physical condition by the time we arrived in Manila about the 20th of May. And this would be to our benefit with what was to come.

We reached the bay in mid-morning, were off the ship by noon, and no sooner had we set foot on dry land than we were whisked away by buses to the Army and Navy club for a reception. The party was gigantic—seemingly every last person in uniform in the Philippines was there, including the two thousand or so who had just arrived. And why all the fuss? Before too long, we understood: those who had already been there awhile were getting nervous about the Japanese, and pretty happy that so many soldiers and pilots had shown up to reinforce the garrison. They were celebrating more able bodies who could held them fight, and we took no issue with celebrating that. Besides, it's not like we could hop back on the *Washington* and flash a return ticket.

Well I can tell you, with a party that size and the fact that we were the guests of honor, our discipline regarding drinking and smoking from the trip across the Pacific went right out the porthole. Free booze, free food. We took advantage of both, and by five or six o'clock I didn't even know my own name. In fact, I ended up someplace I still don't know where it was or who took me there. But in any event, two days later the party was finally over and it was time to do what we'd been sent there for—whatever that was. I suppose I could've flown a plane in a pinch after that party but I wouldn't have bet on it. Mercer and I were becoming fast friends, neither quick to go to bed early or leave a good party. Heck, we were single young men in a new country, not to mention getting free booze at every turn at these parties. It would have been rude not to partake.

We were flown to Clark Field, the principal U.S. air base in the Pacific, on the island of Luzon north of Manila, the island's capital city, but keeping in mind that there are many thousands of islands that constitute the Philippines. I mention the vastness and multitude of islands as it's worth noting when ruminating any war strategy or tactic amidst a indescribably complex series of islands with an even more complicated history dating back to explorers like Ferdinand Magellan, and that whole lot of land grabbers. The colonizers as they were called ultimately found themselves in conflict with the colonized as is often the case, and rightfully so. The Spanish colonizers would cede the islands to the Americans as part of the Spanish-American War resolution around 1900, and it would stay in American "control" until after World War II. With American control of the islands, it was serendipitous to have places, like Clark Field, to store a large number of men, planes, and supplies. It was the only air field within hundreds of miles that could land and store our big bombers like the B-17.

Clark Field was quite expansive—15 square miles—and was the largest airfield of its day in the region, so it stands to reason that it became an important tactical base to maintain, just as it was an important tactical base for the Japanese to overtake. Here I was assigned to the Second Observation Squadron, flying single-wing, single-engine O-46 and O-52 aircraft, which were more or less obsolete by the time I got there. They didn't stand a chance of outrunning or outmaneuvering the premier air combat planes of the time, let alone going head-to-head, but as reconnaissance and delivery planes they did the job, particularly in undeveloped places like the Philippines where often we took off from and landed in the most inappropriate places. As long as it was somewhat level and grassy, these planes could get in and out. We even flew into harvested sugar cane fields. Like I said before, someone had to do it.

Our function in the Observation Squadron was varied. In essence we were the eyes of the operation tasked to identify anything untoward or menacing developing in our midst. Sometimes we were supposed to observe enemy positions and troops movements; other times we flew out to sea to look for foreign shipping and naval activity. Still other times we served as couriers, picking up and delivering messages for the Army when field communications were down, as well as ferrying commanders from one defensive area to another quickly. For those unfamiliar with the geography of the Philippines, or the Pacific Theatre at large, it's probably best to invest in a map to have a look as it is not a simple layout to describe in words. In simplest terms, we're talking about a lot of islands, which means a lot of seas—large ones. The Philippines sits between Australia to the south and China to the north, Japan to the northwest. To the east of the Philippines was the aptly names South China Sea which rode north to China. To the west of the Philippines was the, you guessed it, Philippine Sea—a massive expanse of nothingness, apart from blue water. Sitting there in southeast Asia with Vietnam to its west and the aforementioned countries dotted around it, the Philippines was important, strategic real estate when it came to war, particular when Empire expansion is the stated goal of your aggressive neighbor, the Japanese.

But other than the observation work in the skies, social life at Clark Field was more or less nonexistent, which was probably the way the

Army liked it. Because of increased tension, the Japanese expanding their empire in China and the Pacific, the Germans taking over the bulk of Europe, all military dependents had been sent home, which meant there were no young ladies—at least, no white ones—for us to meet. It was us, the 24th and 29th Field Artillery, and the 26th Cavalry and their horses and mules, some 2,500 in all. The horses, of course, belonged to the cavalry, and the mules were there to haul the artillery pieces. Just lots of men and lots of animals.

Still, life was fairly comfortable. We were up early most mornings and over to the flight line for a lecture, or else going to whatever section we'd been assigned to. Sometimes these assignments made no sense, other than the fact that the command really had nowhere else to put us. Once, for example, I was assigned to the aerial machine gun section. What did I know about armament in general and machine guns in particular, you ask? Nothing. And yet, despite that fact, not only was that my assignment but, being a second lieutenant, an officer, I was technically in charge of all the men who did actually know their way around these guns. Fortunately for me, the sergeant of the section was patient, accommodating, and seemed to understand that I didn't have any more choice in the matter than he did. I got along well by not showing up very often, and by staying out of the way, and making sure not to say anything that sounded like an order, on the occasion when I did show up.

Fortunately, there were times when we actually did what we'd been trained for, which is to say fly airplanes. Each of us got around 25-30 hours a month in the cockpit. Beyond that, on weekends we often were able to borrow an airplane and take trips to various places. It was a simple system: you put your name on a list, and if a plane came available and your name was next, you got the plane, and off you went.

Frequently we would fly to Baguio, a beautiful city in the mountains north of Manila, about a mile above sea level. It took about an hour and twenty minutes by air, and we'd land on a grass field chopped off the top of a mountain—dicey stuff, but when you're young you do such things without even thinking twice. Baguio was officially the summertime capital of the Philippines, owing to the mild climate at such a high elevation. It was colorful and lush, with houses built into the hillsides and lots of orchids and pine trees, and the Army had chosen it for an R&R facility, Camp John Hay, a gorgeous base with gardens, 18 holes of golf, a well-appointed officers' club, even an outdoor amphitheater. We could stay there the entire weekend, play golf, tennis, lounge and sun ourselves, eat and drink, all for the princely sum of $3. To arrive in a plane on its last legs added some humor to the story when you did, hopefully, land on your wheels and come to a safe stop.

One of the things I enjoyed the most at Baguio was the Sunday morning market. It was put on by the Igorot, the indigenous people of the Cordillera mountains. They would come out of the forest with their wares—spears and blowguns, tobacco, fruit and other food, and so on. These were very small people; an adult male would maybe come up to my belly button. They would lay out their goods on cocoa mats and wait, sitting back on their haunches, for a sale. Of course, for me and people like me, which is to say occidentals, this was an extraordinary experience. Among many other things, the Igorot would sell puppies at the market—but not in the way you think. When a dog had a litter, they'd fatten the puppies until they were about two months old. Then, starting on a Thursday, they'd give the puppies nothing but water, so that by Saturday they were starving. Then they'd feed them all the corn meal mixed with animal fat that they could eat, and when the puppies were stuffed as full as they could be, the Igorot would slaughter and roast them, then bring them to the market on Sunday. For a kid from Massachusetts, this was about the craziest thing you could imagine. But there it was.

The other place we spent a lot of time on the weekends, of course, was the capital, Manila. We didn't have to fly there; it was an easy two-hour run down Highway #1, a nicely-paved road. We'd get in early evening, rest for an hour, take a shower, and head out to what for us was the biggest attraction—jai alai. It was a big sport in the Philippines, and we came to really enjoy both the sport itself and the spectacle surrounding it.

There were three viewing tiers for jai alai. The bottom was the peasant tier, ground level, where a ticket cost only 25 centavos (12.5 cents). The middle level, for middle-class viewers, was 50 centavos. And then the upper tier, glassed-in and air-conditioned, with private bar and restaurant, a dance floor, even a 12-piece orchestra, was of course for the upper class, which included us by default. Not only were we allowed to take in the games from the balcony, the jai alai operators were so eager to have us young white Americans there that we got in for free. It was a good deal for them, since we were such a novelty, almost as big a draw as the games themselves. It got to the point where everyone working at the fronton knew who we were, and we could just breeze in past the lines, take the elevator to the third floor, sit down at a table with prime views and have a great dinner while we watched the games. The waiters, in addition serving us food and drinks, took our bets for us as well. The bartenders would give us whole bottles of the best scotch, a couple of tumblers and a little bowl of ice. They didn't care how much whiskey we drank; we could fill our glasses over and over all night long. What they wanted was for us to be there, to have dinner and drinks in spots where people could see us, to make appearances in the ballroom. And above all, to place bets. We'd have ourselves a time, treated like minor celebrities, and it all cost us very little. Then on Sundays we'd get up late, go to church in the old city, the cathedral inside the old Spanish fortress, which was also the home to the 31st Infantry. Now the 31st, interestingly enough, is one of only a handful of regiments to have been formed and spent its entire existence somewhere other than the United States. They also had a pretty nice golf course in Manila, where we would play nine holes in the late morning before heading to the Army and Navy club for a couple of beers, often Japanese beers like Asahi, which was very good stuff. Whatever else you could say about the Japanese, they made good beer. Then it was back to Rais Court for a nice siesta until, when the sun began to drop, we'd get back on the road headed north to return to Clark Field for Monday through Friday. And then we'd do it all over again.

Sometimes I'd get interesting diversionary jobs that basically involved flying money out to small remote islands. I'd take an old 52 parasol wing aircraft and fly down to Nielson Field, where MacArthur's headquarters for the joint command of Filipino and American forces was located. There I would pick up bags of money—actual bags full of cash, like in a cartoon—from the Senior Finance Officer's headquarters and begin the challenging and kind of wild task of delivering money to these outlying islands. The money was payroll for the Philippine Constabulary troops stationed on the various islands, which served as police and security forces.

The entire time, island to island, there was no radio communication whatsoever, and I had to navigate by working the maps and using my eyeballs to find the small grass airfields that had been cut out of the jungle. Borderline crazy, now that I think about it as an older man, but like so many other things, at the time it was a good adventure for those of us dumb enough to do it. I'd fly to where the maps indicated there should be a field, and then I would circle, trying to make out the slightly different shade of green that distinguished the field from the green sea of coconut and pineapple plants. Needless to say, there were no towers, no lights, not even a proper landing strip, just a more or less flat space of grass cut out of the jungle or a coconut plantation. Once the field was identified I would circle a couple more times, looking for any obstacles or other dangers, bumps or potholes, and when I was satisfied with an approach I'd take a breath, point the nose of the old parasol toward the field, and come in.

And once I'd landed, it was the same thing every time—what appeared to be a wilderness devoid of people would suddenly come to life, locals emerging from every nook and shadow, because to them an airplane might as well have been a UFO. Tremendous, teeming interest in this strange flying machine and the white man piloting it. The money was transferred, and then I basically had to wait, sometimes quite a while, a couple of hours or more, for someone to come with a couple of 40-gallon drums of fuel, which we'd pump by hand up into the tanks in the wings. And then I'd be off to the next island to do the whole process again. Madness, really, but it was all just part of the job.

Despite all these distractions, however, life at Clark Field was pretty routine and dull, and the base commander eventually came up with other things for us to do to keep busy. One that I really enjoyed was a horsemanship school that was open to all personnel at the base; I guess the commander thought that with all the horses around for the cavalry, he might as well make use of them. The school took place at the upper post, only half a mile up the road, and so was very convenient to attend. I took twenty hours of instruction, a good part of which was simply matching the rider to a horse of suitable temperament. After we'd graduated from the school, anytime we wanted to go riding, usually on the weekends, we'd have the houseboys bring the horses to the front of the BOQ (that's Bachelor Officers Quarters) and have them ready for early evening, say six o'clock. And then three or four of us would take the horses and head northwest into the mountains above Clark Field for the weekend. The idea, as with traveling to Baguio, was to get to higher elevations to escape the heat—the higher you went, the cooler it got. Plus we could swim in the many fast-running streams in the mountains, which we took advantage of frequently. And on these weekend horseback trips we'd each take a backpack full of goodies purchased at the PX to trade with the Igorots. At the time we thought the things they wanted were the oddest little commonplace things—playing cards, salt, cigarettes. But now that I think about it I realize they probably felt the same way about the things they traded to us, the blowguns, spears, and other hunting paraphernalia. They likely thought our interest in these things, which were so commonplace to them, was odd. But regardless, everyone left these little bartering sessions quite happy, and before too long the walls of the room I shared with Mercer in the BOQ was covered with quite a collection of Igorot hunting items.

So this was life at Clark Field, and while all these things were going on, there were still very few indications that war was imminent. Slit trenches were dug outside the BOQ and all down the flight line, outside the maintenance buildings and the enlisted men's barracks. Decoy aircraft were built using bamboo—really beautiful, artistic renderings, really, I wish I had one now—to give the impression, to any foreign agents or reconnaissance aircraft, that our strength was much greater than the reality (remember, from our discussion of strategy and tactics, that you want the enemy to think you're strong where you're weak, and vice versa). And once a month we'd go to the firing range to take target practice, the enlisted men with their Enfield rifles (a poor piece of equipment, WWI-era) and the officers with their sidearms. And that was it, as far as war preparations went. There was no discussion of how things were getting bad and we'd be in a fight soon. Our commander, Jim Parker, either knew nothing or just said nothing, but either way, no one talked as though there was anything to worry about or prepare for.

And it's important, probably, to point out that none of us were really thinking about the Japanese. As far as we knew and were concerned, the Japanese were fighting the Chinese and that had nothing to do with us. So when my unit was transferred to Nichols Field in September 1941, and over two dozen B-17s arrived at Clark to take our place, no one really knew what they were doing there. Their appearance caused quite a bit of excitement because such an airplane had never been in the Philippines before. The range of the B-17 raised the question: who were we going to bomb? There was no one to the south of us who we'd ever fight, and the only place in range, 400 miles out and back, was Formosa. What was in Formosa, we wondered in our ignorance, other than the Japanese, who were not our enemy?

As far as I and Mercer were concerned, the only significance of the move to Nichols was that we could be to jai alai and the Army and Navy club within twenty minutes of our front door. Little did we know that in a few short months we would be at war.

Chapter 3

BOMBED TO BEJESUS

The Filipino military had no real experience in any of the essential matters of preparation and execution of warfare. The only recent conflict they'd been involved with was Moro insurgencies in the southern islands. They had no military tradition, no officer corps through which to pass down institutional knowledge, no capacity to train and field an army. Put very simply, the Philippines could not effectively protect itself. It relied entirely on the United States for military leadership, money, armaments, food, etc. And this arrangement produced, in both the Filipino government and populace, a kind of laissez-faire attitude, that no matter what the problem, Uncle Sam would take care of it. Not only did they not have to do anything, they also didn't have to worry.

So during the fall of 1940, as diplomacy broke down between Japan and the United States, each new ratcheting up of tension was greeted in Manila with a kind of collective shrug of the shoulders. And it was more or less the same with us, the American servicemen. We read the same newspapers the Filipinos read, and our commanders never mentioned a word about anticipating armed conflict with the Japanese. Whatever the problems, they were for men in suits and neckties to sort out, while we continued with our routines.

U.S. Secretary of State Cordell Hull negotiated with Ambassador Nomura, the Japanese envoy to the United States, over many things that fall. The Japanese had what they euphemistically referred to as the "Asiatic-Pacific Co-Prosperity Sphere," which was a fancy way of referring to territory they had seized by force in the years prior, including parts of China and Indochina, what's known today as Vietnam, Cambodia, and Laos. The problem for the Japanese, which they were trying to solve through empire-building, was they had an isolated island nation of 74 million people that was splitting at the seams, plenty of manpower and energy and drive but almost nothing in the way of raw materials and natural resources, and they were eager to modernize quickly. But to modernize they needed tin, rubber, food, and above all, oil. In October 1941 the United States took the step of freezing all Japanese assets in America, which meant, among other things, since New York was the center of the world in terms of trade, that the Japanese suddenly had no way to negotiate business internationally, and more specifically had no way to buy oil. To guarantee Japan a supply of oil, the U.S. wanted them out of China and Indochina. Neither side would budge, and relations continued to deteriorate, seemingly day by day.

In the meantime, in Europe, Hitler had taken pretty much the entire continent, but balked at invading England. And this was fortunate for the Brits, because they were badly overextended throughout their empire, which the Germans did not fully understand. Kenya, India, Burma, Pakistan, the Mediterranean, you name it...British forces were everywhere but at home. Hitler had the resources he needed to invade: a well-supplied and motivated army, a powerful air force, all the momentum in the world from having just conquered most of Europe in the blink of an eye. Things did not look good for the Allies. And yet, Hitler hesitated, then consolidated his gains and turned his attention east toward Russia.

It was around mid-November that we started nightly blackouts in Manila, streetlights extinguished, all household and building lights off, black paper shrouds on the headlights of cars. Well-intentioned but, in terms of practical effect, it felt more than a little bit silly. Even with the lights off, if the moon was out you could see Manila Bay clearly from any elevation. And yet, the blackouts served a different purpose, really—to prepare everyone mentally for what was coming. To affect that all-important psychological shift from peacetime to wartime behavior, which in certain ways was just as important for civilians as for military personnel. In others words, it may get dark for the Filipinos and Americans on-island, figuratively and literally.

What was going on, behind the scenes, that caused our higher-ups to issue the blackout order? Well, this is educated speculation, but my guess is that the Japanese military tribunal, under Prime Minister Hideki Tojo, had already decided to go to war, and any further diplomatic maneuvering on their part from that point forward was just to buy time to make preparations. And I think there were those in the U.S. government and command who suspected this might be the case, as well. Despite the fact that Emperor Hirohito was at heart a peaceful man, the military tribunal had already gotten the country bogged down in China, committed to war to achieve their national objectives, and they had little choice but to continue and expand that effort. And so the die was cast, and the White House and State Department began issuing directives to commanders overseas to get ready, to be prepared for an outbreak of hostilities.

In Hawaii, both the Army, under General Walter Short, and the Navy, under Admiral Husband Kimmel, had been given very clear instructions to get prepared. The Army followed these instructions, but in retrospect they prepared for the wrong thing—they were worried about some two hundred thousand Japanese-born people in Hawaii, who could get up to all kinds of mischief, including espionage, sabotage, and civil disorder. These were farmers, largely, but if they'd wanted to, with those kinds of numbers they could have created havoc, and so that's where the Army's attention was directed. As for the Navy, it's very difficult to say whether Kimmel was incompetent, but given his utter lack of preparations and the way in which American forces were decimated at Pearl Harbor, it's hard not to at least suspect incompetence was part of the issue. Kimmel had no reconnaissance aircraft out to speak of, which was borderline malpractice with four aircraft carriers, eight battleships, and nine cruisers at anchor in the harbor, all lined up as if for target practice. On Saturday, December 6th, the last bit of good fortune the Navy would experience in the Pacific for some time occurred when Vice Admiral Halsey departed Pearl Harbor with the carriers *Lexington* and *Saratoga*, on a mission to transport twenty dive bombers to Wake Island, fifteen hundred miles to the west. I imagine the salts aboard those ships were pretty mad about embarking on a Saturday, when the rest of the personnel on base were getting ready to have a party. And I imagine that twenty-four hours later, they were very glad they'd left when they did.

At that time, in the far Pacific, along the Chinese coast, the British and Americans had picked up a substantial fleet of Japanese ships heading south. They were shadowed, but no one knew where they were headed or for what purpose. They could have been going to Singapore; they could have been slingshotting around the Philippines and heading for Panama. But Hawaii? Unthinkable. Other Japanese ships had been leaving ports piecemeal for a week, one ship here, two there, so as not to alert anyone to the activity of another large force. These boats assembled in the North Pacific and began moving east—this was the fleet that would attack Pearl Harbor, and the fleet off the Chinese coast heading southward would soon attack Singapore.

In the meantime, we in the Philippines were not ideally situated for a defense of the islands. About 100,000 Filipino men had been inducted into the armed forces in the previous six months. Very young, little formal schooling, no military experience whatsoever. And woefully underequipped. Not enough weapons, little transport capability, no air support. Just warm bodies, thrown into uniform and given the most basic of basic training.

We Americans had the newly-arrived B-17s and about 125 other aircraft: fighters, bombers, and miscellaneous transports. The principal ground force was the 31st Infantry, but it was a skeleton regiment, not fully manned. Remember from our discussion earlier that a properly manned regiment numbers about 1,800 men, but the 31st had been stripped of some officers and non-coms to form what is known in military jargon as a cadre—this particular cadre having been formed for the purpose of helping to train all those new Philippine Army conscripts. In addition to the 31st there were a few signal companies, a quartermaster battalion, all told about 13,000 Americans total between air and ground forces, and most of those were neither trained nor equipped for combat. The Navy, under Admiral Hart, had a heavy cruiser, a light cruiser, a dozen old four-stack destroyers (so named for the stacks that vented the smoke from their coal-fired engines), and twenty-five submarines. Unlike many of the ground and air forces, the Navy forces were ready for action. Admiral Hart was apparently a skittish sort of fella, because when he'd been told to be ready for potential hostilities he'd taken the warning seriously, stripping the ships down into combat configuration, loading warheads onto the torpedoes, and so on. In fact, his ships were already mining Manila Bay. History would show that among his fellow commanders in the Pacific, Hart was among the few who saw the writing on the wall and took heed the warnings coming from Washington. His legacy should be recorded appropriately for his foresight and I believe it has been.

So to sum up: there were a large number of bodies available for the defense of the Philippines, but they were largely conscripts who were as green as could be, underequipped, inadequately trained, lacking air and naval power to back them up. Put another way, what was to happen in the next month was, owing to the utter inadequacy of the island's defenses, almost ordained. There was no way to repulse a Japanese attack with such a force, as we would see.

MacArthur, having been promised all kinds of imminent support from Washington, had imagined that by April he would have what he needed to successfully defend the Philippines. Of course, by April the country would be almost entirely in Japanese hands, with the exception of Corregidor. One thing that indicated the promises of support were perhaps not entirely empty was the fact that as the attack on Pearl Harbor was taking place, another 35 B-17s were *en route* to the south

Pacific, as well as a group of ships, called the Pensacola Convoy, that set sail from Hawaii for the Philippines in late November 1941 carrying thousands of soldiers and airmen, parts of planes meant for assembly, weapons, artillery, vehicles, fuel, ammunition (in short, the stuff of warmaking, every bit of which we lacked). But of course, neither the bombers nor the ships arrived in time, and ended up being diverted after the Japanese landed in the Philippines and it became evident that the resistance we offered was minimal and soon to fail. Later, the B-17s and the dive bombers lying disassembled in the convoy's ships would do superlative work attacking the Japanese fleet and transports roaming the south Pacific as the war went on, which meant that, indirectly at least, they did the job for which they were originally intended: defending the Philippines. Because without those contributions, MacArthur's vow to return may never have been fulfilled.

So, it's Sunday, early December, in Manila, which owing to the international date line made it Saturday still in Hawaii. Since our unit had moved in September, Mercer and I had been living in a private rental apartment instead of at Nichols Field, owing to the fact that the BOQ had been taken over, ironically, by officers with wives and families—the Army didn't want to pay them all the dependents' allowance, so it was much cheaper to send the bachelors like us out into the local rental economy. We had a really nice arrangement at this place, three bedrooms, a full-time Chinese cook, house girls (they were called "girls" regardless of their age) including maids and a lavendeer, a washerwoman to take care of our uniforms. We also had a house boy to take care of the grounds, keep the cars washed, and run errands around town. All in all a great living arrangement, much more fun than living on base could ever be.

Anyway, that night, Sunday in Manila, I went to jai alai and returned home around 11 pm or midnight. I barely had time to get in the rack and get to sleep before I woke up to the phone ringing in the dead of night—or more specifically, at about 3 in the morning local time. I answered, and on the other end was Second Lieutenant George Howe, calling from Nichols Field. The timing was odd, enough by itself to be somewhat alarming, but what confirmed there was good reason to be alarmed was the way George identified himself—as the Officer of the Day. The moment someone says that, you know that whatever they have to say is urgent, because they're using the title deliberately to make clear they're speaking, in an official capacity, for the base commander in the commander's absence. So George asks who he's speaking with, and I tell him Rafferty, and he says "Lieutenant Parker wants you out at the base immediately."

Now, I say that George identifying himself as the OD *should* have been alarming to me, but at first it wasn't. Because Mercer and I had played a pretty dirty trick on George about a month before, and he hadn't forgotten about it and neither had I, and I thought maybe he was getting even with us, making us get up in the middle of the night on the weekend and hustle to the field for no reason whatsoever. It would have been a perfect payback.

So instead of responding properly to the directive, I just said, "Come on Howe, we're even," and hung up and went right back to sleep. But only for a minute. Because the phone rang again almost immediately, and this time Mercer answered and after a moment hung up and said "I think Howe is serious. We better get out to the base."

We dragged ourselves out of bed, pulled on our khakis, and drove to Nichols, and in that short drive the whole world changed, of course. Because when we arrived we got the news from Howe—the Japanese had attacked Pearl Harbor to devastating effect, sinking five or six battleships and at least three or four cruisers, an unknown but likely very large number of dead and wounded, an instantly crippled Pacific fleet, and we in the Philippines, with our utterly insufficient defenses, were very likely next, and in short order. It was an enormous blow, with more to come.

But it was also, on the part of the Japanese, a huge mistake. The seeds of their defeat were already sown in what appeared to be an unqualified victory. Because the nature of the attack—utterly underhanded, occurring even as the Japanese ambassador Nomura was in Secretary of State Hull's office, claiming to have no foreknowledge of the attack himself—galvanized the entire American public, sending a shot of adrenaline through everyone and allowing the government to marshal and mobilize all the latent power of the greatest country on earth, getting hundreds of millions of people into a military configuration in no time at all. Already, people were enlisting so fast that there was no way the enlistment officers could begin to keep up. The entire country wanted to get even with the Japanese for such a vicious and unprovoked attack. That's the way America managed itself in those days, one for all, all for one, just as we had through the Depression and World War I. And I felt this same general way about this, arriving at the base that morning and learning what had taken place. There I was, a very young fella, idealistic, having the thinnest grasp of the forces that were afoot in the world, and all of a sudden, with just a dozen words, the entire trajectory of my life had changed unmistakably.

I felt a tremor go through me, though I had no inkling yet of the brutal realities of war. I also had no idea of the very detailed, multipronged Japanese plan of which Pearl Harbor was only the first step, a plan at that very moment unfolding across the Pacific and headed, of course, directly toward me and my fellow airmen and soldiers and the people of the Philippines. In fact, the plan had been in motion since December 2nd, with all the movement of Japanese naval forces that had been noted but not understood. Admiral Yamamoto, the commander-in-chief of the combined fleet and the architect of the plan that was at that moment being executed, sat on his battleship *Nagato* in the inland Japanese sea, fielding updates and issuing orders. Yamamoto was born into a samurai clan, and his first name, Isoroku, translates (oddly enough) as "56," his samurai father's age when Yamamoto was born. Within the Japanese Navy, Yamamoto enjoyed universal respect and deference, but he had serious misgivings about Japan's ability to win a war against the United States, owing in large part to the perennial oil shortages Japan had begun its aggression to address. But the different branches of the Japanese military were quite cloistered, and Yamamoto realized at some point that the Army was going to drag the rest of the country into this conflict he believed would likely end in defeat. And so, he came up with the only plan he thought had any chance of working—to attack broadly and viciously, and inflict such losses on American forces that they would negotiate a peace before America's vast superiority in warmaking capacity could be brought to bear.

And once the Japanese did commit to the war, Yamamoto entered it with zeal and real ability, hoping to prove himself wrong about the outcome. The attack at Pearl Harbor, in its brazenness as well as its tactical planning, demonstrated that. The U.S. lost 2,400 men, 18 heavy ships, 185 aircraft, and suffered untold damage to military infrastructure as well. Comparatively, the Japanese lost only 30 or so planes and five midget submarines, a handful of personnel. By any meaningful metric, the battle, if you could even call it that, was an absolute Japanese rout, and a crippling loss for the American side.

The reasons for this loss were bitterly debated for years, but when you strip the issue of its politics and look at it plainly, those reasons become simple and clear. For one thing, the American High Command never dreamed the Japanese could put together an effective carrier strike force. We had extensive, though outdated, intelligence from having participated in Japanese war games, and that intelligence indicated they just didn't have the capacity to mount such an attack. That, specifically, was the principal cause of our defeat at Pearl Harbor. More philosophically, we were the victims of our own arrogance. We imagined ourselves too powerful for the Japanese to risk attacking at all. We imagined the Japanese were too feudal and unsophisticated to fight a modern war successfully. We refused to face the realities of 20th-century geopolitics, thinking we could simply wait out what was happening everywhere else in the world, until finally the whole thing exploded in our faces. And so it came to be that the Japanese utilized one of the principles of war—Surprise—to tremendous effect, and caused the United States to finally enter the conflict through a frightful disaster at Pearl Harbor.

In the meantime, back at Nichols Field, what we knew and what was actually happening around us were two very different things. So different, in fact, that it gave the entire experience the feel of not being real. Pearl Harbor was burning, the Pacific Fleet had been crippled in a scant hour and a half—but here in the Philippines, we were drinking coffee and smoking cigarettes and wondering what in hell we were supposed to be doing, if anything. At this point, there was no overt sign whatsoever that we were in Japan's crosshairs. It was 7 in the morning and no one was telling us anything. Our squadron commander was in a meeting with the base commander, but he never came out to tell us what was going on. And in the meantime, remember it's December 8th—the date of the Feast of the Immaculate Conception, which is about as big as a celebration gets in the Philippines, owing to the fact that the island's people had largely been converted to Catholicism by the Spanish some four hundred years prior. One needs to understand, the day-to-day life of the average Filipino was fairly drab. They worked difficult jobs for little money and had none of the things that made life exciting in the United States. So a celebration like the Feast was a very, very big deal, and in all the barrios all around the island that day people were preparing for a fiesta, little girls in their dresses and the streets decorated brightly and people gathered in squares and at churches and markets, eating native foods and sweets, playing music and dancing. That was what was supposed to happen, but what actually did happen on December 8th, 1941, would end up being far different.

Because from that moment, everyone in the country—certainly the populace, the Philippine government, but also us, the American servicemen, enlisted and officers, probably up to and including MacArthur himself (though surely he'd never admit it)—was cast into darkness and chaos. And that chaos was due not just to the actions of the Japanese, but also to the confusion regarding who was in charge of what in the Philippines. They were a quasi-independent state, after all, with a president and a congress. They hadn't declared war on the Japanese. But MacArthur was in charge of all military, the Filipino as well as the American, and whatever limits had been placed on that authority in recognition of Filipino sovereignty, MacArthur no doubt ignored those limits, probably even refused to communicate much with President Cazon, and certainly did not ask for or consider Cazon's opinion about matters.

Even when there's a clear and established chain of command, hostilities, particularly sudden hostilities, have a way of breaking down communications—sometimes this is referred to as the fog of war. But as I just established, we didn't even have the benefit of an established chain of command. And so the chaos started, I think, with a simple and well-intentioned communication from Major General Hap Arnold, the Chief of Staff of the Army Air Corps. In it, Arnold instructed his commanders to not attack unless first attacked. And even though MacArthur, a 4-star General, was not junior in any way to Hap Arnold, he had received the directive and planned to adhere to it. And so when Major General Brereton, who was in charge of Army Air Corps forces in the Philippines, came to MacArthur wanting to take those new B-17s and bomb the Japanese air bases in Formosa, about 350 miles to the north, MacArthur told him to stand down—the Philippines had not been attacked and so they would follow what they'd been told, keep their powder dry.

Except, of course, that by now the Japanese had, in fact, launched aerial attacks on the northernmost tip of Luzon, but remember what I said before about communications in outlying areas—it was almost nonexistent. So no one had any idea the invasion had already begun. And because of that, MacArthur turned Brereton down, and Brereton, for his part, left quite upset. He had his planes fueled and armed and ready to go, and it made no sense to him to wait for the Japanese to attack the Philippines directly. The war was on. There was nothing left to wait for.

And even though he couldn't defy MacArthur, one thing Brereton could do was get his planes in the air in case, as he suspected, the first place the Japanese attacked was Clark Field—he'd heard about all the planes destroyed on the tarmac at Pearl Harbor, and he had no intention of repeating the same mistake. So he told his B-17s to fly from Clark and just circle Mount Arayat, an extinct volcano that sticks up out of a plain like a custom-made landmark.

As Brereton paced and waited and worried, the morning passed without incident at Nichols Field. We listened to the air raid sirens from Manila, and I ran into town to pack my B-4 bag and hustled back to the field, but at no point did we see any sign of Japanese aircraft all afternoon and into the evening. And so MacArthur's order to not fire unless fired upon held, even though the Japanese had by this point bombed Aparri, in the far north, as a test to see what kind of resistance they would meet, the plan being for Japanese troops to land there a few days later. And while it may have been possible for communication to and from Aparri, at least before the attack, none came, either because that capability was destroyed or, maybe more likely, the people in charge there, civilians and bureaucrats, were reluctant to declare anything or make any decisions. Everyone protecting their own position, as it were. Just think—World War II has broken out and everyone's too sluggish or too scared to do anything.

The following morning, still nothing, and by now it was getting a little spooky. I went to the mess hall, then down to the flight line, and waited some more. By this point I hadn't even seen my commanding officer, Captain Parker, in the twenty-four hours since I'd arrived on base. So we're there on the flight line, still listening to air raid sirens from Manila wailing over the landscape. Nine o'clock passed, then ten, then eleven, and it seemed this morning would pass as quietly as the previous one. But then, on toward noon, an Air Corps sergeant watching the sky alerted us all to a large flight of bombers. Three echelons, expanding out from the front: three planes in the front, another three to the right and left of them, and six each to the right and left of them, for a total of eighteen planes. And to the right of that formation, another eighteen in the same formation, and to the left another eighteen. A total of 54 bombers approaching, and all around them, in pairs, circling, zippy little Zero fighters flying overwatch, waiting for anyone to take off and challenge the bombers. They were flying south, toward Clark Field, very low, only 8 or 9 thousand feet, and the sergeant said, "Don't worry, they're heading to Clark but there's nothing there to hit, everything's been sent up—oh wait, look, they're dropping leaflets."

I don't know what made him or anyone else think these were leaflets—it was an absurd notion but also, as I've gotten at, strangely understandable, you haven't yet been in war and your mind tries all kinds of crazy things to make sense of what you're seeing, tells you it can't possibly be that these planes are dropping bombs, and dropping them on *you* no less. So: leaflets. We all looked up, and by this point it was nearly high noon and the planes were crossing the sun and we could barely see them and the small shiny objects they were dropping. And what broke the spell, finally, what got us understanding what was going on and got us moving, was when these objects that we all wanted to believe were leaflets started to whistle as they fell.

Within seconds, the bombs began to land. Understand, these kinds of bombing runs are what's called aerial bombing, as opposed to the precision of a dive bomber. What that means is the bombs are released in strings, ten or so at a time, and they land the same way, one right after the other in a line, bam bam bam bam bam, so that they seem to be marching along and blowing up anything along a very predictable path. And that's what was suddenly happening at Nichols field, except the bombs were marching everywhere, fifty-four strings falling at once, turning the north-south runway into rubble, shattering our planes all lined up nose-to-nose, smashing into buildings and support vehicles and other equipment. Just utter destruction and chaos. Like most everyone else, I just lay down and covered my head with my hands. What else could you do? We weren't in any position to resist or fight back; we hadn't been prepared and did not have the equipment or the training or even the kinds of units that would be useful against such an attack—no intercept fighters, no anti-aircraft guns. At that time my outfit, the 2nd Observation Squadron, was the only one stationed at Nichols, and even if we'd been in the air when the Japanese showed up, we couldn't have done much except try to run. And of course we weren't in the air, so the only thing to do was hide and wait for it to be over and hope you'd still be alive when it was.

It got worse. After the first bombing run, the fighter escorts took their turn, screaming down out of the sky to take strafing runs at low level, spraying everything in sight with machine gun rounds. It was an absolute turkey shoot, no resistance whatsoever, a maddening, hellish thing to go through, everything exploding and burning all around me, and nothing to do but pray to God and talk to our mothers a world away.

All this went on for only forty-five minutes, though if you've ever been through something similar you know that time stretches out impressively, each second an hour, the minutes like days, never seeming to end, such a helpless, terrified feeling. The bombers turned around and came back for another run, and then the fighters took another whack at us.

And then they were gone.

There was a guy on the ground near me by the name of Lieutenant Warfield. He was an observer in the squadron, one of the men who sat in the alternate seat in two-seat airplanes and scouted for enemy positions, troop movement, shipping at sea, that sort of thing, while the pilots like me flew the plane. So we're all still just lying there a few minutes after the bombing stops, and then finally Warfield sat up and looked around and said, "My God, the BOQ's on fire."

I looked up and, sure enough, the south wing of the BOQ was fully engulfed, though it was hardly the only thing on fire at that point—the hangar, other buildings, jeeps, planes and people's private vehicles.

Warfield and I got to our feet and took off like mad, racing to the BOQ, three or four hundred yards, splitting up when we got there, he to his room, I to mine. I grabbed my bag and stuffed it with everything I could get my hands on, coughing like mad as the smoke got thicker and thicker. If you've never breathed in smoke from a structure fire it's hard to explain how awful it is, when your lungs just seize right up and you understand suddenly how people are overcome so quickly in a fire. So I beat it out of there before the place could come down around my ears and met Warfield out in the parking lot, he's got his own bag now crammed with clothes and shaving kit and the like, and our intention, I guess, if we had one, was to run to his car and throw our bags in there for the time being. But as we run toward his car and get closer we can see it's kind of smoldering, not exactly on fire but not exactly *not* on fire either, and when we're only maybe a hundred feet away, all of a sudden Warfield's car blows up like it's been wired with TNT. Another ten seconds and we would have been blown to kingdom come along with Warfield's car. This was the first time, but definitely not the last, that my life was saved by pure dumb luck and nothing else.

By now the hangar had burned down altogether, which meant the Squadron Operations room, which had been housed in the hangar, needed to be moved, set up on the fly somewhere else. A base can't operate without a Squadron Operations room, because it's where the senior officers from operations, navigation, and maintenance get together with the base commander and organize the execution of orders from higher up in the chain of command. Without that coordination, nothing can really happen—or nothing good, anyway, as we're about to see, because the chaos of this disastrous day had only just begun. Anyway, on the eastern side of Nichols field were two or three bomb storage revetments—picture a building foundation, except instead of a building on top there's just a curved concrete roof, like a Quonset hut. The idea being to store bombs and munitions there to keep them from exploding in just such an attack as had just occurred. We learned that a makeshift Squadron Operations room had been set up in one of these revetments, so we booked it out there, again on foot, to see what was what. Still lugging our bags, by the way, I've got everything I own except what's still back in my apartment in Manila, which is no small amount of belongings, by the way. My little 1936 Essex, a real oil burner of a car, golf clubs, furniture I'd purchased, personal records and letters, all the memorabilia I'd traded for with the Igorots—it was all good as gone now, or would be soon.

And no sooner did we make our way across the airstrip to revetment #2, than the Japanese came back and pummeled the bejesus out of us once more, turned the entire base into a shambles. We offered almost no resistance, no planes taking off to meet and challenge the Japanese, only small arms fire and a few .50-cal machine guns at the end of the runway that someone was able to man during the second bombardment. I heard later that we might have shot down two or three Japanese planes; I saw only one for sure, a Zero that hit the runway and exploded as I was running up out of the revetment to ground level. But other than that, Japanese losses, at least as far as we knew, were nonexistent, while ours were catastrophic, near-total.

And we weren't the only ones. I mentioned before the lack of communication and preparedness, the confusion over what exactly was happening and where and when, the reluctance to act. That was happening everywhere, and even where we did act, either the Japanese were observing closely and timed their attacks to when we were most vulnerable, or else they were just lucky as hell. Either way, take what happened that same day at Clark Field as an example of what I mean: recall that the B-17s at Clark had been sent up earlier in the day to circle Mount Arayat and avoid being sitting ducks on the ground. In addition, a bunch of P-40 Warhawks out of Iba were flying cover, had been for hours. Well, those bombers and fighters were up there milling about aimlessly, dog tired by now, the Warhawk pilots having chased phantoms on the one operational radar in all of MacArthur's command since 2 AM, and Clark hadn't been attacked, so it was decided that all these planes would land, refuel, let the pilots rest and eat. So here come the brand new B-17s back to Clark, they land and are lined up in a nice pretty formation, you know, like a parade, the military fetish for neatness and order being what it is. And the Warhawks go home to Iba and sit waiting for the next alert.

It comes around noon, the radar operator spotting a big formation coming in across the China Sea with plenty of time, for once, to get the Warhawks airborne and mount a defense, maybe make the Japanese pay a bit more. Except they make a small but critical mistake: given the heading of the formation, the assumption is they're heading to Manila, and so the Warhawks at Iba, instead of going airborne to fly cover for Clark again, head to Manila Bay.

What it comes down to is, that day at least, the right hand didn't know what the left was doing, and vice versa. People running around like headless hens. No definitive information anywhere, except those blips on the radar. Everyone at Clark Field, the airmen and the mechanics and the cavalry personnel, in the mess hall eating lunch like it was any other day. Iba sent a message to the aircraft warning officer at Nielsen Field about the incoming formation, and in turn the man at Nielsen tried to contact Clark, but couldn't get through—the radio operator was having lunch. Eventually he got a telephone connection and the junior officer at Clark assured the aircraft warning officer that he would pass on the message to the base commander immediately—which he did not do. Meantime, fifteen P-35s out of Del Carmen field, were supposed to be flying cover over Clark but never got the order from Nielsen. And so on, a cascade of failures and miscommunications.

The Japanese formation appeared in the sky over Clark, with the B-17s all lined up for the slaughter below. You had all these American pursuit aircraft aloft but hopelessly tangled because of poor communication and confusion of orders, and they hear the calls of the handful of pilots in the sky over Clark: "Tallyho," "Bandits over Clark." And everyone now heads toward Clark Field, but it's too late. By the time these fighters arrived, Clark was destroyed. Nichols, as we've seen, was also done for, and in short order Iba, after their pursuit aircraft returned from Clark, got caught on the ground in the same exact manner, and were also destroyed.

Of course, communications were out, and so we only discovered the scope of the losses by doing our job—namely, going up in our planes to observe and report. The next morning, Jay Mercer took off in an old 52, one of the squadron's standard observation planes, and flew up to Clark to take a look around. What he found was stunning: of the 17 B-17s on the ground at the time of the attack, only one was undamaged. The remains of thirty-four P-40 fighters lay scattered about the field, and of course the older P-35 and P-26 fighters hadn't stood a chance against the more advanced Zeros. The destruction at Iba was even more comprehensive—so much so that the Japanese had returned to Clark after destroying Iba, looking for more targets for their remaining ammunition.

Hence, in only a day and a half the Japanese had effectively eliminated MacArthur's air power—craft and facilities. Nothing resembling an effective fighting force remained. And this was all done through surprise, and the chaos and forced errors that surprise engenders. Unlike the American forces at Pearl Harbor, we didn't have the excuse of a lack of warning. And in the meantime, other bad news came in. The central pieces of the British naval strike force at Singapore had been destroyed—the battleship *Prince of Wales* and the battle cruiser *Repulse* were sunk by Japanese torpedo planes. This meant that only three capital ships of the Allied forces—the three American aircraft carriers that had steamed from Pearl Harbor less than 24 hours before the attack—remained in all of the Pacific. The Japanese now effectively owned the ocean and the air. And soon, they'd be coming for the islands themselves.

Chapter 4

SURRENDER AT BATAAN

At some point, I'm not sure when, the decision had been made among the Americans and the British regarding the order in which different theatres of war would be supplied. First priority was Europe, the Pacific second. Within these two broad priorities were further hierarchies of importance, but what it all boiled down to was that we in the Philippines would be left to our own devices until further notice. Abandoned, in effect. There were too many needs and not enough to go around, and that meant that, strategically at least, Washington had decided we would be abandoned.

But that didn't relieve us of our duty—not to mention the practical necessity, if we wanted to survive—of defending the Philippines. And so MacArthur, in the absence of any immediate threat to Luzon, set about gathering his forces, such as they were, to move north from Manila up to Lingayen Gulf, because that's where he expected—correctly—that Japanese forces would land. If you look at a map, you'll see that the mountainous terrain to the northeast and southwest of the gulf, largely unbroken elevations of four to six thousand feet, make Lingayen the only logical landing point for an invasion. A long, broad valley, 75 miles wide, given over primarily to cultivation of rice, stretches south from the gulf, offering an invading force a flat and easily traversed avenue for advancement. And so MacArthur made plans to concentrate his defenses there.

In the years since all these events took place, I've had occasion to read the book *American Caesar*, the famous biography of MacArthur, and I believe the comparison in the title is apt. Caesar was, of course, an emperor, but he was also an accomplished general, leading Roman forces in the field for many years and through many conquests in France, Spain, across the Mediterranean, until Rome controlled the entirety of that area all the way to present-day Iraq. In addition to being brilliant tacticians who commanded an almost awed reverence from their subordinates, both Caesar and MacArthur were, I think it's fair to say, megalomaniacs. Certainly MacArthur was a man of grandiose plans. His objective, at all times, without question or exception, was victory. In war, of course, that meant defeating the enemy, and in peacetime it meant achieving some objective that MacArthur had either been given by civilian command or had set for himself.

But more than anything—and I was convinced of this before I read the book, and am even more convinced of it after having read it—I believe the chief feature of MacArthur's personality was paranoia.

This aspect of MacArthur begins with the fact that his own father was an accomplished and powerful Army officer, who himself had been Governor-General of the Philippines during the initial American occupation. Douglas was considered an obstreperous character, and was sent to serve as an aide to his father because people in Washington, at the War Department, wanted to be rid of him. He was given to these grand schemes and if someone tried to interfere he became very brusque and aggressive, tended to trample on people. He also had a habit of flaunting authority in odd ways that highlighted an individualism the military normally tries to hammer out of people—wearing an unauthorized custom uniform, for example, and refusing to wear a helmet even when in the field. In World War I he was very strict about making sure his men always carried gas masks, but very rarely carried his own.

But his brilliance and bravery as a commander was undeniable, and frequently overrode these quirks of personality in terms of keeping MacArthur from being punished or demoted. Through World War I he commanded the 84th Brigade, was wounded several times and awarded seven Silver Stars. This was not a man who sat back twenty or thirty miles from the action and directed things from some castle—he was always right up in the trenches. Like Napoleon, he drove obsessively and unrelentingly toward the objective, with a goal of always achieving victory as quickly as possible. But despite his aggressiveness, he was also very observant of the principle of war regarding conservation of forces. For example, MacArthur lost fewer men in the three years it took to recapture the Philippines than Eisenhower lost in one week during the Battle of the Bulge. This was due to his preparation—there was no detail too small to consider and analyze and manipulate to his advantage, and as bold as he could be, he would not commit forces to the fight until he was absolutely satisfied that he understood the situation completely and could achieve the upper hand. And there's one aspect of his personality that's particularly relevant to the defense of the Philippines—he never believed he got enough men, equipment, weapons, and supplies from his superiors. If there were any limits, in his mind, to what he could accomplish, they always lay with the fact that others could not or would not provide everything he needed to accomplish an objective. So you can see how this tendency of thought would become enflamed in the days and weeks to come, when we in the Philippines were basically left to fend for ourselves by the American command.

As I mentioned, MacArthur knew well that the natural strategy for the Japanese was to land at Lingayen Gulf, then proceed south toward Manila. But even though he anticipated this and moved forces to counter, it turns out that Manila itself simply cannot be defended successfully. Because the city sits at the east end of Manila Bay, it's vulnerable to attack from too many angles. It can be easily invaded from the water by sea forces that blast their way past Corregidor, and there are no topographical features to prevent land forces approaching from both the north and the south in a classic pincer movement, an encirclement. MacArthur suspected this would be the Japanese strategy, and even though he recognized as well as anyone that the city was essentially indefensible, he still determined to move to protect against this encirclement, setting up defenses in and around Tuguegaro and other towns on the southern end of Lingayen Gulf. And when the Japanese did come they had the bulk of their forces land in that area, as well as a separate invasion force at Batangas, south of Manila. But they did not make an attempt to come in past Corregidor, from the China Sea, and attack Manila from the bay side of the city.

Incidentally, and ironically, this was the route MacArthur would use three years later in January 1945, when he approached Manila with a massive armada, over a thousand ships, and sailed right up into the bay. MacArthur himself, still not content to sit back in Mindanao and direct things from afar, was aboard a Navy cruiser with his binoculars, watching with his own eyes as the ships went in and the troops landed. Of course, the previous September he'd come ashore in Leyte, and that force was now making its way north, and there was also a lot more air power at MacArthur's disposal than the Japanese threw at us in December of 1941.

But all that was to come later. For now he was the hunted, not the hunter.

And there was further bad news to come shortly: the British had been defeated with lightning speed in Singapore. This was not one of Great Britain's finest moments in warfare. Considering the manpower they had there, some 90,000 troops, plenty of aircraft and number of heavy ships, they did not do a good job of strategizing. The biggest mistake was thinking the Japanese couldn't advance through the jungle, and subsequently allowing themselves to be outflanked and soundly defeated by a considerably smaller force. This complicated things for MacArthur in the Philippines, not least because the Japanese commander, General Yamashita, needed to leave only a small force in Singapore to round up the British troops and put them behind barbed wire, and in the meantime he was able to place the bulk of his soldiers on transports to assist in the invasion of Luzon.

But as grim as things looked for us in the Philippines, it was in certain ways even worse elsewhere. The Japanese were also invading New Guinea and Papua and faced little or no opposition there. The seizure of Port Moresby posed a particular problem for the Australians, as it could serve as a perfect springboard for an invasion of the Australian mainland. And sure enough, a very large Japanese task force of some 25 transports accompanied by destroyers, cruisers, two battleships and two aircraft carriers were heading through the Malacca Strait near Java. Aerial reconnaissance, processed and analyzed by military intelligence, concluded that this task force was in fact headed for Australia, and the worry was that the Japanese would land at Darwin, and because the Australians had very few forces with which to defend their own country, soon the entire Western Pacific would be in Japanese hands. Most of Australia's armed forces were committed to fighting with the British in North Africa. There were some minor garrisons in Northern Australia, maybe three to five thousand troops, but no armor and only a handful of aircraft. They were in no position to repel an invading force. But perhaps the saving grace of the Australians was the number of B-17s that had managed, almost accidentally, to escape the carnage in the Philippines. Those bombers, along with others already en route from the United States, landed in Australia, and over the coming months would prove instrumental in holding the massive Japanese ambitions in check. Among other things, these B-17s would catch the task force headed for Australia and beat the bejesus out of it, a defeat that is widely believed to have convinced the Japanese that they had overextended themselves and should shelve any plans of invading Australia.

And in the meantime, the Japanese were busy reinforcing their existing garrison in Guadalcanal, with another task force headed to Wake and Midway Islands. In fact, reinforcements were then landing in nearly all of the far-flung imperial holdings of Japan, including one that would feature arguably the most fearsome battle of the Pacific war: Iwo Jima.

All major countries in the world maintain staff colleges, principally army and navy but a few have air war colleges as well, including the United States. Great Britain has an air war college, at Andover, which I attended for a year in 1954. The principal function of the staff college is to examine and analyze the ground, naval, and air forces of all potential enemies—a list that includes many of your current allies. You shouldn't be aghast to learn that Great Britain maintains detailed plans for an invasion of the United States—not that they'd be able to pull it off. At Andover, we were focused on Pakistan and India. There were eighty of us in the class, divided into eight task groups, each of which had its own particular area of focus, for example, Indian air fields. And over the course of our year there, we had to prepare an actual plan and present it to the staff of the college, which is part of the refinement process, the process of keeping all these plans up to date.

I mention all this because you can be assured that the Japanese were doing these same things in the late 1930s, and in fact we had taught them how to make these plans and why they were necessary, during the period of modernization that transformed Japan in the last decades of the 1800s. In fact, Douglas MacArthur had been with his father when he served as the U.S. military attaché to Japan in 1905. And now that knowledge passed to the Japanese was being used against us. The Japanese staff college no doubt told the military command how to best invade the Philippines, and part of that plan included, as all invasions do, deceit and misdirection.

To that end, the Japanese had come ashore in small numbers at Appari and on the southeastern corner of Mindanao, testing responses, trying to divert and confuse. It was now mid-December and we were seeing ghosts. Wild rumors abounded, ship sightings, submarine sightings, ghost flights over Clark airfield. It was all nonsense. The public relations men at MacArthur's headquarters drafted daily briefs full of nonsense about how prepared we were for a defense of the islands. I'm not sure whether this was intended for the Japanese or for us—maybe both—but the reporters would take these briefs and send them back to their editors in the States without visiting the sites or researching the flack. So there were all kinds of headlines back home about how invulnerable the Philippines were. I don't know if anyone bought it, but if they did they would find out in short order they'd been had.

There was more and more of a sense, quiet but unmistakable, that normal life had come to an end and war was about to envelop us. For one thing, Manila was very, very quiet. The streets weren't abandoned but they no longer teemed like normal; the military had seized trucks and buses for official use, and people largely stayed at home, waiting to see what was next. More ships patrolled the bay. By and large the Filipino populace had no real expectations one way or the other; in fact, President Quezon wanted to go to the Japanese and declare his country open, which you can imagine how MacArthur responded to.

By now it's around December 20th, and a convoy of about 80 Japanese ships is spotted by the American submarine *Triton,* forty miles north of Lingayen Gulf. That same day, 5,000 Japanese troops landed at Davao. This was all good, solid intel, confirmed information. But what to make of it? Davao was on the opposite end of the Philippine archipelago from Manila—was that where the Japanese were planning to invade in earnest? Where was the convoy north of Lingayen actually headed? And did it matter, ultimately, given that with the landing at Davao, and the fact that the Japanese now controlled Borneo, the Philippines were surrounded, completely cut off from supply routes of any kind?

In the meantime, MacArthur's abiding sense of inadequate support (which was quite justified in this instance) kicks in, and he's sending wire after wire after wire to Washington, pleading for help—quite a difference in tone, it goes without saying, from the messages of calm assurance being pumped out every day by his PR officers. But even those began to change, with language theatrical even by MacArthur's standards: The Locus of Victory or Defeat in the Pacific Rests Here in the Philippines. Of course MacArthur, being who he was, always believed the locus of victory or defeat centered on him, but in this case he was correct. But for what are probably obvious reasons, he had not been made aware of the decision that the Philippines were not really going to be defended. After Pearl Harbor, the American forces in the Pacific were shattered, and until those forces could be built up again, the situation in the Philippines was hopeless and there was no sense pretending otherwise and expending what few assets remained on a lost cause.

Because here were the cold, hard facts of the matter: those 80 transports in the water off Luzon held the Japanese 14th Army, between 125 and 130 thousand troops under the command of Lieutenant General Homma. And on December 22nd, these men came over the sides of their ships, boarded landing craft, and despite very heavy surf that day, landed successfully on the eastern side of Lingayen Gulf.

MacArthur's plan to hold the Japanese at the beaches proved completely untenable. The 11th and 71st Divisions collapsed almost immediately, and while the Philippine 26th Cavalry put up a better fight, they were forced to withdraw after sustaining significant casualties with no hope of reinforcement.

And in no time at all, the Japanese were ten miles inland and advancing fast down Highway #3. As had been the case in Singapore, the Japanese were outnumbered, but the Filipino forces were simply not capable of going toe-to-toe with a seasoned, well-equipped army. It wasn't their fault—there had been no time to train them. They could do little more than parade and salute. Equipment baffled them. They had no concept of tactics, not even the commanders. And they had no communication infrastructure. They were just warm bodies in some semblance of a formation. Easy pickings for the Japanese.

With no air force or navy, MacArthur had to abandon his cherished strategy of pinning the Japanese to the beaches. Which meant he had to consider the General War Plan from the Army War College. It called for the withdrawal into Bataan and defense of Manila Bay. MacArthur hated this plan—he considered it a defeatist move—but already the landings on Luzon had succeeded and the pressure was becoming too great and the Japanese were pouring south and it became obvious that there was no other choice. So MacArthur called in his staff and ordered War Plan Orange #3 into effect. The hope was simple: a last-ditch defensive effort that could hold out for maybe six months, perhaps long enough for the Navy to send in supplies and reinforcements.

The senior officer in the field was General Jonathan Wainwright, and as reports came in of the various divisions collapsing, abandoning tanks, the 26th Cavalry routed in the foothills, Skinny Wainwright took what is known in military euphemism as a strategic withdrawal. Now, whether it was strategic is open to debate, but it was definitely a withdrawal. He pulled south to the Agno River and set defenses there, hoping that, with reinforcements sent north by MacArthur, he could mount a counterattack against the Japanese.

In the meantime, I'm flying missions in an old 52, which is not much of a plane as far as combat is concerned, but it did have .30-caliber machine guns, just about enough firepower for a good pheasant hunt. We got a report that a bunch of parachutes had been observed on the west coast of the Bataan Peninsula, out near Subic Bay. We flew out there but didn't find anything. And otherwise I was flying straight reconnaissance missions, up the central San Fernando plain, on toward Tarlac, at times near Baguio to check if there were any Japanese troops coming across the hills toward the summer capital. And I flew missions out over the China Sea, looking for groups of Japanese ships. I saw a handful here and there in the distance, but never anything resembling a group heading for Corregidor to attack Manila directly, which was the primary concern in my area of operations.

And speaking of Manila, by now the city was quite subdued. The writing was very much on the wall, only a matter of time before the Japanese came in, and in certain ways things started feeling decidedly apocalyptic. For example, the Navy had ordered the fuel tanks and repair facilities in Kivini, on the south shore, to be destroyed, and those facilities burned for days, filling the air with a thick smoke that made it hard to breathe. People are fleeing, everyone and everything in uniform headed north out of Manila to Bataan.

General Brereton went to MacArthur and suggested he and his staff evacuate to Australia, regroup down there and plan for a return some day. MacArthur is supposed to have said to Brereton, "I hope you'll tell the people outside what we've done and protect my reputation as a fighter."

In the meantime, President Quezon was preparing to flee to Corregidor, and after he did in fact leave and word got around, the feeling spread that maybe the jig was up—when the President heads for the hills, after all, that seems like a pretty bad sign. By this time the streets of Manila were a parking lot, with trucks and buses waiting hours in the hot sun to move, but also strangely quiet—everyone was patient, resigned, nobody blowing their horns or cursing each other out. There was a fatalism to it all. I'd never seen or felt anything quite like it.

The higher-ranking officers, including General Brereton, were evacuating, and at least in the air corps, where our headquarters was being plucked like a chicken, it caused a massive amount of confusion on top of the chaos of retreat—no one knew who was in command. Things at Nielson Field were just as chaotic. What was left of the 27th Bomber Group was told to move to Bataan, the explanation being that Manila had been declared an open city to spare it further bombing by the Japanese. Calls to Fort McKinley, the army base ten miles east of Manila, got no response. So you can see that by this point the entire superstructure of the military forces had begun to disintegrate.

There were some fighter aircraft still operational, but they were severely limited by the lack of airfields—everything that would have put them in range of targets of opportunity had been destroyed. Clark, of course, was a shambles, and the airfield at Del Carmen, the 34th Pursuit Squadron, had been turned to rubble. But the Army Corps of Engineers (which, incidentally, had been MacArthur's outfit for the first fifteen years or so of his career) had somehow managed a feat of impressive ingenuity amidst all the running around and falling back.

About twenty miles southwest of Clark Field was a great expanse of sugarcane fields, and by that time of the year the harvest was in, all the fields cut down and prickly with stubble from the stalks. So the engineers went in with their excavators and scraped the fields level. But what they did next was a real stroke of genius. The byproduct of sugarcane processing is a substance they called centrifuge, a thick, gooey paste full of pebbles and dirt and straw, ultimately not unlike pavement. So the engineers, when they were finished leveling the field, went out with truckloads of centrifuge and poured it onto the field, and in the hot sun it hardened into a pretty good surface for a runway. What's more, this surface kept the dust down, so Japanese planes aloft couldn't see the dust of a takeoff or landing and take a pop at the plane in question.

With the Japanese 14th Army pounding away at the meager defenses that remained, and the Filipinos outgunned and undertrained and lacking supplies and ammunition, and a limited number of Americans and his best soldiers, the 26th Cavalry, having taken massive losses, MacArthur finally had to admit it was over, at least for Manila. The Japanese were advancing at will, almost as if unopposed. The best MacArthur could do was fall back to Corregidor himself, pick a spot on the map that could be reasonably defended, and do what he could to extend the defense of Bataan as long as possible.

Substantial volume of supplies had already been streaming into Bataan for two months—ammunition (though this was always in short supply no matter what), food stocks, bamboo huts that served as barracks, and so on. But now, at a time when it was of paramount importance that the flow of men and materiel be unimpeded, it was suddenly gridlock out on the highway. I mean, just utter confusion and paralysis. Because as the military tried to move north, a flood of civilians fleeing the advancing Japanese army rushed south, cars, wagons, horse carts, bicycles, any kind of vehicle you could think of, people got in it and on it and ran for their lives. And now all those people and soldiers, all those carts and trucks and buses and horse carts, were stuck facing each other out in the open on the highway. Why the Japanese didn't come in out of Formosa and strafe the bejesus out of everyone, I have no idea. That would have been the end of everything, right then and there.

It was now December 24th, Christmas Eve, when a large Japanese force landed at Atimonan on the southeast corner of Luzon, and they proceeded west to Santiago to meet up with another force that had landed at Maubon, thereby cinching the circle around Manila, and that was it for the capital. The only remaining route of escape was to head west toward Calumpit, because the bridges over Manila Bay had been blown up by General Jones, so as not to leave them for the Japanese to use. The problem was that 80,000 people, including all support services, nurses, quartermasters, repair companies, transport companies, tank repair, some aircraft, still had yet to flee. And so everyone barreled in a rush to Calumpit, all 80,000 with their vehicles and supplies counting on one small two-lane bridge to get them to safety. And here's another instance when one has to wonder why the Japanese didn't take advantage. Why didn't they bomb the bridge at Calumpit? If they'd done that, the retreat was so cumbersome and slow the allied forces would have been dead ducks. Maybe the Japanese just didn't realize the opportunity, maybe they were too myopically focused on Manila, which was a fait accompli anyway. But whatever the reason, the bridge remained intact and most everyone escaped into Bataan.

For my part, I flew out the same day Manila fell—Christmas Day 1941. I took off from the little grass field south of Del Carmen, and I landed on the east coast of the Bataan Peninsula. And obviously this mode of retreat was much easier for me than for most, who were stuck on the ground amidst the heat and the chaos, wondering if they would escape before the Japanese descended and it was all over.

Part of the reason Bataan was chosen in War Plan Orange #3 was because it was hilly, rather rugged country, which made it, depending on your perspective, either easy to defend or difficult to attack. My unit, the 2nd Observation Squadron was down to just three planes. That was the bad news. The good news was they were all the same type—old 52s. Which meant that, in the absence of replacement parts, we could cannibalize two of the planes to keep the third one in the air. And these planes were weary, so we indeed had to strip parts from one plane to keep the other ones working. In this way, we were able to keep doing our job, which was, of course, to get into the air and spot the enemy. I spent a lot of my time flying north to look for ships and Japanese troops, because by then a force had landed in the southern part of Bataan, at Mariveles, and command was worried about another pincer move, a landing in the north that would be game over. I never saw any ships or troops, but one day, as I looked shoreward three or four miles, I did see a massive turmoil in the water, almost like a whirlpool. And I thought, that certainly merits a closer look. So I cut in toward the shore and descended from three or four thousand feet, and I saw, as I skimmed in over the water, a building on the shore, two stories with a fifty foot chute extending down into the water. It turned out this building was a slaughterhouse, and all the offal and sinew and hooves and what have you were thrown down the chute, where the sharks were feasting on it. That's what I had seen from three or four miles distant—hundreds of sharks, tigers and makos and reef sharks, all in a frenzy over this endless stream of meat and guts flowing into the water. It was an impressive sight.

Another time, me and Mercer were ordered to fly behind the Japanese lines to Nielson Field, where reports were there might be some operational aircraft. So I jumped into the one functional 52, and Mercer took a real old plane, I don't even remember what kind, but truly decrepit, as befit the overall situation, and we indeed flew into Nielson as if it had never fallen into Japanese hands. Because of course the Japanese, having secured Manila, were largely in and around Bataan, and had no use for an airfield they'd blown into gravel. And we did find one airplane. It was a 19, an observation plane, with corrugated sides and a tin roof, the first all-metal plane in the Army Air Corps, better suited than wood for the climate of the tropics.

By now, the main line of resistance (that's army jargon for the point at which you're going to defend) ran from Agack to LaMau, and we went with our aircraft south to Limac, another dirt field put together by the artful engineers, this one carved into the side of a hill and as a consequence quite scary to get into and out of. And at this point we're down to two meals a day, a preview of the outright starvation to come. And don't think for a second that we're getting hot meals with all the fixings, vegetables and salads and coconut cream pie, all the coffee you can drink. Or even the occasional can of beer. Not so. It being the tropics, our rations were tinned, and we referred to the meat as bully beef. Much of that, because it was British, came from Argentina. We had lots of rice, of course, some of it good, some of it dreadful, not refined or even sifted, you could break your teeth on a hidden pebble. And whereas Army regulations called for each soldier to receive 4,200 calories a day, I'd be surprised if at this point we were getting any more than 1,200-1,400 calories. So out of self-preservation, or desperation, or both, we began scavenging for anything that might be edible.

One time, I ran into some fellas from the 90th Artillery, bedded up in the hills. They really wanted my officer's sidearm, a .45 Colt revolver, why not an automatic like most officers carried I never asked or knew. And so being the hard bargainer I am, I talked them into trading me a dozen hand grenades for the gun. Now understand, this is a serious military offense—you don't give up your arms, not even to friends. But when you get as hungry as we were, and when you're feeling as abandoned as we did, well, those sorts of hard and fast rules suddenly don't seem to apply quite as much. And I had a plan for the grenades—you see, I was going to go fishing. Waded out into the water, a couple other guys with me, pulled the pin and tossed the grenade away, and after a few seconds, BAM, a big plume of water would shoot up into the air, and you could feel the concussion in your legs through the water. And it was the concussion that got the job done, you see. After a few seconds the fish, knocked dead by the concussion, would come floating to the surface, and we'd gather them and have a bellyful of fresh protein. But those grenades only lasted so long, and as time went on, the food situation got worse. Any of the locals who had animals—ducks and chickens, pigs, you name it—didn't have them for long. Those animals were stolen, plain and simple, by the ground troops. Some soldiers killed and ate monkeys, if they could find them. We also, occasionally, would get horse or mule meat from the 26th Cavalry. But mostly it was ducks, in part because of a truly disgusting Filipino delicacy known as balut.

Balut is a fertilized duck egg that's allowed to develop for a couple of weeks, then boiled or steamed and eaten from the shell. What you end up with is a featherless, shiny, translucent little thing that looks like exactly what it is—a duck that hadn't finished developing—alongside a yolk that by this point has become more like a placenta and less like the sunny little yolks you're used to seeing in a chicken egg from the store. Full of veins and such. As I said, disgusting.

A little sidebar story about my introduction to balut. A few months before, in September of 1941, while stationed at Clark Field, I used to go to the upper post frequently, to the quarters of Captain Rago, who was a dentist. Mercer and I and a few others went regularly to play poker. One night after supper, before we played poker, we decided to go down to Angeles, and there was a furniture factory down there owned by one Sol Tinio, and at the end of his furniture warehouse was a little bar. We decided to go down there for a few beers and have a look around, something different to do. When we were leaving, each of us with three or four beers in us, enough to perhaps make it seem like a good idea, someone challenged Captain Rago to eat a balut. They cost ten centavos, or five American cents. Now, Rago's putting on a good show of bravado, waving his hands in a theatrical kind of way, telling us all to stand back and watch him show how it's done. Meanwhile, of course, he no more wants to eat this egg than he wants to cut off his own hand. But the challenge had been issued, the bet made, and we all walked down from the bar to the courtyard to see if Rago could back up his bluster. Finally, Rago cracks the egg, peels it, down the hatch it goes. And the thing with Balut is, you can't just swallow it—remember, this is a half-formed bird in there, with bones and everything, you have to chew it. And Rago's chewing for all he's worth, trying hard to make it seem like no big deal, and then suddenly it all goes sideways on him, the balut and the beer and his dinner all coming up at once. And of course we had a big laugh at his expense. And that's balut for you. I don't think I would have been able to eat one even later when I was starving in the camps.

But we were already pretty hungry in the winter of 1942, food of any kind growing scarce, fresh food nonexistent, so that by the time the Japanese finally overwhelmed the peninsula in April we were already pretty weak, didn't have any stamina or drive, and we weren't starting our time as POWs in a place of great physical health. I say that to give you an idea of why it was so difficult for so many men to survive what was to come—we were already significantly weakened before it even began.

Anyway, on Bataan there was one and only one road that ran along the coast, and in addition to the lack of food and the tropical heat and the general malaise of a terrible situation, one of the things that wore us down was how exposed we were on that road, how easy it was for the Japanese to come in and bomb the hell out of us whenever we had to venture out on that road during daylight. And in the meantime, with almost no functional aircraft left at our disposal, me and others from my unit were instructed to join the infantry. I reported and was sent to take over Second Platoon, C Company, Third Battalion, Sixth Regiment under V Corps under command of MacArthur's headquarters. Now I knew nothing—and I mean not the first thing—about infantry skills or tactics, no grasp of what was going on. The only thing I knew about trench or other infantry fighting was what I read in the newspaper, the same as any other person off the street who had no business running an infantry platoon. Attacking, retreating, maneuvering, how and where and under what circumstances to use the different skills and specialties in a platoon, I had no idea. But the Filipinos, of course, didn't have the leadership from their own officers, and by this time they were ready to run anyway, thoroughly demoralized and anxious to just get back to their villages, they'd had enough of that mess on Bataan and wanted no part of it anymore. Hence the reason for taking us as spares and turning us into so-called infantry officers.

I was in a few engagements—thank god nothing that fierce, but enough to know I could stand up there and take fire from the enemy without either soiling myself or running away. Periodically the Japanese would throw artillery at us, just to terrorize and harass, and we'd take to the foxholes and just sit and wait, dirty and weary, for the bombardment to end. The shells were big, one hundred, one hundred and fifty pounds. And needless to say, it was a depressing feeling. You were thinking, the next one is for me. The next shell is for me. My name is on it. For hours, you'd think this way.

By February 1942 MacArthur has fallen back to Corregidor, and General "Skinny" Wainwright was in command on Bataan. It was around this time that a peculiar example of the kind of psychological tactics that take place during a siege happened. It turned out Skinny was quite a boozer, in noncombat situations, in his downtime (and who knows, maybe all the time, but the rumor was he liked his sauce when he wasn't on duty). Now, Japanese reconnaissance planes regular came in over us, and one time when I was at Lamon one of these planes dropped, of all things, a bunch of beer cans. Inside the beer cans was a little written message (and I wish I had one of these today, it would be quite the little trophy to have) that read, in good English, something like "Hey Skinny, why don't you come over to the Army and Navy club and have a few beers? And a fifth of scotch?" Taunting Wainwright, of course. But it was also intended as propaganda, to make us question our leadership, lessen the will to fight, and kill morale, which given the circumstances was already pretty low.

In the middle of February I was relieved of command of the infantry platoon and sent over to Corregidor to again do the job for which I had been trained and for which I was much better qualified. They had the 19 that Mercer and I had recovered at Nielson Field, and while it was not state of the art, nor was it in terrific shape, it did fly. And so my job was to take turns with another pilot taking this old 19 up and flying southeast along the shore of Bataan province, the south shore of Manila bay, scouting for gun emplacements. Because the Japanese had brought guns in and were lobbing shells at Corregidor, keeping everyone's head under cover and generally making life difficult. And the shellings were erratic, unpredictable, the Japanese wanting to establish no pattern so they might catch people outside, and so there was never a time when we didn't worry that the shells could come screaming in at any moment.

The one place you could go on Corregidor at this time and be safe from shelling and bombing was Malinta Tunnel. If you look at the island on a map, you see it runs east to west, kind of looks like a polliwog. It's about two and a half miles long, maybe half a mile wide, and at the eastern end of Corregidor is Malinta Tunnel, bored out of a hill about three hundred feet tall. A railroad track ran through the main tunnel, and off the main tunnel were about ten laterals on each side, ammunition storage, hospital, repair facilities for trucks and guns, and so on. This tunnel was where MacArthur had set up his headquarters, and because I was in and out of the tunnel frequently

I saw him many times, even spoke with him on a few occasions. He was a very imposing person, with his specially-made field commander's cap, all the braid on it, very non-regulation, but then MacArthur was MacArthur. Always very natty and clean, puffing away on his corncob pipe, his strides long and steady, bent forward a little at the waist, *forever* contemplating some move or another.

On toward the end of March the old 19 was kaput, no replacement parts to keep it functional, so it was abandoned and, my usefulness on Corregidor having expired, I was sent back to Bataan, and I ended up at a small field near on the southern tip of the Peninsula. They had a couple of aircraft that were still operational, but we didn't really do much of anything. There was no fuel most of the time, for one thing, and even when there was fuel there was often no oil, and I guess it goes without saying there were no replacement parts here, either. But I did fly a few times, on up toward Calumpit, north of the mainland, looking for troop movement or transports, any sign that the Japanese were bringing in reinforcements and/or planning to redouble their efforts to finally break through in Bataan. As it stood, they were getting herded into a kind of funnel as they tried to enter the peninsula, and they would get in their own way and bog down, and because they couldn't bring all their forces to bear at once, our defenses were such that we could hold them at bay.

It was around this time—mid-March, the Ides of March, wouldn't you know it—that word started spreading MacArthur had left Corregidor for Mindanao, then had flown on a B-17 to Australia. This news was a terrible blow to us, maybe more demoralizing than anything else could have been. We knew to a man, right then, that the jig was up. By now we could all recite the limerick "The Battling Bastards of Bataan," written by Frank Hewlett, the bureau chief in the Philippines for United Press, and the last reporter to leave Corregidor:

We're the battling bastards of Bataan
No mama, no papa, no Uncle Sam
No aunts, no uncles, no cousins, no nieces
No pills, no planes, no artillery pieces
And nobody gives a damn
Nobody gives a damn.

Because the British had succumbed in Singapore, and the Dutch in Java hadn't put up any fight at all, and the Australians didn't have enough forces to protect their own territory, let alone mount any kind of offensive against the Japanese, the Japanese were in turn, with

Tokyo's approval of course, comfortable moving forces from Singapore to help with a final push in the Philippines. They were landing at will in Lingayen—just pouring these troops in under General Yamashita. And when he arrived with 30,000 additional troops, Yamashita took over command, brought in all the supplies and armament and ammunition they needed, and then, when he had everything arranged the way he wanted, he mounted a massive attack against what was left of us in Bataan. This was the 28th of March, and the assault was so overwhelming that after months of holding out, it was all over by April 2nd. Our defenses crumbled, the Japanese poured through at will, and on April 6th Skinny Wainwright went north up the perimeter highway flying the white flag of surrender.

Over the next several days there was still sporadic fighting as Wainwright and his aides discussed terms of surrender with the Japanese. Except the Japanese weren't acquiescing to any terms—they were determined our surrender be unconditional. One day during negotiations, a Japanese aide said to Wainwright, in good English, "What do you think we are, barbarians? You don't have to demand these things of the Japanese." He was, of course, lying through his teeth, because they were a murderous bunch of monsters, as we would soon find out.

And the truth is, the victory came at a great cost for the Japanese. They lost about 14,000 men, and most of their remaining soldiers were just as beset as we were with beriberi, malaria, the diseases common to the tropics. For us, the sickness was due to malnutrition and lack of medicine. The Japanese had medicine and so recovered faster, but overall their forces were in pretty poor shape by the time the end came.

Needless to say, life for Filipinos changed radically, overnight. In my limited time there prior to the war, six months or so, I observed life as being casual, slow-paced, and serene. It was island life—there were plenty of customs that governed behavior and expectations, but little in the way of official or legal guidelines.

For example, the concept of "cunsha" was widespread. Our Chinese cook would go out in the morning to buy us 3 rolls for ten centavos. His "cunsha" for the transaction—"cunsha" means percentage, but you can think of it almost like a commission—was one free roll for himself. He brought the baker a little business, and he was rewarded. So you see what I mean by customs—the baker knew what was expected, our cook knew what was expected, but there were no rules or laws governing cunsha, just the understanding between them of how things were done.

Similarly, in the Philippines there were really no banks. Banks existed in Manila, of course, but not like a branch bank, the kind of place where regular people could go in and deposit or withdraw money. Instead, if you lived in a barrio and needed to borrow money, you went to the local Chinese, who usually controlled private lending. They usually had a little shop, and often their currency was rice. Rice being a seasonal crop, many Filipinos were out of work for three or four months of the year. They would go to the lender, and he would give them a ten-kilo bag of rice. When those same Filipinos got their share of the crop the following year, they would repay ten kilos and pay ten more kilos in interest. All these unofficial, socially run systems of getting by were wiped out by the Japanese.

The Filipino Peso, meanwhile, quality currency backed by the American government, was removed from circulation before the Japanese victory. The paper money was burned, and the coinage was brought to Corregidor and buried until after the war, when it was recovered. So the Japanese brought in their own Peso that they turned out in a printing press somewhere in Japan. It was worthless, of course, with nothing backing it but the promises of the Japanese government. Certainly the Filipinos had zero confidence in it. But they needed some kind of currency to work with, something to exchange for goods and services, so it was accepted but scorned. And it was through this phony money that the Japanese immediately began looting the Philippines, as they had other countries in the Pacific. This thievery was the real work of their so-called "Co-Prosperity Sphere," which was only about Japanese prosperity, of course. They used their worthless money to buy up all the resources in the Philippines, engaging in a systematic and purposeful denuding of the country. And though they "paid" for everything, or most everything, the money had no actual value, so everyone involved, the Japanese most of all, knew the whole charade amounted to nothing more than mass theft.

It's worth mentioning, too, in contemplating the transition of power from the Americans to the Japanese, that the Filipinos were very loyal to us throughout the war. America was in charge, we were a colonial presence, but we did not exploit and abuse the Filipinos the way others had—the Spanish, for example. All the European colonial powers in the Pacific, particularly the British, had a well-earned reputation for taking whatever they wanted and offering little in return but disdain and maltreatment. So by comparison, at least, America seemed pretty good to the Filipinos. And because of that, they held out for five months against the Japanese, and that as much as anything was an essential part of slowing the Japanese takeover of the Pacific down so that America could gather itself for the purpose of fighting back. Even though the Philippines succumbed, we owed them a debt for having held on as long as they did. It cost the Japanese troops, supplies, and time, three things in very limited supply to them.

I should also discuss briefly, for the purposes of understanding the different elements at work during the Japanese occupation, the social structure in the Philippines. At the top of the heap, of course, were the Spaniards, the old-time families that had been there since the conquest some 300 years prior. They were the absolute upper crust, not unlike the Boston Brahmin. The Spanish families were very wealthy, owning beer breweries, import/export and shipping, heavily into pineapples and gold mining, the production of lumber and hardwood goods. Below the Spaniards, small in number but powerful due to their money lending system, were the Chinese, who were also invested in coconuts and lumber. Below the Chinese were the mestizos, which was the Spanish word for "mixed"—people of Spanish and Filipino or Chinese and Filipino ancestry. They had large holdings in agriculture and other businesses. Below the mestizos were the petty businessmen, who were not too numerous, and below them were the great mass of peasants and blue-collar workers. And superimposed on this whole caste system was the fact of indentured servitude, which meant you worked for ten, fifteen, twenty years, and at the end of that time, in theory at least, you became free to move around and decide your own fate. But there was a catch, and a wicked one at that. Because the son had to assume the debts of the father, and so on down the generations, so there was effectively no way to free oneself of the obligation to work for someone else for next to nothing.

Now the Spaniards and the Chinese and the mestizos, being wealthy and well-educated and connected in Filipino society, suddenly found themselves in pretty grave danger once the Japanese took over. Because the Japanese knew where the power was and, like any dictatorship, they meant to clear out the power structure, just as communism first attacks the pulpit. You take out the clergy, then the businesspeople, then the intellectuals. This was what the Japanese meant to do, so the rich, by and large, fled the country. If they couldn't get off the island they went to the hills, where they could hide successfully because the Japanese had relatively few troops on the island and no natives loyal to them.

These were the backdrop circumstances under which my time as a prisoner of war began.

Chapter 5

DEATH MARCH

The Japanese aide's protest to Wainwright notwithstanding, these were not a humanitarian people. They had been brought up in the belief that the white man was a devil. And to a certain degree, when taking in the colonial history of that part of the world, this attitude squared with their experience. There's the Englishmen in Hong Kong, the Spanish and then the Americans in the Philippines, the Dutch down in Java, the British again in New Guinea, and of course the Australians and New Zealanders. Such omnipresence of the white man. Europeans and Americans in Asia were the reason Japan could not expand the way it wished to, the way it needed to. Every place they went, they were bumping into a white man. There was a deep-rooted resentment of this within the Japanese, and that motivated a lot of their inhumane behavior.

Plus, they were people in a hurry, the Japanese. And remember, when Bataan surrendered, Corregidor was still fighting for more than a month—they had artillery and a substantial number of troops. And because the Japanese were in a hurry to put an end to that, they couldn't be bothered with those of us on Bataan. They wanted to build up their troops and entrenchments on the peninsula, and they didn't want us in the way while they did so. And as such, out of Yamashita's headquarters came the order to get us out of there, on the double, as it were. So we got our instructions for surrender—we had to go to predetermined spots, turn in our weapons and ammunition, stack it all up and move to the southern tip of the peninsula, Mariveles, from which began what became known as the Death March.

The Death March was called that not because of the distance we had to travel—it was relatively short, only 65 miles give or take for most men, a distance a reasonably healthy man could conquer in his boots under normal conditions. It was the conditions, however, under which the Japanese forced us to march that turned it into a de facto massacre. We were given no food or water or medical care, just driven like cattle up that perimeter road, summer coming on and daytime temperatures reaching over one hundred degrees, no cover. We weren't allowed to wear hats to protect us from the sun—just about everything the Japanese could think of to make us miserable, they did, and did with an evil kind of glee. Mind you, this was the hot season in the Philippines, the kind of heat ready-made to inflict mental and physical anguish when put into the hands of these monstrous Japanese guards introducing their codes of Japanese superiority. This "sun treatment" as we'd soon call it would become routine. The Filipinos marched in front, followed by enlisted American men, with the officers in the rear—all a means to degrade the American soldier and his senior officers. And by the way, you learned quickly not to announce that you were an officer, because we were the ones to get it in the neck first. Not a slap in the neck with an open hand, rather a bayonet quite literally through the neck. So a typical group would be about a thousand or fifteen hundred prisoners, only twenty or so Japanese guards to push the group along, with a sergeant who would be in charge of the whole group. Starting from Mariveles on that southern tip of the Bataan Peninsula in the Philippines, they would march us deliberately in the heat of the day.

On the first day of the march, they rounded us up at about 9 am, shoved us into a column formation and then we wouldn't move for an hour, but you weren't allowed to sit down, either, and if you did that'd be the end of you. People fainting from exposure, from exhaustion, and we'd have to hold them up or one of these sadistic guards would come by and pop the guy, put a bullet right through his head. They seemed to think this was a good way of getting everyone else's attention.

"We're in deep shit, sir," said the young man from Oregon who looked every bit of 15 years old, scared and overwhelmed. To be fair, we were all scared and overwhelmed, myself included.

"Be prepared for the worst and focus on the best-case scenario," I advised.

"They'll kill us all," he said. "The Japs murder Americans like a fish swims—it's what they do."

For the first day on the march we were introduced to starvation and what life is like without water. No food at all, and no water; the only water available to us was from puddles on the road, and even that we couldn't really access because anyone who fell out of line for even a few seconds—for example, to stoop over and drink quickly from a puddle—a guard at the back of the column would aim his rifle and *zippo*. I couldn't sleep a wink that night as we settled into a night under the stars. The thirst follows you to bed, maybe it's even worse at night because you're stationary and consumed in tortuous thought about water. Time barely passes at night on account of the thirst, and each second is a dastardly reminder that you are, without debate, dying of thirst. At the end of the second day or marching up to Lamao, the thirst overcame me. I had, of course, felt thirst in my life to this point, but having this feeling of approaching death due to thirst was new and unbearable. Unfortunately, it would become a more familiar reality as this journey for us captives was only beginning. I had to get moisture in my mouth or I was going to pass out or run towards a guard's gun to eat a bullet and put me out of my misery. So on occasion, we'd see the roadside puddle formed despite the heat. It was more like a muddy pile of slop than a puddle, but it housed dirty water and had moisture. From under my brow-eyes always cast downward per order of the Japanese captors I spotted a mud puddle approaching, let's say about twenty feet up at 2 o'clock. It was partially occupied by a dead horse and dead Filipino soldier, but I didn't care. I had to drink something. Two other American soldiers soon knelt beside me, one taking a bayonet straight through his heart within two feet of me for daring to hydrate. Before the guard could raise his bayonet and stab me dead, I shot up like a spooked pheasant and hustled back into the columns of dying men and blended into the pack. He either chose to not pursue me or couldn't find me. I sure did hope another prisoner did not pay the price in a case of revenge or mistaken identity.

We marched until one in the afternoon or so the first couple days, at what would be considered a moderate pace if not for the heat and how weak and sick we all were—understand, there were many of us already so weak on miniscule rations leading up to this fiasco that even a few steps at any pace seemed impossible, and yet we walked, and kept walking, long after we thought we couldn't possibly go on. And those who reached their breaking point, those who literally could not take another step, were shot in the road, or else run over by trucks following the column, or simply left for the wild dogs, what have you. I suppose they could have tried to march us into late afternoon but I suspect they wanted to have a few survivors for reasons beyond me. The formula, it appeared, was to march from about 9 am to 1 pm and have a significant number of men die, but not all.

Perhaps now is a reasonable time to recall a particularly horrible experience from the march as it happened here on Day 4 as we headed to Balanga. Please understand that I have kept these memories to myself for good reason and I don't mean to horrify anyone so I will not detail everything I saw in the march. But for starters, I had never seen a fella murdered in my life. That, in itself, was all new to me on those first few days. I had seen the occasional bruised eye or beaten up ego, of course, in my travels around my Boston neighborhood, but I had never seen a man killed. We'd have the fisticuffs in those days back home as kids and I admittedly had to insert myself on occasion from the culture conflicts of the time and place, but no, no one was ever killed. The Italians, Polish, Irish etc. in Boston were parochial types, and we lived in neighborhoods with cultural alignment, but we ironed things out usually without much physicality on the occasion that we crossed paths and had issues with other groups. We did have a boxing match in the street here and there, but from what I recall, a fight stopped right away when the lesser man said it was over. There was a principle to it. I most certainly had never seen a boy physically assaulted to the point of nearing his death. That was foul play, of course. You can imagine then, to my horror, what it was like to see a young soldier buried alive that day. This poor soul had been buried up to his neck with only his head left unburied. I couldn't definitively tell if he was buried horizontally or vertically, just his head showing.

I will not soon forget, ever forget, that young man screaming for his life through his agonizing tears. A mother's child screaming for my help. The moral dilemma twisting inside of me was a matter of life and death, and I was prescient enough to know what would come if I attempted to assist him. Every Christian cell in my body was compelling me to veer out of the column and help this boy. Doing so was suicide, though, immediate lights out. Perhaps it was this maddening helplessness that nearly—I recall, *very* nearly—caused me to lose my own life in that moment when I spotted that sharp-tipped shovel and thought briefly about taking a guard's life with it. A one for one trade, I contemplated, as the boy screamed for help. But I decided my life was worth more than the guard's life—no deal. I let the shovel be and the guard lived for now. Those of us who wanted to live would grit our teeth and cast our beaten eyes downward as we marched up this road. The young man buried alive would die that day. There was no chance of survival in his case. No funeral, no record of his death unless someone in the columns knew him by name and saw what happened. A mother back in the US would probably never know the horrors of her son's death, and maybe that is a good thing. I can't say. All I know, it was a death in ways that future generations may not quite appreciate, not as much as we did on that damn road, marching and dying for the ideals and freedoms of the United States of America. But that's all we knew then, let's face it. We had to march on or die that day. Nonetheless, the face of that soldier buried alive and the wretched sounds he made that day are not an abstract, fuzzy memory for me. They are crystal clear.

Like most of the fellas in this wicked situation, I began to think about what lay ahead, odds, likelihoods, and such coming down fast on a young man. Each train of thought ended in a bad place, generally with a vision of loosely scattered dirt over my lifeless body. I decided it was time to adjust my thinking. Japanese prison camp awaited me, and it didn't take a Harvard man to deduce that reality and what would be coming with it. I would be in for some hard time, that seemed the best case. The worst case was death, and potentially in a cruel and painful way. The question to be asked—no, the adjustment to be made—was how I could turn this hardship into an elevated plane of thought. To be diligent about living a life of observation and thinking, to "tire of everything but understanding" as Aristotle would advise in my college philosophy books, perhaps could get me out of this thing alive and not go mad as a loon by the time I get home. *Get smart, son,* just like dad would tell me when I misbehaved as a child. My mind must be occupied by a thinking man's narratives, not the desperate or unrealistic thoughts of a broken man being tortured by his enemy.

So at this beginning stage of this march and now living life as a prisoner of war, I had begun to make this necessary adjustment in thinking. I was beginning to gather some strength of mind, in fact, as I did so. Now on about day 5 or 6 of the march, still shuffling onward to an unknown destination, I still had all my belongings which created a fleeting sense of being alive, in that way that having "stuff" creates an illusion of existence and worth. I had everything in my B-4 bag, clothes and personal items and letters and such. But that had become too heavy to carry on the march and I was forced to start abandoning things. The first thing that went was my flying jacket, a beautiful coat, gorgeous doeskin, really a prized possession that I certainly wish I had today, so many experiences embedded in that jacket—and I just tossed it on the side of the road like it was nothing. I had never had a jacket like that growing up in a modest home with kids living on top of each other in tight space. Discarding it went against everything I had ever been taught to appreciate. Thinking intelligently under duress is not easy and I wondered in real-time if I was being foolish to discard it, but I knew that leaving the jacket was the only course of action available to me. It had to be done. The second-guessing came more with my canteens. I had gathered two canteens of water off fallen men, and one of them I tossed if you can believe that after much internal deliberation. Weight like this, even a pound or two, was life and death. We marched, got more and more weary, and you just get rid of things, just don't care anymore. After a while, a five-pound musette bag, a shoulder bag, became unbearable, so burdensome you could think of nothing except being rid of it. As the bodies of once-fit, capable men starting lining the roads in motionless, broken forms of the dead, the notion of material belongings having any value or use went out the window for me. I was after very simple things now—water, food, and putting one foot in front of the other while not giving the hairy eyeball glance that I so desperately wanted to give these Japanese guards who were getting increasingly agitated and murderous. That can happen, I suppose, when brainwashed armed men take control of larger, unarmed enemies.

The Japanese had promised us, on several occasions, that there would be transportation of some kind, but it never materialized, of course. Keep in mind that we're still fighting a war, and we'd caused them a lot of misery and losses and they hadn't forgotten it. Which is not to excuse the way they treated us, merely to explain the situation and what I think was at work. I don't need to condemn these men and the way they treated us; history will condemn them for the abuse they visited on all those they conquered. And I knew that they'd ultimately be judged by war tribunals and, I would imagine, in some instances, their own conscience if they had such a thing. My purpose here is merely to report accurately what happened and how we were treated and, where I think it's possible to say, why we were treated that way.

And part of what happened was not malevolence, but simple incompetence. For example, the Japanese underestimated how poor the condition was of most of their prisoners. We were severely malnourished at the start, sick with malaria and dysentery, and by contrast the Japanese were relatively well-fed and healthy. Further, they had no idea how many people they would be dealing with. They thought around 35,000; it was more than double that number. So as the soldiers, sailors, marines, and airmen began turning in their weapons and collecting at the tip of the peninsula, the Japanese quickly became overwhelmed. And it wasn't just military personnel—there were around 25,000 Filipinos, none of whom lived in Bataan, who drifted down the valley in front of the Japanese invasion and now had to be dealt with, had to be moved out of the way as surely as we did. So all in all, the Japanese had about 100,000 people on their hands, and their plan, insofar as they had one, did not provide for transportation for those kinds of numbers. So they were going to do whatever they had to do to move us, and whether or not we suffered, whether we lived or died, was not a primary concern. All the promises the Japanese brass had made at the surrender table, the oaths to observe and obey the Geneva Conventions, were not a concern. Speed was the concern. Efficiency was the concern. They were bringing in troops as fast as they could, tanks, artillery pieces, preparing for the bombardment and assault upon Corregidor, and everything else, including us, did not matter.

Take for example at one point, at a makeshift hospital along the march, chock full of the sick and wounded (which was just about all of us), wholly inadequate facilities and supplies and medicines, wounds that refused to heal, no food, everyone weak almost to the point of death, the Japanese came in and ordered everyone out of the place and told them to make their way as best they could down to the road about half a mile away. Half a mile may as well have been the distance to the moon for these men. But the Japanese said the trucks couldn't negotiate their way up the wooded area to where the prisoners were sent. So the prisoners would now have to walk down, but it was promised that if they made it there would be trucks waiting to take them to a nicely outfitted camp. And so everyone struggles out of bed, many too weak to make it the half mile through the woods and so being carried on blankets and shelter-halfs. And when they make it to the road, of course there are no trucks waiting at all. They're told to form up in a column and march. Deception, cruelty, and plain incompetence; at a certain point, it stops mattering which is which, because the results are the same. Our men were dying in droves and I had a front-row seat that I wished I didn't have.

Sprinkled amongst the incompetence and evil behaviors, it's worth noting that the Japanese were fierce looters. On one occasion, before the collapse and surrender, when I was in charge of the infantry platoon, a Japanese soldier was captured and he had four wristwatches in his possession. So even in the midst of combat, they looted. A despicable practice, of course, to steal from the dead, but they were given to that, many of them, because they were far from wealthy or worldly people. Kids, really, from the hundreds of little islands in the Japanese archipelago, the sons of poor fishermen who had only ever seen a wristwatch on a wealthy man, if at all.

So they gave in to these temptations and did some frightful things, out of greed, and also out of cruelty. They'd perform shakedowns, frisking the prisoners like a policeman might do if looking for stolen goods on a person. They would stick their hands right into a fella's pockets and take whatever was in there, from lint to coin. Once I watched a guard rifle the pockets of a man, find his wallet, remove a picture of the man's wife and children, and tear it up. Just to be devilish. Another time, a guard got upset about something and took the glasses off a prisoner, put them on his own face, and made a cruel pantomime of being blind, putting his hands over his eyes and laughing wickedly. Then he took the glasses, bent them up, and tossed them on the side of the road, and the man had to carry on without being able to see. There was no recourse we could call upon, which made these situations doubly unbearable. You see a friend's glasses get smashed and you want to take an action, but no, you cannot. You simply cannot. Action in that circumstance was action against the Empire and it comes with a death sentence. The number of times I looked upward to the sky and took a deep breath while muttering a quick prayer are beyond a count. They like to say the Irish boys like me can have a quick temper and maybe there's a little something to that in the rare circumstance where tempers will flare, but I never considered myself or my neighborhood friends to be the quick-tempered type, frankly. I would admit, however, that watching a friend be tortured can make a decent, peaceful man turn to thoughts of violent revenge.

In the meantime, while we're marching northward with boys dying at a rapid, regular pace, remember that the assault on Corregidor is still going on, the Japanese pouring troops and resources south and throwing everything they had at trying to finally take that little island. Sometimes we could hear the guns in the distance, big coastal guns on the island intended to protect Manila Bay from attack. But a couple of those guns could be turned far enough to reach the western side of Bataan, and now the Corregidor defenders were using them on the Japanese. And these were massive, fearsome guns, 14-inch, tossing projectiles that weighed nine hundred pounds. I remember one night watching from a rice field and looking across Manila Bay to Corregidor, watching the great blasts of flame coming out of the guns as they pummeled Japanese positions. These muzzle flashes were silent, at first, owing to the distance between us and the guns. It would take a minute, maybe more, before the sound would reach us. And at night we couldn't see the shells. We would see the muzzle flash, silence, the blast would reach us, more silence, and then we would see and hear the massive explosion when the shell landed on its target to the west. During the day you could trace the path of the shells through the sky as they tumbled, end-over-end, a terrible, impressive sight. And after weeks of this, what had been a beautiful and lush peninsula when we arrived, with plenty of thriving agriculture, banana and coconut trees as far as you could see, acres and acres of pineapple plantations, and lots of wild native plants and trees, was pretty much laid to waste by all the shelling, everything broken and barren, all that lush life gone.

The road we were walking was topped with crushed shells, clams and crustaceans that had been pulverized and laid down as the driving surface, and we were passed all day every day by columns of Japanese troops heading south to the fight, riding trucks and tanks and artillery units, and kicking up an ungodly cloud of dust from the crushed shells that just hung in the air constantly, coating your skin, getting in your eyes and throat, getting down into your lungs. We were stark white from all the dust, not having shaved in a week, my god we were a sight.

And the further we got from Mariveles, which again was the origin point of the march, the crueler and more vicious the Japanese became. This was an army that historically used everything it came across for itself, looting and stealing and laying waste, and this was no different. The American army, by contrast, did not take from the land it passed through. Of course, American soldiers took food here and there in France and Germany—and stored wine, probably—but we did not live off the land as a matter of policy like the Japanese did. The American armed forces were supplied from the United States, or supplied from abroad with funds from the United States Armed Forces. We did not forage and denude the countryside and starve the natives. The Japanese soldier, however, was wired to take all for himself and the Empire. After all, they were in an expansion mindset and had long-since concluded that they rightfully owned whatever land they happened to desire. It was a disgusting sight to watch the guards not only torture us, but also ransack the land and animals in their path.

I mentioned that it was not the distance of the march that did so many of us in. It was, rather, the pace, the unrelenting expectation that we would keep moving from point to point, town to town, without food or rest or respite from the sun, that caused thousands of soldiers to falter and die. This was not how I planned to spend my birthday that year but there I was. Nothing to celebrate this year. Before reaching Balaga, I found myself obsessing about a couple nights ago in Lamao where we had camped for a night in a dried-up rice field, because that was where some things happened that smartened us up real quick, helped us understand what a mess we were in and how we might survive it. It was in that rice field in Lamao three hundred or so of us just sitting there waiting for instructions to move on, relishing the opportunity to sit when the sun was down, and suddenly the guards came through unannounced and began making people turn out their pockets, empty their musette bags and suitcases, and let the Japanese rummage through and examine what they were carrying. If they found any Japanese money, or a Japanese uniform insignia, or any article that indicated the man in possession of it had taken it from a Japanese soldier, that man would be shot dead on the spot. And that certainly got our attention. You'd look around and see guys taking things out of their pockets when the guards' attention was directed elsewhere, trying to destroy these items or otherwise hide them, desperate, not wanting to die. So you see, some Americans had done looting of their own. Thank God I wasn't given to that sort of thing, because when caught, it turned out to be fatal.

As we neared Balaga, of course not knowing where we were going, there were all kinds of horrors along that road, of course, and it's amazing how you can become not just used to but almost bored by the most awful things when you see enough of them. Mostly what we saw were bodies, some beheaded, some with entrails hanging out. Even where they made efforts to bury the dead, the Japanese couldn't keep up with the amount of corpses they produced, and so the road was just littered. And by this time, it became difficult to distinguish between a dead American and a dead Filipino. Not that it mattered, really, but I mention it just to give an idea of what it was like. Because you see, lying in the tropical sun for a few days, it doesn't take long for a body to bloat up and turn coal black, and the only way to distinguish between an American and a Filipino at that point, generally, was by size.

The worst thing of all remained—the thirst. I was managing okay with getting a few calories ingested. I had a few tins of rations with me at the beginning, and I got by on that for food, and then north of Limay we were fed once, a concoction of rice and water called muguai. An old wives' tale has it that muguai will cure anything—not so, but we ate it with gusto and could have eaten much more. In any case, a man can go for a long period of time without food, living off the fat in his body for a month or more. But water—three days, at most, and it's a slow and painful death, which I saw firsthand. It was driving us mad, the thirst. You sit in a field, scorched, no water. Other times, the Japanese would make us sit by water, in the sun of course, but not allow us to drink, which was even worse. Along the road I saw men trying to drain fluids out of dead animals, even dead people, to drink. The thirst was so insistent, so compelling, that you'd do absolutely anything.

But still we continued on and by the 15th or 16th of May we'd made it to Abucay, which is getting up toward the throat of the peninsula as it curves to the northeast around the bay. The group I was in was sitting on the bank of a dried-up river (this now being the dry season). And there was a rivulet of water still running down from the Mariveles Mountains that we were allowed to drink from, and this was a blessing unlike any I had ever experienced, cool, clean water, straight from the mountains, it seemed like a miracle. We spoke aloud to our different Gods and saints as we guzzled what we could. The dried shoulders of the stream were about seventy-five or a hundred feet of sand, and that's where we camped for two days. Coming on the tail of such a blessing, the stream water, I guess I should have known something bad was about to happen, but I did not know I was about to have the worst experience I ever had.

The Japanese came through and rousted us, shouting, slapping, stirring things up, screaming at us to hurry, hurry. *Apmati! Speedo, speedo!* But many of the men were, by this point, actually dying. They hadn't been fed, were so sick with malaria and dysentery, no medicine, days and days of marching, many of them wounded, beaten, oozing gashes from mischievous bayonet poking and stabbing, they just could not go on another step, couldn't even get to their feet. I would guess most reading this have never had malaria, but the effect of it is almost nonsensical. You sweat and sweat and then have these periods of chill when you shake so hard it seems like your teeth will fall right out of your head. You can be sitting directly in the sun on a hundred degree day and shivering as though you're sitting on ice in mother's freezer chest.

So that's what was going on with these men, at this point. They were dying, they could not get up. But the guards were insistent. They would come through and kick a fella, and if he didn't move, the guard would gather up three or four other Americans and order us to take the guy and put him in a blanket or a shelter-half and drag him down to the stream. Then they gave us little shovels, the kind of collapsible shovels issued to infantry men for various uses, to dig foxholes, fill sandbags, use as a weapon in close quarters in a pinch. We had to use these shovels to dig a shallow grave for the fella and put him in.

More than once, though, we would hoist a man into his grave, and then he would start moving. And I would look at the Japanese in a pleading sort of way, like *There's some life left in him, let us carry him for a while,* gesturing to that effect, trying to get the guard to demonstrate a little humanity and not make us bury our comrade alive. And the guard would just point his rifle at us and indicated, *Scopu, scopu*. Our choice was to either bury him or die ourselves. Maybe I should have made a different choice, maybe I was weak, but all I can do is tell you what I did: we shoveled and scooped the sand as fast as we could, smothering the fella and trying to kill him quickly with suffocation. I remember looking down at where his hands were, saw the sand move and ripple a little. He was trying to push his hands through and get at the air. And that there was the worst experience I had ever had.

He was not the only one. There were quite a few buried alive at Abucay. And there were more than a few that I buried personally. I had my own little prayers and messages that I would try to impart on the soldier pleading for his life, but none of it soothes a thing to this day. I put dozens of men to their rest, and there is no easy way around this fact as I can see it. I had to kill to live so I killed. My only rationalizing thought is that these men were going to die in short order and I helped them die sooner and with less pain. In another way, if I was dying, a sick American soldier halfway around the world from my dear mother and father, I would prefer an American soldier to put me to rest with some remorse or love in his eyes. Some of us were upright and able to do this terrible task and that is what we did.

It's impossible, probably, to understand why the Japanese did what they did during the march. Maybe it's foolish to even try to theorize; some things just are, and there's no explanation for it. The logical thing is to blame it on their leaders, which is in fact, eventually, what happened—the higher-ranking Japanese officers on Bataan were tried after the war and, in some cases, held responsible and executed for the actions of their subordinates. I had the distinct displeasure of meeting some of these characters and felt their wrath as an unarmed, malnourished soldier, but these fellas would mostly go on to serve their sentence of labor after war tribunals did their analysis. It was occurring to me that so many of these soldiers behaved the way they did because of a Japanese concept called Bushido, which translates as "the way of the warrior." It's an indoctrinated code infused early into the Japanese soldier's training.

In practice, Bushido is a system of discipline and obedience that is followed without question. We must cast our modern sensitivities aside to understand Bushido, which effectively means the Japanese are a master race, not dissimilar to Hitler's approach in Germany. A core mission of Bushido was, therefore, oppression of the white race. Oppression translates to every horror one could imagine, from torture to rape, to outright murder of anyone not part of the expansion plans of the Japanese empire (see: Rape of Nanking where the Bushido code led to over 200,000 deaths amongst their Chinese enemies—civilian women and children included—in only six weeks). To consecrate the code, Japanese sergeants would slap soldiers, lieutenants would smack sergeants, great, cracking blows that knocked them to their knees. It was allegiance and obedience all the way up and down, from the guy on the bottom all the way to the Emperor. And because Bushido encompassed everything and was followed without even a smidgen of doubt or question, it could justify all kinds of terrible behavior—

particularly against people who had no Bushido, which is to say no code, no honor. American soldiers, mind you, were a hearty lot. We believed in our own codes, so there was the rub. What developed was this unspoken battle of codes that we Americans (and Filipinos) had to fight quietly as unarmed captives. And despite this battle of codes, I had yet to see an American (or Filipino) soldier outwardly *beg* for forgiveness or break because their code failed them. Perhaps it was the gumption of tough American kids taken captive, but I do believe that most of us would much rather get buried on the road than look Bushido in the eye and blink—I would never do so, most wouldn't. Still, we had a formidable enemy with their rock-solid code of how they would treat us. In the end, their greatest honor was to die for their Emperor and it was sub-human, despicable to surrender to the enemy according to their code. In fact, the Japanese soldier (the samurai as he is called) was honored to die for his Emperor and would gladly accept death if imprisonment loomed. This Bushido code, supported by a nationwide campaign of propaganda and censorship similar to Hitler's campaign in Europe, actually *demanded* death before surrender for its own soldiers.

American soldiers, white men slotted well below the Japanese race as a starting point, were destined for severe punishment as captives who had surrendered. It stands to reason that nearly thirty percent of POWs in the Pacific theatres of war would die in the hands of their Japanese captors, an appalling statistic that speaks to the broad scope of war crimes the Japanese deemed righteous by way of Bushido. The Geneva Convention that had been signed in the late 1920s to protect prisoners from abhorrent treatment was, of course, bastardized by the Japanese as they added an addendum that effectively gave them free reign to punish prisoners as they saw fit. Hanging a man alive by wrists from a tree limb, starving him, beating him senseless, sun treatment, solitary confinement in a wooden crate—all acceptable and encouraged behaviors to bolster the strength of the Empire and to send a message to the enemy. When our Major General King had negotiated our surrender before the march, he was given assurances that his men, both the American and Filipino soldiers he commanded, would be treated with dignity and not fall prey to this type of behavior. That was a lie.

As we moved north out of Abucay, the communities grew larger and larger the closer we got to Manila. Which meant we often had an audience as we marched through a town. Most of the Filipino men were gone, and the older girls and the grown women, to keep them from the attentions of the Japanese, were either hiding or with armed resistance forces. But when we came through, it was the women who showed great bravery in offering us assistance. They knew what brutes the Japanese were, and in spite of that, they emerged. One time, a girl ran out and handed me a banana leaf—this was how Filipinos would wrap food. No paper bags or wax paper. They would take a banana leaf and roll it up over a piece of sugar cane, or a rice ball, or a gorgeous piece of brown sugar. Other women offered water, filled containers with water for us. And in their faces you could see a look of support, of comradery. There was, in the end, a real rapport between the Filipinos and the Americans. These women were looking for their own people as we marched through—a husband, a brother, a son—but when they didn't find them, when all they saw were white faces, they still stepped forward and offered mercy, at great personal risk. Brilliant humanity and bravery. Meanwhile, the Japanese guards, generally with their short, stocky builds and stumpy legs, walked noticeably taller as they paraded us by the onlookers. We were, by design, helping to announce to the world that Nippon supremacy was upon us and had conquered the Americans.

Finally—I don't know on what date—we arrived in San Fernando. It must have been about nine grueling days since we had started the march. Those of us who survived that far were rounded up and placed in various spots for holding—I ended up in the county jail, which was, incidentally, the second time I'd been in jail. Not to be smart but the first was after I'd graduated from primary flight school in Tuscaloosa and we were sent down to Montgomery. Four of us rented a car and went back to Tuscaloosa, which was the site of the University of Alabama, where we'd gotten to know some people during our time in flight school, to see if we could get dates with some of the girls we knew. We had to drive to the next county over with these girls, because Tuscaloosa County was dry and we couldn't have that. We went to a dance hall, a brown bagging affair, BYOB, and after a few hours it was time to bring the girls back. So we're dropping them off, and after having been up at 5 for parading and reviewing, I fell asleep in the back seat. Some may argue it was being responsible. Anway, some time later I come to and found a big old Tuscaloosa copper shining his flashlight into the back seat, and there's a bottle of whiskey there. It was probably empty but it was enough evidence that I had been behaving badly. I got hauled in and spent the night in the local bastille. And the way it got sorted out was odd—the desk sergeant told me to go down to the H&W drug store where we would hang out on the weekends and speak to the manager and tell him you've been locked up and are going to be fined. So I do that, and the H&W man says, "It's a common thing, gonna cost you fifty bucks. Get it together and bring it to me and I'll call the sergeant." He did that and late afternoon I went back down to the station, got my wallet and offered my watch to cover any difference, and I was loose again.

So anyway, halfway around the world, there I am in jail again. And this time the situation's a lot more serious and it's going to take more than fifty bucks or a poor fella's timepiece to get me out of this one. In a cell that was really suited for just two people, they shoved twenty-five of us. It was awful, so tight some of the guys were smothering, no room to move, to turn, to lift your arms, and definitely no room to lie down. I dare say I'd almost rather be marching in the sun. No toilets; when you had to go, you just went, right where you were standing. And we stayed in that pen for three days. And when it was time for them to feed us, the Japanese brought a wheelbarrow with rice in it. Imagine that. Feeding us like pigs at a trough. But we ate it, with great relish, and it was delicious. To this day I like rice. I really do. And I think maybe I got to like it so much right there in the San Fernando jail. That rice kept me alive and tasted fine.

After three days, they came and unlocked the cell and let us all out into the street again. We were joined by others who'd been held elsewhere, and in a column we marched. But not far this time—just through to the other side of town, where we found ourselves in a railroad assembly yard. Guys were falling down around me and a few expired there on the spot, but I was enjoying some deep breaths up my nose. This was a big operation, I could see. I saw multiple rail lines coming into and out of the yard, because San Fernando was the largest city in the rice and sugar plain north of Manila. It was the provincial capital, the place where all the agricultural products from the surrounding area were gathered and redistributed. Which meant San Fernando had the kind of transportation infrastructure to handle moving tens of thousands of people at a time. Finally, it seemed, the promise of transportation that had been made repeatedly by our captors was coming to pass. But there's good reason they tell you to not get complacent.

Because this was a narrow-gauge railroad, understand. There were no American-sized boxcars in the Philippines, or anywhere else in the Orient, for that matter. These cars were maybe a third of the size, only seven feet high, eight feet wide and thirty feet long. Fifty men per car would have been a very tight fit, but our guards screamed and slapped and jabbed us with their rifles and bayonets until one hundred or more of us were crammed in—then they slammed the doors shut. Claustrophobia is a term I've heard to describe that feeling folks gets when trapped in a tight space, so I think a clinical term like that probably applies well here. I did not take a bayonet jab during this particular trip, but I observed what a serious wound compounded by this claustrophobia could do to a man. Hideous results.

The Japanese by this time were even more brutal and impatient, completely disorganized, no real idea what to do with all of us. They were tired of the whole thing, didn't want anything more to do with this kind of duty, the ugly, boring business of dealing with prisoners. And the truth is, an officer doesn't put his best and brightest on POW guard duty. Mercer, the smart Duke graduate, was certain that they used the dummies to guard us, the ones without the imagination to be enterprising, to think, to try to do the right thing. And like any soldiers, if they're going to be far from home, hungry, sick, tired, in a place that's ungodly hot and teeming with bugs, at the very least you want to see some action. No matter how dumb, if you get stuck on guard duty you have to know it's because someone doesn't think much of you. So that makes you behave badly, too. You look for action, a bayonet jab or a trigger pull at a prisoner's head.

It's difficult to explain how terrifying a feeling it is, to be packed so tight into a space that you can't move, can't lift your arms, can't turn around, can't sit or lie down, can't even breathe. Immediately, the interior of the boxcar became so hot that men began passing out. Others were screaming, to God, to our captors, begging incoherently. The fellas in the ends of the boxcar, jammed against the unyielding metal of the walls, suffocated. And then the train began to move, slowly, too slowly to circulate even the faintest hint of fresh air. It smelled to the heavens in that pressure cooker. The car was like a rolling oven, and it took four hours to travel the 25 miles north to Capas. I don't know how many of us died, in part because it was so difficult to even attempt communication in the cars. We all died a little, I'm sure of that. On the march, we could at least see each other and offer each other the occasional update or word of encouragement. None of that on the train. When the train pulled into the station hours later, those of us who had survived managed to climb out, those who hadn't survived fell where they stood. The car had been packed so tight that they'd been dead standing up for hours. By this point, seeing a dead comrade was regrettably common. In this instance, they just looked like stacked sacks of potatoes in that train cart. Dead weight on dead weight. The exaggerated inhale of fresh oxygen I took getting out of that damn boxcar is a memory. The temperature would have been akin to an unbearably hot day at the beach, nearing one hundred degrees I'm sure, but having the fresh air hit our skin and lungs was a tremendous feeling.

Once enough trains had come in and a sizeable number of prisoners had been gathered, wouldn't you know it, we started walking again. By now, even though it had only been a week and a half or so it felt as though this was going to go on forever—we would just keep walking and sitting and climbing onto and off of trains and watching our friends die and walking some more, until we ourselves finally gave out, until every one of us was gone. The Japanese continued to cull those who were limping along, or who fell off the pace or looked like they were sick, and it became evident they were trying to eliminate all but those of us who were still relatively healthy, the idea being that we were about to be transferred to work camps and the weak and infirm had no place there.

Eventually we reached Camp O'Donnell, a hellish place where many unfortunates would stay and die. Of course, no one will ever know how many died, how many whose bones have turned back into the soil, so many unnamed and unmourned. Many of us thought, despite the chaotic nature of the march, and how disorganized and unprepared the Japanese were, that the cruelty of it was preplanned and deliberate, coming from the top. The abusive, cruel attitude of the soldiers may well have been official policy beyond that Samurai code. When I was in the Pentagon, many years later, I read a report about one of the admonitions against surrender in the Japanese Army's field manual. It made clear that to surrender or be captured was among the worst disgraces that could befall a soldier. Not only did you shame yourself and your outfit, you brought shame upon your family, and they would have to live in disgrace forever afterward for your cowardice. So always save the last bullet for yourself, was the instruction. And maybe given this, they thought we were despicable because we'd surrendered and allowed ourselves to be imprisoned. Maybe they thought that in light of this, we deserved all the abuse and cruelty they heaped on us. They were constantly belittling us, accusing us of having no discipline, no honor. Pretty rich coming from men who treated us as they did.

The time at O'Donnell for the 10,000 or so men who were sent there was short but notable as my first real placement into a prison camp. It was a strange set-up there at O'Donnell. They had the customary barbed wire fence as you'd expect, I suppose, and there were bamboo guard towers looming above us from the corners of the lot. Within each tower, more stocky Bushido warriors draped in khaki and sour looks. The optimistic amongst us believed we'd start to be fed and get access to water. But we were wrong. We were starved just as we were for most of the march and water was limited to a single spigot to serve many thousands of thirst-stricken men. The barracks were bare—simple cots with a dirt floor, bamboo enclosures. Sleeping in the barracks was a real chore. No mattress, blankets or pillows to speak of. Worse, we were not afforded mosquito nets to protect us from incessant buzzing and biting throughout the night. Before we'd head out to our next location, over two thousand more men had perished while at O'Donnell. It was altogether too common and expected at this point, not to mention the burial duties becoming routine.

In any event, after a couple of weeks at O'Donnell, I and hundreds of others were ordered onto trucks and driven two hours through the countryside to Cabanatuan, a former Philippine military training facility now being used by the Japanese as a prison camp. More or less the same setup as O'Donnell—nipa palm barracks all in a row, a headquarters building, a couple of dirt roads through the center of the grounds. This was where the work began. Our first task was to build the fence that would hold us in. We were separated into labor gangs and would go up into the foothills, cut down a tree and drag it back, use the log as a fencepost. And in between these fenceposts we built bamboo panels, taught by Filipinos how to interlace the pieces of bamboo to make a structure that was almost unbreakable. Later the fence we built was replaced with barbed wire, but for now, in a pinch, the Japanese decided bamboo would suffice.

And they were right. In fact, they probably didn't even need a fence of any kind. Where were we going to go? All that was likely to happen was you'd wander around for a bit, then run into a Japanese patrol and get your head cut off for your trouble. Besides, we'd been so terrorized on Bataan, through the siege and the surrender and then, of course, the march itself. At least here we got fresh air, we had running water and some food, if not enough, never enough. And it occurs to me now that whether they intended it or not, the Japanese had conditioned us quite well—we knew how miserable things could get, so anything just a tick or two above that in terms of living conditions seemed pretty great by comparison, and we weren't likely to make a fuss or try to run. For what it's worth, I never heard of a single man escaping from Cabanatuan.

Once the fence was erected—it was a lot of work but it didn't take too long—we went from builders to farmers, and fell into a reliable routine. At seven in the morning we'd form up into groups of 75 or 100 men, go out and work the fields. We harvested cane sugar, and my god was that dreadful work. I don't think it's possible to walk through a field of sugar cane without being slashed by the leaves—they were like razor wire. In fact, they're supposed to be planted a certain distance apart so you can walk between them without getting sliced up, but of course that wasn't the case at Cabanatuan. When we harvested sugar we got cut to ribbons, but the tradeoff was being able to sneak pieces of the raw cane, get a bellyful of sugar, which probably saved a bunch of lives including my own many times over, just the calories. We also raised camotes, a kind of half-wild sweet potato, purple, very starchy. These you could plant just by cutting some of the ground cover from a plant and sticking it back in the ground, and voila! It starts another little hill of camote, like peanuts in the ground.

We worked for weeks and weeks on end, every day the same. There was no sign of American military forces whatsoever, and over time most of the Japanese were gone, too—the war had moved on to somewhere else, and while we and our situation were still related to the war, we no longer had any real part in it. The Japanese had left just enough men behind to run the camp, which at the time held about 15,000 prisoners. The guards who remained were real beauts, terribly abusive characters—again, probably in part because they felt as abandoned and forsaken as we did. One of these fellas would walk around bare-chested with his cap on, a real cock of the walk, carrying a three-foot-long stick. And anyone he thought wasn't working hard or fast enough, speedo-speedo—he'd walk up and crack him with that stick across the back. He gave me a shot to the elbow once, and I was pretty sure my arm was gone. Our nickname for him was "Fireball." He was a monster.

Incidentally, Corregidor finally fell on May 6th—somehow the defenders of that tiny island held out for another month after we were finished on Bataan. Those who survived were taken on barges across the bay to Manila, where the Americans were separated from the Filipinos. The Filipinos went to some camp, and the Americans—because the Japanese wanted to humiliate and make an example of them—were marched through the city, ragged and tattered, thin from months of not having enough to eat. Some of them were detained in Manila and became part of the infamous rat packs on the piers, loading and unloading Japanese ships. This probably sounds awful but the truth is, of all the places and situations one could have ended up in as a POW in the Philippines, being on a rat pack was probably among the best. Because the sailors of the Japanese Navy had nothing to do with the combat on Bataan and Corregidor, of course, and so they didn't share the soldiers' animosity and resentment of us. So while these fellas worked hard, they were treated and fed very well—probably due also, in part, to being right at the spigot, as it were, of the supply chain. I ran into some of them in Bilibid Prison in Manila, where I was shortly to arrive, and was stunned to hear about how well they fared.

It was General Wainwright who was commander at Corregidor, and when he finally made the decision to surrender, he did so with no small amount of doubt and regret. When he'd made up his mind, Skinny ordered the guns on the west end of the island to be destroyed and the remaining ammunition blown up. The guns were loaded with a charge and then packed full of sand, and when they fired the monsters it blew the barrels apart. The ammunition depot was blown up, trucks were destroyed, all in keeping with the kind of scorched-earth philosophy most commanders will employ when they know they're about to be defeated—the idea is to leave nothing of use for the enemy. Wainwright himself was still in the tunnel, destroying money—he was knee-deep in money, the story goes—when the Japanese overran the topside of the headquarters, the barracks area and such. And so, with the Japanese closing in, Wainwright wired his last message to President Roosevelt: "With a broken heart, and with a head bowed in sadness, but not in shame, today I must arrange terms for the surrender. There is a limit to human endurance and that limit has long since been passed. Without the prospect of relief, I feel it is my duty to my country, and to my gallant troops, to end this useless effusion of blood and human sacrifice. If you agree, Mr. President, please say it to the nation that my troops and I have accomplished all that is humanly possible and that we have upheld the best tradition of the United States. May God bless you, preserve you, and guide you and the nation in the effort to ultimate victory. With profound regret and continued pride in my gallant troops, I go to meet the Japanese commander. Goodbye, Mr. President."

But the news wasn't all bad. Around the time we arrived at Cabanatuan, an extraordinary thing occurred, and though we wouldn't be aware of it for some years, and though in terms of tactical effect this event was of little significance, it nevertheless would end up being of great significance to the morale and courage of both the United States and its allies. A B-25 pilot named Jimmy Doolittle had been training with about two dozen other pilots in Florida, practicing short takeoffs, trying to devise a way for the 25s to take off from a carrier deck. Now the B-25 was a dual-engine bomber, not at all designed for use from an aircraft carrier. I flew them for three years when I was at the Pentagon post-war, and I can tell you they like a nice, long runway from which to launch. And as far as landing on an aircraft carrier, you could forget about it. So once the crews were trained and ready for the mission they'd devised, their planes had to be lifted onto the carrier with a crane. This was Admiral William "Bull" Halsey's task force and with the B-25s aboard, it launched from Hawaii and sailed across the north

Pacific, intending to return the nasty surprise the Japanese had visited on Pearl Harbor.

The intention was to sail within 100 miles of the Japanese coast with a cruiser, several destroyers, and the carrier *Hornet*. This range would allow the bombers to take off and bomb targets in Japan, then continue on to China, where they could land—remember, no way to land back on the carrier, so the only way was to make it to friendly air bases after the bombing runs. But the ships only made it to within around 500 miles of the coast before they were picked up by a Japanese picket ship—that's a vessel set apart from the main group for the purpose of exactly what happened, which was to provide early warning of enemy activity.

So Admiral Halsey decided that surprising the Japanese was out the window, and he gave the order for the B-25s to take off. Now I can tell you, as a pilot myself, that launching bombers from a carrier would always be at best a dicey proposition. And these were less than ideal conditions, very heavy seas. The problem was timing the takeoffs so the bow of the *Hornet* was pointing correctly—the bombers couldn't get up enough speed to recover if they were angled down when they left the carrier deck. So every takeoff was a combination of skill, guts, and dumb luck, but somehow they all got airborne.

Doolittle himself was the first to reach Tokyo, and he flew in unopposed over the city. The reason for this was simple: the Japanese didn't believe anyone could reach them. They thought the home island, and Tokyo in particular, were well out of reach of their enemies. Manchuria, Indochina, the Philippines had all been subdued. The Japanese controlled Okinawa and Iwo Jima. Australia, Alaska, and Hawaii were too far for a round-trip for any bombers of the time. And the Russians had their hands full in the west. And so, as the Japanese looked around 360 degrees, they believed, with reason, that they were safe.

And then here came Doolittle and his raiders, each with three 500-pound bombs and one incendiary bomb. Another reason they flew through without so much as some anti-aircraft flak was because people on the ground mistook the American insignia—red, white, and blue concentric circles—for the Japanese insignia of the Rising Sun. Doolittle and his men dropped their payloads, which didn't do a whole lot of damage, but the point had never been to actually inflict meaningful losses on the Japanese. The point was to puncture their sense of invulnerability, make them worry, bring the war home to them in a way it had not been before. And in this, the raid succeeded completely. Through the rest of the war the Japanese would never again feel safe from attack, and they had to commit 60 aircraft and two regiments of infantry to Tokyo at a time when those forces would have been better used as part of consolidating their gains elsewhere in the Pacific. What's more, the raid had a galvanizing effect on the morale of the American public, as well as our allies. Up to this point, things had looked about as grim as they could get—the Philippines, Singapore, Burma all fallen, American forces decimated in Hawaii. But the Doolittle raid, inconsequential though it might have been tactically, was a shot of adrenaline to the Allied people around the world, at a time when they desperately needed it.

Of course, those of us in camps around the Philippines had no idea any of this was happening. Later there were men who came to Cabanatuan and managed to smuggle a radio in, to listen to radio broadcasts and get a sense of what was going on in the war. For us, in early 1942, we might as well have been on the dark side of the moon.

Chapter 6

DAPECOL DOUBLOOS

I was still at Cabanatuan, harvesting sugar cane and sweet potatoes, in the summer of 1942 when what's widely considered to be the turning point in the Pacific war—the Battle of Midway—took place.

The Japanese got greedy, you could say, and wanted to take Midway Island so they had a place from which to attack Hawaii—Midway Island being located between Japan and the west coast of the US, over 1,000 miles northwest of Hawaii in the Pacific. What they didn't know was U.S. Navy cryptologists had broken the Japanese coding system for communications, which meant every detail of their plan for attacking Midway was known to the Americans, who set an ambush in response.

And the Japanese walked right into that ambush. They attacked the Marine base on Midway with aircraft from four carriers, unaware that U.S. Naval forces were just on the other side of the island, waiting for their planes to return to the ships to refuel. When they did, U.S. carrier aircraft launched and caught the Japanese nearly defenseless, sinking all four of their carriers. As far as naval warfare is concerned, I don't think we've seen a more decisive, consequential win by the United States in history. The added psychological lift for the Allied forces was to have sunk the Japanese carriers that had inflicted a major blow to the United States just six months earlier at Pearl Harbor. Revenge tastes sweet in these theatres of war.

This was a horrendous loss for the Japanese—so much so that old Admiral 56 was ashamed to bring the news to the war ministry in Tokyo. The Japanese people were never told of the defeat, and I wonder whether they even told the Emperor. Bushido punishes its own, remember, with top-down punitive repercussions for failure to support Japan's quest for expansion. The fact was, Japan couldn't replace the ships and planes they'd lost, at least not nearly fast enough,

Young airman Patrick Rafferty in his Army Air Corp uniform following enlistment to serve his country. (Photo courtesy of Rafferty family)

Rafferty seen here outside his family's Brookline, Massachusetts home. (Photo courtesy of Rafferty family)

Rafferty often trained in the BT-14 and the T-6 Texan while in Tuscaloosa and Montgomery, Alabama before boarding a ship carrying him and other young pilots to the Philippines. (Photo courtesy of Rafferty family)

Rafferty ready to see the world as a young pilot trainee, not long before he would be captured by the Japanese. (Photo courtesy of Rafferty family)

A photograph taken of Battleship Row at Pearl Harbor soon after Japanese aircraft had departed following their attack on December 7, 1941. Burning furiously, USS *Arizona* can be seen nearest the camera. To the left of her are USS *Tennessee* and the sunken USS *West Virginia*. (Photo courtesy of USNHHC)

The strike on Pearl Harbor underway, as seen from a Japanese plane during the torpedo attack on ships moored on both sides of Ford Island. A torpedo has just hit USS *West Virginia* on the far side of Ford Island (center). Other battleships moored nearby are, from left to right, *Nevada, Arizona, Tennessee* (inboard of *West Virginia*), *Oklahoma* (torpedoed and listing) alongside *Maryland,* and *California*. On the near side of Ford Island, to the left, are the light cruisers *Detroit* and *Raleigh*, target and training ship *Utah* and seaplane tender *Tangier*. *Raleigh* and *Utah* have been torpedoed, and *Utah* is listing sharply to port. Japanese planes are visible over both Ford Island and the Navy Yard at right. (Photo courtesy of NARA)

Japanese soldiers celebrate the surrender of Allied forces after the Battle of Bataan, April 1942. (Photo courtesy of Getty Images)

U.S. Major General Edward P. King negotiates surrender with Japanese officers prior to the Bataan Death March. (Photo courtesy of Bettman/Getty Images)

Under Japanese guard following the surrender of Bataan, American POWs are pictured sorting captured US equipment, April 11, 1942. Following this, the Japanese commandeered the material and the POWs were marched to prison camp. (Photo courtesy of USNHHC)

A Japanese soldier overlooks captured Allied soldiers at the onset of the Bataan Death March in April 1942. (Photo courtesy of Bettman/Getty Images)

Japanese troops guard American POWs at the beginning of the Bataan Death March. (Photo courtesy of NARA)

American POWs with their hands tied behind their backs on the first day of the Bataan Death March, April 9, 1942. They are identified as, left to right, Private First Class Samuel Stenzler, Private First Class Frank Spear and Captain James Gallagher. All three were bound for having been found in possession of Japanese money, photographs, or similar items. None of these three men survived captivity. Gallagher was killed later the same day that this image was taken; Stenzler died in Camp O'Donnell on May 26, 1942, whilst Spear was executed in a POW camp in Japan on July 9, 1945. (Photo courtesy of USMC)

A group of American prisoners under guard during the Death March in April 1942. Note the guard in the center with the fixed bayonet. Captain William Dyess, commander of the 21st Pursuit Squadron, survived the Death March, but later recalled the Japanese behaviour: 'Their ferocity grew as we marched … They were no longer content with mauling stragglers or pricking them with bayonet points. The thrusts were intended to kill.' (Photo courtesy of USMC)

With temperatures reaching well over 100 degrees, the lack of water and food deteriorated the captives' spirits and their ability to continue marching. (Photo courtesy of Department of Defense/ Wikimedia Commons)

Japanese guards did not hesitate to murder or severely injure captives using bayonets and pistols, even as the POWs faced exhaustion and the effects of tremendous heat and thirst. (Photo courtesy of Bettman/Getty Images)

American men were forced to bury their comrades alive on the roadside. Refusing to do so meant death. (Photo Courtesy of US Army Signal Corps/ Wikimedia Commons)

A burial detail of American and Filipino prisoners of war uses improvised litters to carry fallen comrades at Camp O'Donnell in 1942 on the Bataan Death March. (Photo courtesy of NARA)

The *Oryoku Maru* "Hell Ship" prior to its sinking by the American bomber USS *Hornet* in Subic Bay in December of 1944. (Photo Courtesy of Record of the Office of Chief of Naval Operations, RG 38)

Japanese ship *Montevideo Maru* was the first of the Hell Ships to be sunk by the US Navy. (Photo courtesy of US Navy Archives)

As Hell Ships listed or sank under the fire of US bombers, American soldiers were forced to fight their way abovedeck and jump overboard in an attempt to make it to land through shark-infested waters. (Photo courtesy of Department of Naval Warfare)

Quinn, David L. , Chpln Lt, 63952, USN, 16th Naval Distr, District Chaplain, USA, 1/13/45, I, , , , Crisfield, Maryland

Radcliff, Elgin Gilbert, Capt, O&023558, ENG, 803rd Engr Bn (Avn), , USA, lived, II, Fk-1, , Jinsen, Norristown, Pennsylvania

Radosevich, Joseph R. , 2nd Lt, O&890153, CAC, 515th CA Regt (AA), D Btry, USA, 2/7/45, I, KMH, , , Gallup, New Mexico

Rafferty, Patrick H. , 2nd Lt, O&406334, AC, 2nd Obsn Sqdn, , USA, lived, II, Fk-1, , Jinsen, Brookline, Massachussetts

Rahe, John E. F. , Pfc, 6938046, AC, 24th Purs Gp, Hq & Hq Sqdn, USA, 1/11/45, , , , , Dyersville, Iowa

Raider, Jerome L. , 1st Lt, O&390078, Inf, 102nd Inf Regt (PA), , USA, 1/22/45, I, , , , Milwaukee, Wisconsin

Ramsey, Herman G., 1st Lt, O&361069, Inf, 1st Inf Div (PA), , USA, 12/15/44, I, , , , , Ohio

Patrick Rafferty listed as one of the few, fortunate survivors of the sinking of the *Oryoku Maru* and Japanese prison camps. (Photo courtesy of USMA Archives)

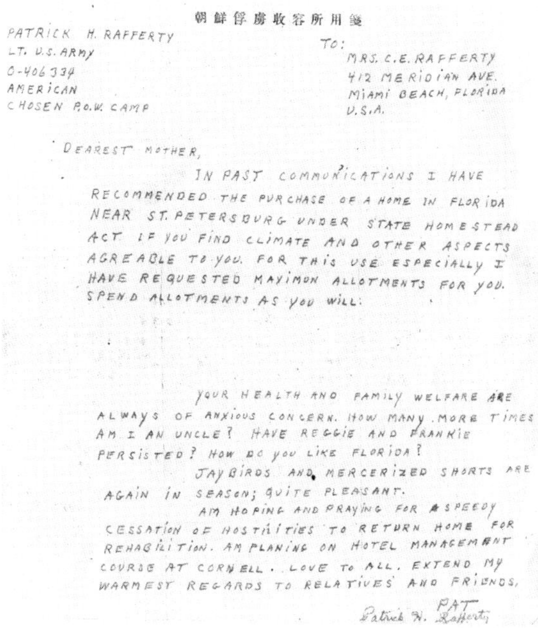

朝鮮俘虜收容所用箋

PATRICK H. RAFFERTY
LT. U.S. ARMY
O-406334
AMERICAN
CHOSEN P.O.W. CAMP

TO:
MRS. C.E. RAFFERTY
412 MERIDIAN AVE.
MIAMI BEACH, FLORIDA
U.S.A.

DEAREST MOTHER,

IN PAST COMMUNICATIONS I HAVE RECOMMENDED THE PURCHASE OF A HOME IN FLORIDA NEAR ST. PETERSBURG UNDER STATE HOMESTEAD ACT IF YOU FIND CLIMATE AND OTHER ASPECTS AGREABLE TO YOU. FOR THIS USE ESPECIALLY I HAVE REQUESTED MAXIMUM ALLOTMENTS FOR YOU. SPEND ALLOTMENTS AS YOU WILL.

YOUR HEALTH AND FAMILY WELFARE ARE ALWAYS OF ANXIOUS CONCERN. HOW MANY MORE TIMES AM I AN UNCLE? HAVE REGGIE AND FRANKIE PERSISTED? HOW DO YOU LIKE FLORIDA?

JAYBIRDS AND MERCERIZED SHORTS ARE AGAIN IN SEASON; QUITE PLEASANT.

AM HOPING AND PRAYING FOR A SPEEDY CESSATION OF HOSTILITIES TO RETURN HOME FOR REHABILITION. AM PLANING ON HOTEL MANAGEMENT COURSE AT CORNELL. LOVE TO ALL. EXTEND MY WARMEST REGARDS TO RELATIVES AND FRIENDS,

PAT
Patrick H. Rafferty

Seen here is an original letter written from Patrick Rafferty to his mother spending a winter in Florida. Note the postscript about 'Jay'birds and 'Mercer'ized shorts, a clever way to let his mother know to tell Jay Mercer's family that dear friend and fellow POW Jay Mercer was also still alive. (Photo courtesy of Rafferty family)

The famed B-29 bomber had returned to the Philippines, a sight for sore eyes of the many prisoners who were nearing their bitter end if not for rescue in 1945. (Photo courtesy of Public Broadcasting Service)

The American bombers were notorious for humorous nicknames, like the one Rafferty recalled seeing fly over the prison camp named *Slick Dick*, and they were not shy about putting a personal message on the bombs that were dropped on their enemy. (Photo unknown)

General Douglas MacArthur was the US commander at the time of the Japanese capture of the Philippines in 1942, but also returned as liberator at the end of the War in the Pacific. This photograph of MacArthur smoking his famous corncob pipe was probably at Manila in August 1945. (Photo courtesy of NARA)

A portrait of the former Japanese prime minister, Hideki Tōjō, taken whilst he was in US custody in 1947. (Photo courtesy of NARA)

A session of the International Military Tribunal for the Far East underway in the former War Ministry building, Tokyo, Japan, on January 6, 1948. In the dock at right is former Japanese Prime Minister General Hideki Tōjō, guarded by US Army military policemen. (Photo courtesy of USNHHC)

Former Japanese Prime Minister General Hideki Tōjō testifies during his trial before the International Military Tribunal in Tokyo, January 6, 1948. (Photo courtesy of USNHHC)

Patrick Rafferty walking the aisle with Dorothy O'Neil upon returning from the War, introduced to Dorothy from his fellow POW, Jay Mercer. (Photo courtesy of Rafferty family)

A noteworthy military career would follow imprisonment, leading Rafferty and Dorothy to various Air Force bases home and abroad as they raised their six beloved children together. Tenure at the U.S. Pentagon marked the late stages of Rafferty's military career.
(Photo courtesy of Rafferty family)

Due to illness stemming from his time as a prisoner, Lieutenant Colonel Patrick Rafferty was forced to stop flying and retire early from active duty after 21 years of service. Rafferty would settle in Duxbury as proprietor of Mr. Donut in Marshfield, MA before retiring to Falmouth, Massachusetts on Cape Cod. (Photo courtesy of Rafferty family)

Rafferty seen here celebrating his Irish roots with daughter, Patsy, and son, Brian, on St. Patrick's Day circa 1960. (Photo courtesy of Rafferty family.)

Patrick and Dorothy Rafferty's children. L to R: Oscar, Regina, Helen, Patsy Joan, and Brian. (Photo courtesy of Rafferty family)

Patrick Rafferty with grandson and co-author, Chad Godfrey, in Duxbury, Massachusetts in early 1978. (Photo courtesy of Godfrey family)

Gravestone as seen at Otis Air Force Base on Cape Cod, a final marker to a life and military career full of adventure and resilience. Rafferty is the last recipient of full military honors with a ceremonial fly-over at Otis. (Photo courtesy of Rafferty family)

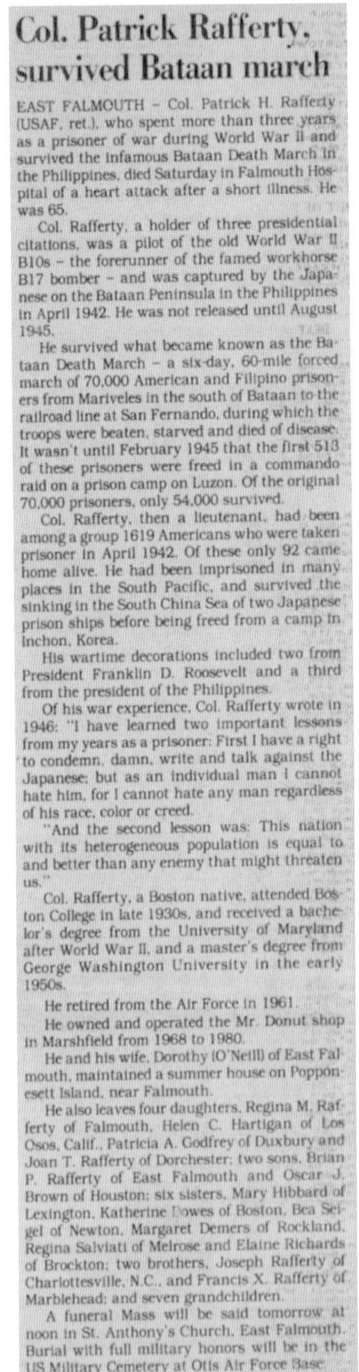

Col. Patrick Rafferty, survived Bataan march

EAST FALMOUTH – Col. Patrick H. Rafferty (USAF, ret.), who spent more than three years as a prisoner of war during World War II and survived the infamous Bataan Death March in the Philippines, died Saturday in Falmouth Hospital of a heart attack after a short illness. He was 65.

Col. Rafferty, a holder of three presidential citations, was a pilot of the old World War II B10s – the forerunner of the famed workhorse B17 bomber – and was captured by the Japanese on the Bataan Peninsula in the Philippines in April 1942. He was not released until August 1945.

He survived what became known as the Bataan Death March – a six-day, 60-mile forced march of 70,000 American and Filipino prisoners from Mariveles in the south of Bataan to the railroad line at San Fernando, during which the troops were beaten, starved and died of disease. It wasn't until February 1945 that the first 513 of these prisoners were freed in a commando raid on a prison camp on Luzon. Of the original 70,000 prisoners, only 54,000 survived.

Col. Rafferty, then a lieutenant, had been among a group 1619 Americans who were taken prisoner in April 1942. Of these only 92 came home alive. He had been imprisoned in many places in the South Pacific, and survived the sinking in the South China Sea of two Japanese prison ships before being freed from a camp in Inchon, Korea.

His wartime decorations included two from President Franklin D. Roosevelt and a third from the president of the Philippines.

Of his war experience, Col. Rafferty wrote in 1946: "I have learned two important lessons from my years as a prisoner: First I have a right to condemn, damn, write and talk against the Japanese; but as an individual man I cannot hate him, for I cannot hate any man regardless of his race, color or creed.

"And the second lesson was: This nation with its heterogeneous population is equal to and better than any enemy that might threaten us."

Col. Rafferty, a Boston native, attended Boston College in late 1930s, and received a bachelor's degree from the University of Maryland after World War II, and a master's degree from George Washington University in the early 1950s.

He retired from the Air Force in 1961.

He owned and operated the Mr. Donut shop in Marshfield from 1968 to 1980.

He and his wife, Dorothy (O'Neill) of East Falmouth, maintained a summer house on Popponesett Island, near Falmouth.

He also leaves four daughters, Regina M. Rafferty of Falmouth, Helen C. Hartigan of Los Osos, Calif., Patricia A. Godfrey of Duxbury and Joan T. Rafferty of Dorchester; two sons, Brian P. Rafferty of East Falmouth and Oscar J. Brown of Houston; six sisters, Mary Hibbard of Lexington, Katherine Dowes of Boston, Bea Seigel of Newton, Margaret Demers of Rockland, Regina Salviati of Melrose and Elaine Richards of Brockton; two brothers, Joseph Rafferty of Charlottesville, N.C., and Francis X. Rafferty of Marblehead; and seven grandchildren.

A funeral Mass will be said tomorrow at noon in St. Anthony's Church, East Falmouth. Burial with full military honors will be in the US Military Cemetery at Otis Air Force Base.

– WILLIAM P. COUGHLIN

Patrick Rafferty's obituary highlighting his regarded words about decency and the power of diversity in the United States despite his POW experience. (Photo courtesy of Rafferty family) and meanwhile the United States' great manufacturing capacity was just beginning to get up to speed, pumping out ships and planes and tanks and weapons just as fast as you like. Yamamoto knew the one chance the Japanese had—to eliminate the U.S. Pacific fleet, and force a negotiated peace—was now gone. But it would take a lot more bloodshed before Japan, as a nation, accepted that fact. In addition to losing the planes and carriers, a good portion of Japan's most skilled aviators were also killed at Midway.

And now MacArthur, as the overall commander of Allied forces in the Pacific, immediately saw an opportunity to bring naval, air, and ground forces back to the Philippines, and began making plans for exactly how to do so.

At the same time, the European theater was still the #1 priority, which meant that men and materiel were not exactly pouring into Australia, at least not as much as I'm sure MacArthur, that old glutton, insisted on having. Hitler had to go first, then the Japanese. But on the other hand, given the victory at Midway and how it weakened the Japanese, Roosevelt and his commanders had to do something in the Pacific. Now that they had momentum, had an advantage, they couldn't just stand pat while they dealt with the Nazis. So MacArthur gathered himself and attacked New Guinea. This was not easy territory to assault—rugged and mountainous, almost no roads to speak of. Civilization existed on the perimeter of the island, but the interior was nothing but tangled jungle. While this made attacking difficult, it also meant that if you controlled just a couple of key points—a strait, or a fort—you would in effect control the whole island. The highlands all over the Pacific were so impenetrable, in fact, that there were native peoples who had never seen a white man. There were tribes of Filipino natives who had never seen anything of the outside world, save for an occasional airplane going overhead, which they could not understand or analyze. This, maybe more than anything, gives an idea of the kind of territory we're talking about. You lived near the ocean, where one could navigate, or else in the lowlands to grow crops. Otherwise, the jungle reigned supreme.

MacArthur's campaign in New Guinea did not start well—the terrain proved unforgiving, bogging down advances and snarling up supply lines, and the 32nd Infantry was inexperienced to the point that MacArthur sacked many of the division's officers. But the Australian units proved capable, and after the shakeup the 32nd got its act together, and before too long New Guinea was in Allied control.

In the meantime, life at Cabanatuan continued uninterrupted, unchanging, except that the death rate among the prisoners went way down. Not that conditions improved, really, but—and there's no delicate way to say this—by this point those who were still alive were the hardiest, the strongest. It was pure Darwinism, a thing most people fortunately never have to experience. So those of us still alive stayed alive, for the most part, because we were lucky enough to be hardy and to not have a bullet drilled into the back of our heads. Darwinism and luck, equal parts. It certainly had nothing to do with merit, or virtue. Just dumb luck often, to have a hardier constitution, or stronger natural immunity to tropical disease, or whatever. A man cannot fight these diseases on will alone. Sure, the hardiest can fight longer, harder, but a tiny parasite or disease could take down any man it chose to take.

We worked every day except Sunday. Why they gave us Sunday off I don't know; the Japanese didn't know Sunday from Tuesday, so it must have just been a coincidence that the day off happened to be the Christian Sabbath. And there wasn't anything to do on our downtime, in any event—no books, no radios, no newspapers, nothing to connect us to the outside world—but the guards grossly understated the morale lift we had every Sunday amongst the fellas. You see, we had a diverse group of talents in the prisoner population as you would in any group of military men, I suppose. We all came from different cities and had different interests and talents, and I personally found my social interaction to be good exercise for the brain. It's healthy to learn and think about what you learn from the other men, whether it be a nuanced story from a dude who fixed up an old Model T Ford in his garage, or maybe a nostalgic sportsman who can explain with great detail how he caught a game-winning touchdown pass from Notre Dame's Angelo Bertelli when they were on the same high school football squad.

And then, in December, some 1,500 of us were selected, myself among them, and sent to Manila. They put us on trucks and it was a dreadful ride. But I suppose anything was better than Cabanatuan, with the isolation and the sense that the rest of the world had disappeared. This was when I ended up at Bilibid prison, a brick-and-stone structure built by some Conquistador three hundred years prior. The building itself was in-the-round, the wings of the prison like spokes on a wheel. The entire facility was ringed by a fifteen-foot-tall wall, rising in some places to 25 feet, topped all the way around with barbed wire. I was only there for about a week; the prison itself was mostly a place for the sick, had both American and Japanese medical staff, and otherwise was just a transportation hub for moving prisoners from one camp to another, or else putting them on ships to other penal colonies, or the home island of Japan.

At Bilibid I ran into some old buddies from Stotensburg and Clark Field, Bill Montgomery and Bill Challic, who'd been at Bilibid all along, what a dreadful, horrible, depressing place. There was more to eat there than at Cabantuan, though, and a sense that the world hadn't disappeared after all, and so we had that, at least. The sleeping conditions being concrete slabs without a sheet or blanket made for a miserable, long night but that was the situation and we had to endure or succumb and die. And then after a week the 1,500 of us were taken to pier 7—the longest pier in the world at the time, by the way, it could dock five or six ships at once on one side—and loaded onto transports for we had no idea where, except the certainty that it would be yet another awful place. It was a good three, maybe five, mile walk down to the harbor so it was always good to see some new sights and hear some different sounds. Maybe I was different in that sense, but as I've mentioned before, the desire to absorb and think about the world around me was a critical survival tactic of mine. As we boarded, you could look out across Manila Bay and see that it was a shambles just as the buildings were for the entire walk to the pier through Manila. Destroyed structures and buildings of all shapes and sizes—rubble. War, it was clear to me, could inflict horrible damage on beautiful architecture. As I looked out to the sea, I quickly counted no less than 60 ships in various versions of destroyed: stern up out of the water, broken propeller, the bow up in the air and the stern sunk, ships floating on their sides. And this destruction was oddly heartening, because the only thing you could conclude was that someone was spanking the Japanese. It wasn't the Filipinos. It wasn't the Chinese, or the British. It had to be Americans. They were somewhere. Coming back, we hoped. This was now about a year of captivity, at this point.

But as we set out on the transports there was no sign of American forces. I should describe these ships as they would become fairly important in our adventures: these were not ferries transporting a handful of families, these were ocean freighters or "maru" as they were called. These monsters were seven thousand tons or more—massive, weighty ships designed to carry obscene amounts of cargo and people. The put us prisoners down below, into the hold we went. Now, I will say that this particular trip was not as distressful as we anticipated. Yes, it was hot—it was always hot—but we had a bit of elbow room and would catch the occasional whiff of the ocean through the hatches. But here was the real kicker: we were fed like human beings, not like our time in the prison camps. A well-portioned heaping of meats like pork, soups, greens, and, of course, rice. But I should not confuse things too much. We were still prisoners and defecating in leaky buckets, wrestling to piece together a couple hours of sleep each day. At least we had that long-forgotten sensation of a full belly on that haul.

For two weeks, maybe three, we made our leisurely way down through the Philippine archipelago, San Bernadino straits and down the east coast of Mindanao to Tumbao. Tumbao was not what you'd think of as a great port, but it was a good anchorage for naval forces. And it was the location of DAPECOL—the name a mashup, or abbreviation, of Davao Penal Colony. This place had just been hacked out of the jungle in the early 1930s, and had served as the principal federal penitentiary for the Philippines until the Japanese took over. Now it was a prison camp.

When you try to picture this place, the emphasis should be on the "colony" part. It was not like Concord or Walpole prisons in Massachusetts, places with massive walls surrounding grey, hard buildings where men are meant to feel closed in and small while incarcerated. DAPECOL was an open prison. They had no need of walls because there was nowhere to go. Step off the beaten path here and the jungle would swallow you up, and that would be the last anyone saw or heard of you. No wall built by man could ever be as effective at keeping people in as an untouched jungle.

DAPECOL was in fact a prison, but in terms of how it functioned it was more like a farm—a farm that you couldn't leave, of course. Fifty square miles, a massive tract of land, with thousands of acres of bananas, even more of abaca, a kind of banana tree cultivated not for its fruit but for its leaves, which are stripped, pounded, and dried on racks in the sun to become the famous Manila hemp, the finest in the world. Coconuts, soybeans, casava—anything that could be grown was grown there, and grown well. There were water buffalo for plowing the fields, several thousand chickens, a pig farm. They had a breeding farm, a hospital, a machine shop, a rice mill. The rice-growing area was bigger than any other, and even had its own name: Mactan. It was reached by narrow-gauge railroad three miles from the central compound.

By the time we got there, the place had been decimated by the Japanese—remember, the Japanese army lives off the land. And having eaten everything, now they wanted to grow more food, for which they need labor. Thus, our presence. We 1,500 from Cabanatuan were joined by another 500 who had surrendered at Del Monte, so generally the strength at DAPECOL at any given time was 2,000-2,200 men. We were divided in the central compound according to what kind of shape we were in. Section 1 was the workers, those of relatively sound mind and body; section 2 was the barracks with people who had broken more or less mentally; section 3 housed the sick and the lame; and section 4 was reserved for the dying. Threading themselves through sections 3 and 4 were the scurvies, malarias, beriberi, oh just dreadful inflictions on a man down to 90 pounds standing over six feet tall. As for malaria and the other diseases carried by mosquitos, you'd have to count to near infinity to understand the number of mosquitos in DAPECOL. Although there were not that many deaths in the 15 months we were there owing to the fact that we grew and raised enough food that we were fed three times a day. No one was getting fat, of course, but we ate enough to survive. And there were only two suicides: one a Navy dentist who I remember was from New Orleans, the other an Army lieutenant. I say "only" two suicides not to diminish the tragedy of these two deaths, but only to say that given the conditions and the fact that we were well into our second year of captivity at the hands of these monsters, you would have expected this to have more of an effect on our heads. It did not.

Our captors numbered about 150, the senior officer being a Major Mita. On the second or third day there, the guards came and rousted us out of our barracks and outside into this large parade-grounds type area. Once we were assembled, Major Mita came out and got on this little stand and said, with great seriousness, "America—you do not come here to lazy." We knew better than to laugh, but it was damn hard not to. A big, baritone southern drawl on the prisoner next to me whispered "you best not come here to lazy, Rafferty" and I just about lost it. The Major gave us a pep talk about how decent the Japanese people were, propagandizing the hell out of us. The Japanese are very good and generous, the war will be over soon, we will all be able to live together peacefully when America respects Japan's place in the world, etc. Of course, we didn't take a word of it seriously. It took effort to fake any real consumption of this horseshit, but a little effort we still had. We still had fight as a group, strength in numbers, and down to the man for most of us.

By the time we had arrived at DAPECOL, the original population of Filipino prisoners was mostly gone, of course. This was before the Japanese had taken off, but after Filipino authorities stopped caring about things like keeping the prison running—they had bigger problems. So most of the prisoners had made it back to their home islands, but there were still about 500 or so who had been living at the prison when the Japanese showed up. These were known as Pensionados. After ten years of incarceration, and assuming good conduct, most prisoners were allowed to bring their family onto the compound and set up a household. He was given 2.2 acres of land, a hectare, and could grow his own crops, and all that was expected, aside from a certain number of hours of work a week, was that he couldn't just up and leave of his own will. The reason so many chose to stay on as Pensionados was the plain fact that life at the penal colony was better in every conceivable way than it would have been at home in some tiny fishing village, working like a dog for a couple of pesos a week. Here they got medical care, good food, had the run of the massive plantation. So as we were organized into work details, it came to be that we ended up working alongside the Pensionados, and in this way we found out that there were two ways in and out of the colony if one had a mind for escape.

The first way out, I schemed, was in the northeast corner of the plantation, where it touched the Davao River, a wide, very swift part of the Davao. But there was no way to swim across the damn thing—the current was too fast, and you'd almost certainly end up dead five miles downriver. But there was a kind of ferry, or gondola, that ran along a rope from one bank to the other. The other point of egress was all the way in the opposite direction, to the western boundary of the colony, another river with a similar ferry setup. We didn't know this at the time, but there was in fact a third way out—a road—which I'll tell you about later.

For now, and for the foreseeable future, we were on the penal colony, like it or not. We settled into various work details, not unlike at Cabanatuan. My first job was on the logging detail. The Filipinos would top the trees, these were monstrous Filipino hardwoods, teak mostly, beautiful, magnificent, 250 feet tall and 20 feet wide at the base. Can you conceive of a tree 20 feet at the base? A fire engine is only ten feet wide, so imagine a tree you could drive a fire truck through, and that's your Filipino teak.

We had only axes, no saws at all, certainly no power saws, and we would start cutting away at the base, chopping and chopping and chopping, for hours, days—hell, I remember one tree that we must have hacked away at for three weeks. And when it finally fell, the sound was like an armada of bombers had come in overhead and dropped their payloads on us all at once. You could hear the crash echo through the forest. I found a degree of pride as that big sucker fell, even more so a jolt of enthusiasm as a fella said "the whole empire will fall like this big bastard." Our minds could still be ours despite this back-breaking prison labor.

From there, we had to cut the tree into 6-foot lengths (and remember, this thing is really thick all the way through, cutting it into segments was just as time-consuming as chopping it down in the first place) and then roll and push and otherwise by hook or crook move these segments down into the river. The logs would float down to Davao Bay, a brackish harbor where we'd lash the logs together with chains, hundreds of them, and they'd float and cure for a couple of years, then be brought ashore and arranged in piles to dry for another couple of years, then finally slabbed and shipped off for export.

What made this long, difficult, drawn-out process worthwhile was, of course, the quality of the wood. It makes the most exquisite furniture. It was out of those trunks, years before, that the largest table on earth was hewn, the dining room table in Malacanang Palace, the home of the president of the Philippines. It accommodated something like 200 people, one solid, unbroken piece of wood if you can imagine that.

It didn't take long before life became an unending routine, just as it had at Cabanatuan. We settled in, we weren't going anywhere and there was no use fighting it. You lived mostly in your head and gave yourself over to the routine because you had no choice. Up in the morning at daybreak, some vegetables for breakfast, get into formation for work detail, out the gate and onto the narrow-gauge flatbed cars for transport to the job. I worked the logging detail, I worked details hoeing fields, planting, harvesting. We had a lot of work to do because the Japanese, as was their custom, took and took but didn't replenish anything. They were not given at all to sustaining the plantation. They wouldn't breed the chickens, but they were happy to eat all the eggs. They would not breed the caribou, instead eating the young ones before they could reproduce. It fell to us to figure out how to keep the plantation productive, and to do the work to make it happen. This kept the Japanese happy, which in turn kept us alive. And we did get one nice luxury during that time being served at DAPECOL and that was the Sunday entertainment amongst, and by, the troops.

We had the great fortune of having dramatic, theatrical types amongst us—a few actors and singers that could really do the trick in front of an audience. I would spend my time in prayer on a Sunday morning, but boy did I appreciate the performers doing their acting and singing on a Sunday afternoon. There was one performer, a guy from that shoreline of New Jersey, who did an Eddie Cantor-esque vaudeville routine, and there wouldn't be a face without a smile in the entire group of onlookers. He nailed it and we'd practically beg for more. Mercer would clap as if he'd just seen a brilliant play on a big stage in New York City—he just loved it and I loved to see that. My favorite, though, was a guy whose name I won't recall who was a Bing Crosby doppelganger. I mean, he looked the part like you could hardly believe with the blue eyes and all. I could damn near have tears rolling down my cheeks listening to him do Brother Can You Spare a Dime.

They used to tell me I was building a dream, so the song went, and I found a real beauty to the sadness in that number, and I welcomed the sad emotion, frankly. Human beings, particularly those held in a harsh prison environment, require connections and emotions, most helpfully laughter and a spiritual rigor. But sadness was good, too. It's not good to keep things bottled up inside—we human beings are not airtight vessels. We need to release the pressures that build up inside us, and that can take the form of sadness sometimes, and that's okay. So did these gifted fellas ever provide that release for us, regardless of how sick and tired they may have been themselves as they exerted their energies to perform on Sundays. Like the priests and doctors whom we admired beyond words, the performers on Sunday were downright critical to our survival. People would comment on my nice smile as a young man and I liked to get that compliment, so I was committed, deliberate to not let the Japanese treatment of me take that away.

During the eighteen months I stayed at DAPECOL, though my health was overall quite good, like most of us I suffered many bouts of malaria. On such attack occurred after working in the rice fields at Mactan, a complication called Blackwater Fever, which in those circumstances (poor medical care, no effective drugs) was often fatal. I have no memory of going to the hospital section of the compound, but I was there for a couple of weeks, and I'm glad I don't remember it, because no doubt it was miserable. What saved my life, I think, was simple saline solution. I basically lived on an IV drip of saline while my body somehow managed to fight off the sickness and right itself.

The other thing that could be dangerous, even if you were in good health, was getting cut or otherwise having sores. In that climate, without antibiotics or proper sanitation, a cut could take months to heal, get infected of course, and if this infection spread to the rest of your body, as it did for some, that could be the end of you. Add to the mix that we shared sleeping quarters with an evil army of lice and bed bugs that could just about drive a man to kill himself with the itchy rash they left behind after feasting all night on your skin. Having our open cuts in and around that feasting was not a pretty sight indeed.

Another thing that I think helped my health and that of others had to do with the way we harvested and processed rice. Among the prisoners was a M.D. named Major Waco, who told us that if we could eat rice brown instead of white, that would be very beneficial to us, owing to the fact that most of the nutrition in rice is in the brown hull surrounding the white core, which is polished off in processing. Now understand, in the Philippines and Japan and probably other places in the Orient, no one eats brown rice. It's just not done. Not even the most destitute person would be caught eating anything other than white rice. And so certainly the expectation from the Japanese was that the rice we produced at the colony would continue to be polished white. The plantation had a rice mill for this purpose. And sure enough, one day somebody, I never found out who, while the rice was being poured for polishing, took a big hunk of scrap metal, iron or steel, and threw it down the chute. Now the milling stone was substantial—three or four tons, probably, maybe more, fifteen feet in diameter and a foot thick. It took a long time to get it spinning, and once it did spin, of course, it did the job quite nicely. But all that spinning energy, when the piece of scrap metal hit the stone, shattered it irreparably, just as whoever threw it down there intended. There was no fixing it, and it wasn't like you could just find another stone, so we ended up with brown rice and were pretty elated. The Japanese, on the other hand, were just sick about it. They had to bring in their own white rice thereafter, couldn't believe we would actually eat it brown. I'm sure it did nothing to improve their opinion of us as unrefined.

And speaking of food, the person in charge of the prisoners' mess hall was a Marine named Lieutenant Winterhalter. Winterhalter had somehow survived even more, on balance, than the rest of us, including a disease that had attacked his lower body. At one point he'd been in a wheelchair, though he was back on his feet now. He was a good guy, and really tough, among the toughest people I'd ever met. And he had to be, because part of his job was making sure everyone got their ration of food, no more or less. Which meant he was constantly policing guys who tried to take more than their share. This wasn't considered stealing, really, though maybe it should have been—it was just part of surviving. Anyway, Winterhalter had a sharp eye and took his job seriously, didn't let anyone slide. Which may have been part of why the story I'm about to tell you happened.

Winterhalter had a dog, a little mongrel that followed him everywhere he went. I'm not sure where she came from, but there was no question she was his dog, and he loved her and she him. In the barracks I was in, we divided up into groups of 8 men per bay. My bay was all guys who had been pilots at Clark Field—Perry Franks, Bill Challic, Mercer, Alsabrook, some others. We all got along very well. There was a respect and humor amongst our group that served us well. Not much talking, you know, occasional bits of conversation, but that feeling of ease when you know and understand other people and nothing much needs to be said. One day—and I don't remember who came up with the idea—we got it in our heads to catch Winterhalter's dog and cook it up. Listen, we were men terribly in need of protein.

It'd been so long since any of us had had meat and I guess maybe also some of us resented Winterhalter a bit for being so good at his job. In any event, we came up with a plan like it was some kind of big military operation, you know, Perry Franks giving everyone a job and outlining logistics one night, "Okay, Mercer you distract Winterhalter so he doesn't notice the dog isn't around, then Challic and Alsabrook you grab the dog when she's wandering through the barracks looking for a place to pee." And that's just what they did. Alsabrook grabbed the dog, put his hand over its muzzle, brought it into the barracks and whacked it with a right hand hook like a prizefighter might do. Two others had the job of butchering the dog, and two of us, me being one of them, had the job of collecting wood scraps out on work detail and stashing it under the barracks. I think part of the reason I got that job was because I never turned down a work detail; it was the only way to break up the monotony of imprisonment, this tortured, subdued life, and besides, there were all kinds of opportunities, if you were at all enterprising, to find something extra to eat. Wild bananas, sugar cane, maybe some frogs or toads in the rice fields, little crustaceans, water snakes—the Filipinos had taught us how to behead a snake and strip it and get the poison out and they were delicious, like a kind of fishy chicken.

Anyway, back to the dog. I was also on the cooking detail. We had some rice, let it dry and pounded it into a powder, which made the mixture in the pot like a gravy, a kind of mongrel stew. We each ended up with about a canteen and a half of the stuff. And it was such an unusual taste, even as hungry as we were and as many strange things as we'd eaten by then, it felt strange to put a dog in your belly. Mind you, we've long since been on nothing but bland vegetables and rice, and it wasn't like we had a pantry full of spices and condiments to make the dog more palatable. So by the time I got halfway through my share, I realized I couldn't take any more. I was beginning to get the blahs. So I decided to go and give the rest of mine to a friend, Father Bahmen from Pittsburgh. So I went up there to Father Bahman's barracks and I said, "Hey Father, look what I got." And he said, "What have you got there?" in that way that means not so much, "What is that?" as it means, "How can I get some for myself?", you know. And I told him, "Never mind that, Father, this is good chow, help yourself." So he got out his spoon and had a bite and said, "Goodness, this is great stuff, where did you get it?" And I said, "Please don't ask." But he kept eating and asking, and finally I said, "Father, that's Winterhalter's dog." And with that, Father Bahmen dropped his cup, ran outside, and threw up on the dirt walkway. With years of watching sick men having to vomit, I cannot say that I've ever seen a fireworks display quite like what Bahman put on that day and I regret to say that I recounted the story to our friends for many weeks thereafter. Those were desperate times but there was a little humor in there for us.

If you did your work and didn't draw attention to yourself or otherwise start trouble, it was easy enough to get along with the Japanese at DAPECOL. They abused us, but not the way we were abused on the march and in the days after. The truth was that in a weird way, we were all in it together, the prisoners and the Japanese. They were just as sick and tired of being there as we were. They ate poorly and were dirty all the time and dealt with the same persistent tropical diseases we did. They felt forgotten, same as us. So while I wouldn't go so far as to say we bonded, there was an unspoken understanding that came to pass, and as long as you kept your nose clean and did what you were told you could pretty much get along. They weren't running around beheading people, though there would be beatings. I caught a few myself. It could be as simple as not being able to understand a command in Japanese—although we all picked up enough Japanese to get by, certainly, it was funny how quickly you could learn another language when not doing so meant you got the butt of a rifle to the nose. Giving a guard a stern look, even a glance out of the corner of your eye or putting a little firmness in your voice—that was a way to get a good beating. Another way of getting whacked was to walk up to a guard, who were almost all short in stature, five or six inches shorter than us, and look down at him with contempt. On a bad day, that could earn you a bayonet in the belly.

I mentioned that work details were good for finding miscellaneous things to eat. The best was the rice detail. You have no idea—anything that crawled, we'd eat. We had a system worked out for the locating and distribution of found food, which we referred to as "qwan." I don't remember where the word came from or how we picked it up, but basically it was a filler word that meant anything material. A bunch of bananas were qwan. Wild bird eggs were qwan. And so on. The rice detail was thirty men, each of us planting or harrowing or seeding or harvesting. It was piece work—when your row was completed, you were finished for the day. So the thirty guys on the detail, the same guys each day, would look for things to eat in addition to working their row. Whatever was found, no matter who found it, it went to the two guys who were next in the rotation to receive qwan, and those two would have an addition to their meal when we got back to camp, and the next qwan would go to the next two in the rotation, and so on.

One day out at Mactan, we had all finished work and were just resting under a nice alder tree, it looked like a sycamore, big broad leaves, it was gorgeous. And then we all notice an airplane overhead, at maybe 2,000 feet. No one had seen an airplane in months. We had no way of knowing, of course, but by this time MacArthur was north of New Guinea, fighting in New Britain and the Marshall Islands, and the Navy is making its way across the Pacific, hopscotching from island to island, had the Japanese on the run. But here's this big Japanese plane, maybe a transport, flying over us, and there are maybe sixty of us prisoners at least and one Japanese guard all watching it go. This guard was a guy who had a reputation as a big talker, always boasting about everything Japanese, which according to him was always the biggest and strongest and best. He sees this plane and starts in with his routine: "Ah, cocoki Nippon…" Nippon meaning Japanese. "Ah, very big…" So someone takes the cue and begins taunting the guard to give us a long list of all things Japanese and how great they all are. "Menny Japanese takous…ahhhh…" And so he goes down his list of everything Japanese, going on and on about how all of it is big and strong and many. And while he's explaining that everything Japanese is better than anything else in the world, he reaches down kind of absently and scratches himself. And Alsabrook, the dog killer, who was from Austin, Texas and a real wag, says to him, "What about Japanese crabs?" "Ohhh, ahhh…biggo, strongo, toxcan…" And my god, it wasn't that funny but we all started laughing, those big deep belly laughs you can't stop even if you want to. I hadn't had a laugh like that in two years. All of us just roaring. And the guard was laughing along, at first. But it didn't take too long before he realized the joke was on him, and now we've really done it, because the one thing you don't want to do is make a Japanese feel like he's lost face. He got this look, and he stepped back and reached into his belt, pulled out a clip of bullets, put them into the breech, slid the bolt, and pointed his rife at us. Now in the meantime, as we're watching him do all this, we'd shut the hell up. Not even murmuring to each other anymore, absolute silence. We couldn't tell if he was actually going to shoot us, but there was absolutely nothing stopping him from doing so, and if you looked closely you could see *he* didn't know whether he was going to shoot us either, which was not reassuring. So we were just sitting there, still and silent, wondering if this was finally it for some of us, if this was how it all ended. And then the guard got onto one of the little two-foot-wide walkways built up between the rice paddies and started backing slowly away, as if he was frightened of us, as if we'd somehow threatened him instead of just laughing at him. When he got about fifty or sixty feet away he pulled a whistle from his jacket and blew it, loudly. Just as with the Boston police, among the Japanese when you heard a whistle, that was a summon for help. And sure enough, way off in the distance we can see these little guys running toward us with great urgency, negotiating the walkways between the rice paddies, rifles at the ready, and boy it sure seemed we might be in trouble on this one. About six other guards showed up, jabber, etc. We just waited in silence, no idea how this was all going to shake out—what was he telling them we did? How would they react? Were we going to be shot dead right here in this rice field? Would anyone ever find us? Would our families know what happened to us? And then finally, the senior Japanese GI ordered us out from under the tree, into a single-file column—and off we went through the rice paddies, three Japanese to the front, three to the rear... speedo speedo...hurry. They got us out of there double-time fast, put us on the little narrow gauge flatbeds, and brought us back to the main compound. Thank goodness, that was the end of that, and if it wasn't forgotten—the boastful Japanese guard was decidedly less friendly with us after that—at least it didn't cost us our heads.

We weren't the only ones who played a little fast and loose with the rules while out on detail, though. The guards themselves were forever trying to barter with us out in the fields, away from the watchful gaze of their superiors. The Filipinos stayed out of it—we had nothing they were interested in, or couldn't get for themselves. But the Japanese always had some goods and some angle. The principal currency of the prison camp was tobacco, and the principal denomination was a hand, fifteen or twenty leaves knotted together with a string of bamboo and left on a hook to dry. Understand that the tobacco the Japanese brought us was atrocious—they saved the good stuff for themselves, of course, and we got the lousy stuff, rotten, full of moths. But it was still tobacco, and tobacco was the medium of exchange. I'd get a hand from someone on detail and take it back to the camp, and it was so bloody strong you couldn't even make a proper cigar with it, except maybe one of those terrible Italian cigars, the ones that are so strong they make you feel like you're going to pass out or vomit, or both. To take some of the strength out of it you could soak the tobacco in water, wring it out just like a mop, and let it dry a second time before chopping it up for smoking. As bad as it was there were those who would trade for it, so it was always a great boon for me to get this tobacco. Most often I'd use it to trade for food; even with the farm and the qwan system we were forever looking for something more, or something better, to eat.

I never had anything of real value to trade with the Japanese—remember, I'd thrown everything I had on the side of the road during the march when it got too heavy to carry—but if you had something they really wanted, a fountain pen or some jewelry, say, you could get actual cigarettes. These were excellent Japanese smokes called Akebonos. They would have been considered very good quality under normal circumstances, when you could just go to the store and buy yourself anything you wanted to smoke, and so a pack of Akebonos in the camp was a genuine treasure.

A big part of staying healthy, or at least giving yourself the best chance of staying healthy, was to take great care with personal hygiene and grooming. Not terrifically easy to do in such a hot, sticky, muddy climate, but it was worth the effort in terms of survival, not to mention self-regard. I had a full G.I. kit, G.I. meaning "government issue," by the way, when you first enlist everything you get is considered G.I., your socks and underwear and uniforms, of course, weapons, everything. The kit, though, had a canteen, a dish, a cup, a fork, a knife, and a spoon, all of which went in a web belt to hang everything on. The set I had—I don't even remember where it came from—was marked 1918, which meant it was issued, or at least manufactured, during WWI. It was made of very high-quality steel. I was able to knock the half-inch curved tip off the knife and, using a little four-inch portable whetstone (again, don't remember where that came from, one of the fellas had it) I was able to hone the knife down. It took some work, and you had to get the angle just right—20 degrees is the ideal angle for sharpening an edge, you measure it best you can by eye from 90 degrees, which is of course the edge straight up and down on top of the whetstone, and after a while you just get a feel for it and don't have to use your eyes at all. With some practice I was able to put a superb edge on that knife. The edge was good for about half a shave, and then I'd have to do some more sharpening and lots of stropping, I'd found a strip of leather for that and was able to use it to polish the blade. And in this way I was able to shave every day. In fact, I used to shave other guys for a cigarette a pop. And this was the way life was lived, you see. I do this for you, you give that to me. Everything had a value and the economy among everyone there, us prisoners at least, was fair and above-board. That may have been the most remarkable thing about the entire experience—I never once heard of anyone having lost anything of value. There was never any stealing (well, except maybe for that poor dog). Everyone was unfailingly respectful of everyone else.

I mentioned that DAPECOL had a hospital, and though it probably goes without saying, understand that this was not a hospital in the way you think of a big multi-wing building with all sorts of state-of-the-art equipment and doctors and nurses everywhere and clean beds and sterile operating rooms. No, sir. I call it a hospital because that was in effect the function it served, but really it was just four barracks with exceedingly insufficient medical supplies and equipment. This was a makeshift, make-do facility at best, although the one thing we did have—the most important thing, probably—was half a dozen really good doctors among the prisoners. They were all among the prisoners who had come in after the surrender at Del Monte. So we were very fortunate for that.

I had two operations while at DAPECOL, one a circumcision and the other, six months later, for piles. I have little idea how a circumcision would be performed at a proper hospital stateside, but I can tell you—trying to be delicate here—that where and how and why I had it done in prison was probably less than ideal. It starts with the medical tech taking a razor and cleaning up your pubic area. That's the easy part. Then the doctor comes at you with a four-inch-needle. I still shudder thinking about it even today. There's nothing gentle about it, no sense trying to be sensitive—he just grabs your organ and plunges that needle right into the top of it. Oh God, what an experience, I thought I was going to go insane. This is a local anesthetic, of course, and once that's done they perform the operation and if you're smart you find something else to occupy your attention while they work but good luck doing that. Fortunately it doesn't take long, but in my case it was a mess for a while afterward. But I was lucky to not have any infection, and I recovered. Then later on, the piles became so unbearable I had to have that dealt with. That recovery was harder, in part because one still has to take care of one's most basic functions and there was no proper medication to help things along, like mineral oil. Just a long and lingering several weeks, wondering if it was ever going to get any better. Eventually, thank goodness, it did.

In addition to the medical personnel, we were lucky enough to have two dentists in camp. Of course, as with the medical facilities, there was no equipment or materials for anything like bridgework or any fancy capping. For an infected tooth, the method of treatment was extraction, plain and simple, and you counted your stars that there was local anesthetic around for that. Incidentally, to even get into the Army, at least before the war when I signed up, you had to have excellent dental health. They even had a minimum number of teeth, below which you could not be enlisted. For example, if you were missing more than two teeth you wouldn't be accepted into flight school. And you had to be in excellent physical condition as well. The point is that, lucky for me, more than two years after first enlisting in the Army, my teeth were still in very good shape, despite it all. But I still had some work done at DAPECOL. The dentists actually had a piece of field equipment that was made for working on soldiers' teeth on the front lines, a simple machine with pulleys and wheels. It looked an awful lot like a sewing machine. And just like a sewing machine, the way it worked was the dental tech would pedal, like the foot pedal on an old Singer, and the belts and wheels would spin and that in turn would make the dental drill do its thing. It was pretty slow, so to have a tooth filled was quite an ordeal. Anesthetic was in too short supply to use when someone just needed a filling. So it was just open up and hang on for your life.

A funny thing that happened at DAPECOL that relates to all this talk of medical care was—and there's no other way to put this, really—I went into business manufacturing counterfeit medicine.

You recall I wrote about how the Japanese were constantly trying to barter with us. They were after what for them were high-value items like pens, rings and other jewelry, a nice leather wallet. Decorative things, mostly. So we were entirely accustomed to having guards kind of sidle up next to us in the fields and try to cut deals, very secretive and cloak-and-dagger in a way that was kind of comical.

One day I was in the rice fields and a real little guard came up and said to me, very quiet: "America, doubloo, doubloo." Well, I had no earthly clue what he was talking about. I just stared at him, and he said it again, his hand out to me: "Doubloo, doubloo." I just shrugged my shoulders at him and said, "Nai, nai," and went back to my work.

And later I was still puzzling over this, so once I was back at the barracks I mentioned it to a couple of the fellas I bunked with. What is this "doubloo" business, I asked them. And they didn't have any idea, either, so at least it wasn't just me. We were racking our brains trying to figure it out—in part because it was clear that whatever it was, the Japanese guard wanted it badly, and would probably be willing to part with something pretty good to have it. I mentioned to them that the guard had held out one of his hands, palm-up, and with the index finger of his other hand had drawn a little circle on his palm maybe half an inch in diameter. And that's when Bill Challic pipes up and says, "I think I know what it is. He's talking about sulphapizol." We didn't have any idea what he was talking about, and anyway, what was the connection between sulphapizol and "doubloo"? Well, Bill told us, sulphapizol was the drug the medics gave to guys who got the clap—gonorrhea. And it was made by Winthrop Pharmaceutical, and as such featured a "W" sort of engraved on the face of each pill. In Japanese, apparently, W translated into "doubloo." And we all sure had a laugh at that, but we also got to thinking—how could we get our hands on some doubloo?

Our first idea was to gather as much qwan as we could and use it as barter with one of the guys working in the hospital, see if he couldn't find us some doubloo. Out on details we gathered as much as we could find of all kinds of little wild fruits, there were these bitter little orange-like things, and we also came across a tree of wild alligator pears, which I couldn't stand at the time but plenty of the others liked them well enough. Today they're called avocados, but back then we knew them as alligator pears, I'm not sure why. Anyway, we got together a good collection of all these different kinds of fruits, hidden under someone's cot in the barracks, and one day when we thought we had enough we brought it to a G.I. in the hospital section and prevailed upon him to get us some doubloo, and he tried but for whatever reason couldn't get the drugs out of the infirmary.

And that was when I somewhat accidentally went into the fake drugs manufacturing business. Because the next idea was to take a package of plaster of Paris—again, we'd try and get it from the hospital, where of course it was used to cast broken bones—and use it to form little pills we could sell to the Japanese as doubloo. Perry Franks was pretty handy whittling with a little pen knife, and he took a piece of bamboo and carved a bunch of little circular depressions in it, even making a little raised "W" in the center of each one. And we took the plaster of Paris and some water, mixed it with a little rice paste, and filled in each of the holes. When it dried and we popped them out and smoothed them down, we had some pretty convincing little fake doubloos right down to the little W, maybe good enough to try and fool the Japanese with.

I say "maybe" because the pills weren't so great that everyone was clamoring to be the one to try and sell them to the guards. God only knew what would happen to you if they realized you were trying to pull a fast one. There were no volunteers among us, but someone had to try it. Finally Franks pointed at me and said I was the logical choice, since the guard had approached me about it in the first place. Everyone else thought that made a whole lot of sense. So I was stuck.

On the next rice detail, I took a couple of fake doubloos with me—not a fistful, because they weren't uniform enough in appearance to sell a bunch of them at a time; all it would take was a good look at four or five together and you'd realize they weren't the same at all. So during the izamay, which is a little rest period during the day, I went up to the same guard who'd approached me and reached into my pocket and held out the two pills. And he was ecstatic. Then he told me he needed twenty of them. Twenty! I didn't see that coming, and I wasn't sure exactly what to do, so I just shrugged and told him he could have two more the following day.

The thing was, all these Japanese guards had gone out into the nearest town and gotten themselves into, shall we say, social trouble. And they couldn't go to their own clinic; it simply wasn't an option. If they turned themselves in with a case of the clap, they'd catch a frightful beating. Therefore when it came to doubloo, I was in a position of supreme advantage. The next day I went out with five pills, which was maybe a little risky, and I negotiated with the guard and held out for—you won't believe it—thirty packs of Akebonos. Thirty packs! It was like finding gold. I went back to the barracks that day like I'd won the lottery.

But even though this was a bonanza of heretofore unimaginable proportions, there's an obvious question that's probably on your mind—what happens if and when the Japanese realize they've been had, that the pills aren't working? Certainly that question occurred to us after it became evident how valuable the Japanese considered our fake doubloo. I in particular, being the face of the operation with the guards, had my neck out about three yards. This was dangerous. So the guys in my bay had a powwow and talked it over. Obviously the pills were not going to cure whatever ailed the guards. The question was whether they would suspect the reason the pills didn't work was because they were fake, and if so, what they would do about it. And we pretty quickly reached the conclusion that they would, in fact, do nothing. Because there's nothing worse in Japanese culture than to lose face—which in a way was demonstrated by the fact that they'd come to us for medication in the first place. The deal was, basically: if you're stuck, don't admit it. If you've been had, don't admit it. It mattered a lot more to the Japanese not to be embarrassed over something publicly than to get even or otherwise remedy a situation where they were foolish and taken advantage of. So our wager was the guards would never say a word about the ineffective doubloo, because to do so would be to lose face tremendously. And indeed, they never did. After a week of dealing doubloos, they stopped coming to me for them. It must have become obvious the pills weren't working, and so that was the end of the enterprise. But we got one potload of cigarettes out of the whole thing, let me tell you.

By now it was early 1943 and over the holidays we'd received something that was an even greater boon than the doubloo cigarette haul. The Red Cross had sent out holiday boxes to the POWs, and you'd think someone had made us millionaires overnight when those boxes arrived. We didn't get all of them, of course, the Japanese stole what they wanted. The boxes weighed about twelve pounds piece—even just the weight of them, before you even opened them up, was such a delight, so heavy with wonderfulness, it really was like Christmas. Each one contained powdered milk, powdered coffee, chocolate, condensed peas, condensed beans. Two cans each of Argentine bully beef, which was superior stuff—nice and red, a little fatty, but it was delicious, and oh, talk about a Thanksgiving dinner. We'd supplement what came in the boxes with what we could gather and scrounge, and made some terrific meals. In the eighteen months I spent at DAPECOL we got two shipments of boxes, about eight or nine months apart.

And incidentally, along with the food boxes the Red Cross also sent us about a thousand books. In fact, that was where I learned to love reading, right there in the prison camp. Among my favorites was *Gone With the Wind*. I read it probably half a dozen times. There were all manner of books—Spanish grammar, French grammar, math books, nonfiction and novels. It was something to do to keep my head going, keep myself from either getting stupid or going crazy. I studied Spanish while I was there, and even brushed up on my high school algebra. Completed an entire algebra textbook, did every last problem. You don't realize how much time there is in a day until you're stuck in a prison camp for a couple of years, let me tell you. Even better than having the books around, a select few men were starting to receive mail from home which was an awfully fun thing to watch. Imagine getting a fresh photograph of your best girl or your infant that had grown to walk by now. Just fabulous to enjoy those moments with some of the boys, yet in such a devilish place.

While we often bartered with the Japanese, trading items for items, they also frequently tried to pay us in the fake Philippine yen they'd created. I mentioned before that this money was worthless—it wasn't backed by anything of real value, just the Japanese government saying "This is your money now." So no one really cared about it one way or the other, except insofar as there needed, I suppose, to be some kind of currency for people to conduct their business. Anyway, the Philippine yen was even more worthless to us than to regular people, given that we were never in a position to spend it anywhere. Yet the Japanese often used it to pay us. It was terrible, printed on slick oily paper, crude artwork, all kinds of errors in the English. So we used it as cigarette paper, to roll our raw tobacco in. It smoked badly, tasted like hell, would turn black and curl up like a dog's hind leg. We took to calling those cigarettes "awfuls". You'd say to a fella, "Let me borrow a few rolls to make some awfuls. Next time I get some, I'll pay you back."

Later on, by the way, after I left DAPECOL and ended up, of all places, back in Cabanatuan again, there was no wild tobacco growing up there. So we had to rely entirely on the Japanese for cigarettes, and they took advantage, like they always did. They would bring us hand-rolled cigarettes from the outside, stuffed in some crude package with the end open, and they had the gall to write "Camel" on them. What a joke. They must have come from the rear end of the camel, because they were somehow even worse than the awfuls. And the size of the cigarette depended on the dexterity of the roller. One pack would have six cigarettes in it, another thirty-six. Although they did come in the prettiest colors, pastel blues and pinks. It turned out they were often rolled in wallpaper, which I'm sure did nothing for the quality of the experience smoking them. We called them awful-awfuls.

When we worked the rice fields, we did so in nothing but our g-strings. That probably sounds funny, but it was just a matter of practicality—the fields were sodden, often flooded, and there was no point in wearing clothes; you'd only get them soaked and dirty. So when we took the train out to the rice fields the first thing we all did was go to one of the portable buildings that held the rice threshers. There were three of these buildings, always being moved around to wherever they were needed at a given time. No walls, just a corrugated metal roof and steel columns and a platform where the threshers sat. The way it worked was you took rice stalks to the thresher and the machine would separate out the rice itself so it could be bagged and sent back on the train. Anyway, when we first arrived at the fields we would go over to the rice thresher building and take off our clothes, strip down to our g-strings, then gather up in our work gangs and get ready to go out into the fields.

One day, we were in the midst of this process of stripping down and some of us found these little packets we didn't recognize sitting at the base of some of the steel columns, very odd and curious. A fella near me found one and opened it up and discovered some basic medicines, aspirin and a few other things, but also some .45 caliber bullets. Stamped into the end of the bullets was "1942," to mark the age of the ammunition. Well, it didn't take long before some of the guards noticed us all clustered around and murmuring, and they came over to see what the fuss was about. One of the guards pushes his way through the crowd and grabs the packet, and when he sees those bullets he just about loses his mind. Jabber jabber, whistle whistle, and you'd have thought there was a gun in the packet, too, the way they all came running and rounded us up and sent us right back to camp with our clothes still in a bundle in our laps, back behind the barbed wire. Maybe there was a gun somewhere, too, though I never saw it. The moment we get back to the compound they run over to their little headquarters to report the discovery of this ammunition.

Basically what it meant was, they couldn't defend all the islands of the Philippines, and I think they knew it, which was why their reaction to discovering the ammunition was so dramatic. They knew how tenuous their position was, 7,000 islands to watch, no way to know if we'd been stockpiling an arsenal somewhere waiting for the right moment to arm ourselves and slaughter them all. The Japanese knew American submarines were lurking all around, and they'd even rendezvoused with intelligence operatives, Filipinos mostly, taken them to the States and trained them in guerilla tactics, espionage, how and what to destroy to hurt the Japanese most, and then brought them back to wreak havoc, make the Japanese worry every time they came around a corner, make them sleep with one eye open. The idea was less to foment an actual uprising and more to just keep the Japanese on edge, never knowing where this stuff was coming from or how, never knowing when a communications facility might explode. In this case, with the packets of ammo, they never did figure out how it got there. I only found out after the war how the Filipino operatives were being trained and used. But it's possible the reason some prisoners got it in their heads to actually attempt escape was because they had contact with these operatives.

Chapter 7

AMERICAN BOMBERS

Escape is, of course, always on everyone's mind when you're a POW. Who wants to stay in such a situation indefinitely, working the fields, smoking lousy cigarettes, barely staying alive, having your teeth or worse worked over without anesthetic, eating little other than boiled vegetables and rice, reading the same books over and over again, catching beatings more or less at random? No one. But the reality was, escape was near impossible. We had no guns, we had no equipment, we had no food. The jungle was everywhere around us, and that's enough to stop anyone; not even a snake could penetrate that jungle. And the Japanese knew all this. Hell, even the Filipinos knew all this; it was the reason they'd built DAPECOL where they did, and the reason it didn't need any walls. If anyone was foolish enough to try and run, the jungle would take care of them before they even got out of earshot.

Still, you can't help but think: *God, wouldn't it be great to somehow get out of here.*

There were many, many work details around the colony, and the ones my group never saw were dealing with the live animals—the chickens, pigs, cows, and water buffalo—and working in the kitchen. There were two of these details that went out on Sundays—two and only two. The first was a group of four men who went to the Japanese kitchen in the front of the compound and did the slave work, walloping pots all day, scrubbing and rinsing and drying. The other Sunday detail, which dealt with the steers that were used for dry farming, was a group of eleven men led by a Navy Lieutenant Commander named Red McGuire. Red was a brilliant guy, had graduated first in his class at Annapolis in either 1932 or '33. I used to play chess with him. He taught me how to play, and then he would play blindfolded and still beat me. I used to talk to him about celestial navigation, naval gunnery. Just a very smart, entertaining, capable fella. But in all the time I spent with Red, he never once mentioned to me anything about trying to escape. Maybe the fact that he never brought it up, when the rest of us talked idly about it all the time, should have clued me in.

The job assigned to Red's detail was to move the steers' grazing position—these bulls were tethered to an area through the rings in their nose for a week, during which time they'd eat through everything in that spot and then, of course, had to be moved. So these fellas would go out on Sundays and move each of them to new overgrown patches to chow down. What no one knew was that Red and his group had been working very secretly and silently on a plan to escape. They traded with a guy named Sammy Gracio, a second lieutenant and pilot with the 3rd Pursuit Squadron. Sammy worked scrubbing pots in the kitchen, and he would steal food for the Burma Steer detail and trade it for whatever they had to offer. And they in turn—unbeknownst to Sammy or anyone else, these guys kept a real tight lid on things—were storing that food in the fields when they went out to do their job.

And then one early morning, when they'd decided they had enough food and were otherwise prepared to make their escape, they just got up out of their bunks, went out to the road that ran through the compound, right past the Japanese headquarters, and walked away. They had all this food stashed in the fields, wrapped up and ready to go, and they took three of the steers and threw these sacks of food and supplies over their backs, and off they went.

One time early in our stay at DAPECOL, we'd come across on some detail a couple of Filipinos who'd helped build the colony, cut it right out of the jungle. They told us about a secret road that led out of the colony, to the south; I don't even think the Japanese knew about it. And that road was where Red and his comrades were headed.

So it gets on toward later in the morning. This is a Sunday, and so the steer detail is supposed to be leaving anytime now. Remember, this is an eleven-person crew, one leader and ten workers. The Japanese guards assigned to the steer detail show up at the gate, waiting for Red to show up and lead his men out into the fields to change the position of the steers. Some time passes, no Red. The guards start to get squirrelly, wondering where the hell Red and his crew are, and they go and check the barracks and look around the compound and then before you know it, whistles, guards running everywhere, jabber jabber. They know something's wrong, obviously, and a few of them run to the headquarters building and come back with a fella named Wada, who was the Japanese interpreter. Wada was a small fella, about 5′3″, a little hunchback character in his brown army uniform, no insignia, and the usual horn-rimmed glasses. He came through the gate on the double and sought out the American commander to find out what was going on. Our commander knew nothing, not that he would have said anything if he did know, but I think he was telling the truth; Red and his men, as I said, kept a tight lid on their plans. Wada goes around, talking with others, American and Japanese, and establishes that Red is nowhere to be found. Now all the Japanese are very worked up, Wada most of all. Because now they were starting to lose face. The embarrassment of having been duped was sinking in, and as I mentioned before, there's nothing worse you can do to a Japanese than embarrass him, particularly in front of his peers. And so Wada ordered us all, quite angrily, to the barracks. There was lots of yelling and shoving, prodding with rifle barrels, smacks to the back of the head. They were taking their embarrassment out on us, trying to make themselves feel better by pushing us around a bit. They got us inside the barracks and told us in no uncertain terms—Wada speaking to us in clear English so there's no confusion—not to come back out or we would be shot.

So Monday comes, we're still inside, no news, nothing. Tuesday, the same thing. No work details, we all remain confined to the barracks except for chow or to go out back to the latrines. And then around midday on Wednesday, a Japanese lieutenant came in with Wada and ordered us all to get outside in front of the barracks in a tenko formation. *Tenko* is the Japanese term for roll call, meaning you count off, left to right and front to back, to make sure everyone is present and accounted for. And this settled it, finally, that eleven men were missing. I don't know why they waited three days to do this, or whether the decision had something to do with what happened a couple hours later. Because that afternoon they got us back out into tenko formation, and this time three Japanese guards came in with these long bamboo poles, and on each pole was a severed head. There's no other way to say it except how it was. Three of the escapees had been beheaded, and the Japanese paraded them around in front of us to make an example. I recognized two of the faces, but the third was too badly beaten up for me to tell who it was. They threw the heads on the ground and let them stay there for a few hours, then removed them to the other side of the hospital, which was the burial area. The message, of course, was clear: anyone else tries this, and they'll end up the same way or worse. But the Japanese weren't finished making sure we all got it.

A couple hours later two of the escapees were brought back into camp alive. One was a fella named Bucavinsky and the other's name escapes me after all this time. And with all the guards in camp present, every last one, they took us outside the barbed wire—there were two rows of barbed wire eight or ten feet tall all around the perimeter of the camp, and guard towers at each corner—to this level area the size of three or four football fields. We were separated into formations and arranged around this area so every man had a clear line of sight to what was about to take place.

At this point, Bucavinsky and his companion were cut loose—their hands had been bound behind their backs—and given trench shovels and ordered to start digging. And the moment that order came down we all knew, of course, that they were digging their own graves. It took about half an hour, everyone watching as they slowly dug the holes they would die in. I'd rarely seen something so heart-rending, and felt so helpless watching them dig. This was certainly as desperate as it gets. When they were finished the Japanese tied them up again, at wrist and ankle, and forced them to kneel at the edge of the graves they'd just hollowed out. About twenty feet away were six guards, locked and loaded, their rifles pointed at the two men. Now as I understand it, when someone is executed by firing squad it's customary to give the members of the firing squad guns that all have blanks except for one, so that nobody knows who actually killed the prisoner. But the Japanese did away with this gesture of civilized behavior. Each one of them had live rounds, and the lieutenant said, "Ready, aim, fire" in Japanese, and they just blasted these two guys in the back. Not in the chest—the back. And of course the two men toppled over dead into the pits, and that was that. No last words, no prayer reading, no calling out to a wife, mom, or child by the executed. A few of us were selected to bury the bodies and I can tell you that this sequence of events had a very lasting, very vivid effect on us all. I can see it today, in great detail. I can reconstruct the entire scene with absolute precision, as though it were still happening right in front of me. Alas, we all knew: if you had any thoughts of escape, you better have a good plan and adequate supplies, you better be in good shape and good health and be ready and able to trot or run that whole first day, to put many miles between yourself and the camp. You better know how to hide and where to hide and when to hide.

And it turned out that, during the rest of my time there at least, no one ever felt as though they had all of those conditions lined up satisfactorily, because no one attempted to escape ever again. That display of cruelty put an end to any serious consideration of breaking out, and we very shortly thereafter returned to the same dull, grinding routine we'd lived every day up to that point—though there was one more act of cruelty by the Japanese, related to the escape attempt, which I'll get to momentarily.

You'll notice that I've accounted for only five of the eleven men who ran. Six of them were never captured and, I would learn later, had in fact escaped to freedom, including Red. And it's worth mentioning that, true to what I knew of him as a person, a brilliant and deductive and very cerebral fella, Red had organized the entire operation with great skill, and had selected his men carefully based on what they brought to the group in terms of skills and abilities. For example, there was a three-stripe sergeant who had been an auto mechanic and who, on the colony, was responsible for among other things maintaining the diesel generator that provided electricity to the rice mill. Red learned that this sergeant had a genius for machines far beyond working on diesel engines and the like. So Red had him fabricate, of all things, a water distiller, a little machine that could take marsh water or sea water or anything else that couldn't be consumed and make it safe to drink. Where they found what they needed to make such a contraption I have no idea, but it goes to show the ingenuity people were capable of in places like this. Everyone on Red's detail had a skill that complemented the job they'd been given, a job Red had determined they'd be well-suited for and that would help the group as a whole escape. As I said, the man was a bona-fide genius. And he and the five others who escaped made their way up into the hills, to rendezvous with Filipino operatives, who informed them of the nocturnal, clandestine visits American submarines were making to the islands. The men went with the operatives to meet one such sub, and in this way completed their escape to freedom.

But they also still figured into six other ugly, violent deaths.

It's important to note that the Japanese had no patience, generally, for punishing only those individuals who had broken a rule or otherwise incurred their wrath. They went in for mass punishment, both to avoid the time and trouble of finding out who did a particular thing, and to discourage anyone thinking of doing something similar in the future; knowing others will be punished for your actions had a discouraging effect that fear of being punished yourself did not, and Japanese knew that and used it to their purposes. They even had signs posted around the camp that read, "If you try to escape, you will cause ten of your comrades to be shot."

So immediately following the escape, after the five had been captured and killed, our rations were cut as punishment. And then, about a week later—my guess is that what they planned to do was so extreme that they needed time to clear it with some headquarters elsewhere—we were lined up outside the barracks and from our formations six men were selected by the guards. Six men, taken apparently at random, to pay the price for those who had escaped. Two of these men, if you can believe it, turned out to be brothers. And we stood at attention in the sun, watching as they dug their own graves and then were shot. And that was that. The Japanese had gotten their paltry, petty revenge for having been embarrassed.

In a very short period of time, however, it was back to work details and back to the grinding, pointless, soul-crushing routine. We were allowed to have religious services on Sundays, I should mention. We had about a dozen chaplains in camp, oddly enough. Father Bauman, Father Vanderheiden, Carberry, Gallagher. Bauman and Carberry were diocese clergy, Bauman from Pittsburgh and Carberry from St. Louis. Vanderheiden was from Wisconsin, and belonged to some order I can't recall anymore. Gallagher, I remember, was a Jesuit. And then there was Father Brown, who stands out in my mind as the most remarkable of all of them. Brown was a Franciscan, from Mescalero, New Mexico, an extraordinary man. He hadn't joined the military until he was in his mid-fifties, and how he managed to be allowed in at that age I'll never know, but he did, and there he was at DAPECOL with the rest of us. A very generous, warm man of God, who provided great leadership and was not afraid to work out on detail. Because work was all he had known previously, back in New Mexico, work among the Mescalero Indians, in the 20s and 30s, taking care of his flock, and he had a big garden that sustained the clinic and school and orphanage that he oversaw. He was very skilled at planting and harvesting, drew from a great base of knowledge about horticulture but also understood it intuitively, and he loved to do the work, thought nothing of getting out on the rice detail. He never hid behind his cloak or collar; he dressed in the same tattered clothes as the rest of us, with only a small silver cross to indicate anything about his spiritual or religious life. I don't want to speak badly of the other chaplains, men of other denominations, but it must be said that they did not provide the same leadership as the Catholic priests. Too frequently they seemed preoccupied with their own problems, worrying about their wives and children, worrying about when we'd get out of there and whether they'd be promoted if and when we did. Old Father Brown, by contrast, was in there day after day, offering counsel and encouragement to anyone who needed it without any thought for or word about himself. And on Sundays he gave the most delightful, uplifting sermons. For my part, I used to serve Mass myself every Sunday to the Filipinos. And through the Japanese the chaplains were able to get ahold of small amounts of wine for communion. Father Bauman had a little pint bottle, the kind you'd put in your jacket pocket, and do you know how he portioned it out into the chalice each Sunday, to make it last? With an eye dropper. One drop, every service, he would bless and consecrate one drop of this lousy Japanese wine. We did what we had to do to get by and observe some semblance of the lives we'd known, the chaplains in particular.

There were, however, signs that things were changing. By now it was late 1943, and enough news was filtering through to our captors for them to know things had turned in the war, it was very bad for the Japanese. The time was approaching when they were going to have to leave DAPECOL, rounding all of us up and taking us with them. And what do we know by now, about how the Japanese conducted themselves with regard to the resources of other people's lands? They took and used it all without a thought for either those they had conquered or a thought for the future in general. So given the bad news, they started eating the caribou herds, because why not? They certainly couldn't take the 200 caribou with them. They had the Filipinos do the slaughtering. The Japanese took most of the meat, the Filipinos got a little for their trouble, and we ended up with the stripped carcasses, just skin and sinew and bones by the time it got to us. But boy, it was still quite a bonanza. If you've ever cooked down a carcass, say a chicken carcass for stock, you know how much flavor and even how much edible meat you can get once it's been simmered for a while. The fellas who worked in the kitchen had access to these big kuali pots, three or four feet in diameter and two feet deep, in which it was possible to cook fifty pounds of rice at a time. One caribou carcass and three or four of the kuali pots and we were in business, able to make a delicious soup and lots of it. The bones were mixed with a kind of moist rice, making for something not unlike a stew, with a strange but fantastic meaty taste.

Before too long, though, the end of DAPECOL came, sometime in the fall of 1943, when events in the war were such that the Japanese knew their hold on the Philippines was tenuous and likely to end sooner rather than later. It'd been six months since the Allies had taken Guadalcanal for good, and the island-hopping strategy was in full effect, Japanese garrisons cut off, neutralized by air and naval power, and left to starve in New Britain and elsewhere. A two-pronged attack on Japan's territories was gathering momentum, MacArthur leaping from island to island in the southwest Pacific, and Nimitz invading Tarawa in the Gilbert Islands. And in the face of all this, orders had come down for our captors to gather us up and get on the move. There was no forewarning that such a move was imminent. On a morning like any other we heard the rumble of diesel engines approaching, and the next thing we knew the compound was full of trucks, more trucks than we'd seen in one place in probably three years. And we were loaded into the trucks with the few meager belongings we had, a blanket and a scrap of tenting, maybe, some personal items. The sides of the cargo areas where we sat had been built up so you could barely see out even on your feet; we were warned not to try to see out once we got underway. We drove northwest until we reached the Duval River, then we waited. And waited. The ferry could only accommodate one truck at a time, and there were enough trucks to carry 1,400 of us. It was a torturous experience, just standing there in the sun waiting for our turn to cross, which seemed like it would never come. Luckily our numbers had been reduced by 800 several months before, when a good chunk of men had been taken (I would find out later) to Horo, a long snake-like island in the southwest corner of the Philippine archipelago. Horo was nearly uninhabited, just a few tiny fishing villages, and these men had been brought there to build airfields. Their principal job was grading, of course, the hard way: with picks and shovels. Others had to pulverize shellfish to create the dusty, gravelly material that covered the airstrips, the same material we'd been coated in an inch thick during the march following our capture. So thank God there were only 1,400 of us instead of 2,200, because it still took an incredibly long time to finally get us out of that forsaken place.

On the other side of the river, finally, we stopped in the town of Duval, which turned out to be the headquarters of a very large military outfit. I snuck a peek through my blindfold here and there and saw troops all over the place, tanks, artillery pieces, cavalry and horse-drawn equipment, ships in the harbor. Every kind of military activity you can imagine, all of it double-time. It wasn't exactly a panicked feel, but it definitely felt urgent and rushed. I'm not sure if the Japanese were being evacuated, but we definitely were. We got aboard a freighter and in no time were sailing north, up the coast of Mindanao to the San Bernadino Straits. We sailed into Cebu City harbor and sat at anchor for two days while other freighters and tenders loaded various agricultural products onto the ship: sugar, rice, some other things. Again, the Japanese looting on their way out the door.

There was a bit of excitement during our stay in the Cebu harbor—three men jumped overboard on that first night. Maher, Mahan, and Magee were their names, three classmates from West Point who stuck together like glue and had all been commanders on Bataan. The three of them waited until dark and then all went overboard together. The Japanese heard the splash and were firing their rifles, but somewhat randomly; there were no lights and no way to see a thing in the inky darkness of the harbor. I found out later that the three men managed to find some resistance fighters and were returned to American forces to fight again. I appreciate that returning to fight after their ordeals seems unthinkable, but it was so. West Point men, indeed.

Next we sailed north through the islands to Manila, where we prisoners disembarked. We were marched through the city—the old humiliation technique, again—and I knew some Filipinos who lived on the route they took us through. A man named Luis Boretto, who'd been a pilot in the Philippine Air Corps, was a friend of mine, and through Luis I'd met the rest of his family, including his sister Baby Boretto. Whether they saw us as we were marched through I don't know; in fact, I didn't know then and don't know to this day whether Luis survived the war. I didn't see anyone I recognized, and besides, you're too downtrodden and humiliated to spend much time looking at anything but your feet. There's no laughing or waving or anything like that. And anyway, the Borettos were of Spanish descent, the top of the social order, and Luis had been a businessman, in the lumber business, so most likely he wasn't even in the city, if he was lucky he'd fled to the hills when the Japanese took over.

Once we were out of Manila proper and into the suburbs, and the Japanese were satisfied that we'd been properly humbled again, they loaded us onto trucks and buses and drove us further north, eighty or ninety miles, and where do you suppose the buses come to a stop and let us off, but at Cabanatuan. I was back again. And nothing had changed—it was the same routine, up early in the morning, working in the fields, day after day. Well maybe our outlook was changing. I can't speak for every man but I was personally allowing my thoughts to drift beyond getting my next meal. Perhaps, just maybe, we might be getting closer to a return home to a warm, clean bed with sheets.

Time passed, and sometime around September of 1944 we were out working in the cassava fields. Cassava is a little tree about eight feet tall, the roots of which grow like sweet potatoes and are used to make tapioca. Anyway, we're out harvesting cassava and all of a sudden, to the east over the mountains, comes a flight of about 60 aircraft. There was only one other time in my life when I'd ever seen such a formation, and that was the Japanese bombers when they came in over our heads at Nielson Field two days after the war started. So this flight, the larger planes were in flights of nine—three to the front, three to the rear right, three to the rear left. Circling these twin-engine planes were smaller pursuit aircraft in pairs, and these moved up and down and under and over and stayed out in front of the larger birds. They were heading due west, about 6,000 feet or so, and their appearance didn't seem to cause our guards any alarm. So the assumption among the prisoners was that these were Japanese planes. It turned out that the guards were making the same assumption, but had no actual knowledge of what these planes were or where they came from. So we kept working away for about twenty more minutes, and then we felt this earthshaking rumble, and a few seconds later the *thump thump thump* of bombs. And right then and there we realized those planes were not Japanese. This was one penetrating moment in our experience of being prisoners up until that time. Because in three years we, or at least I, had never seen any indication that American or any other forces were giving the Japanese a run for their money. From our perspective it was unchallenged Japanese hegemony everywhere, forever. And so to see they were vulnerable, that something was happening out in the world that indicated strongly not only were the Japanese not invincible, they might even be losing—well, it just really put a charge into us, an energy we hadn't felt in a very, very long time. It turned out that this flight had bombed Clark Field, which was occupied by the Japanese, and when we saw them coming back, we were intrigued, of course. We strained to see the insignia on the planes but we couldn't make them out. The other bit of intrigue was that, to our knowledge, there was no place for these planes to land east of the Philippines, at least not for several hundred miles, which would be beyond the range of such aircraft. This was before jets, and bombers like these, with reciprocal engines and propellers, could carry five or six hours of fuel, at most. So they had to have come from carriers. And on the return trip the pursuit escorts tangled with some Japanese fighters that had been sent up to intercept. We probably should have been frightened, should have been looking for cover, but it was such a spectacular sight and we were so thrilled by it all that we just stood there looking up and watching the drama. We saw two Japanese fighters go down. One plummeted to earth in flames; we heard it crash and explode in the distance. The other vaporized in mid-air after a few rounds hit its gas tank.

We were also able to see, on one of the pursuit planes that broke from the larger flight to meet the Japanese, an insignia we didn't recognize. The only American insignia we knew were the concentric red, white, and blue circles. This was totally different: two flags, each about a couple feet long, with some white lettering and symbols we couldn't make out. But it definitely wasn't an American insignia any of us recognized. We would find out later that these planes had come from Bull Halsey's task force. Halsey, you'll recall, was the Admiral who had saved the day at the battle of Leyte Gulf, keeping the Japanese naval force from getting in among the hundreds of American ships assembled for the assault and wreaking havoc. So

Bull Halsey was at it again, doing what he did best, which was to be a thorn in the Japanese's side. And after that one day in the cassava fields, we would hear and see large flights of aircraft more and more, and we could even sometimes hear, forty miles distant, the sound of air raid sirens going off at Clark. Sometimes, usually at night, we could feel the *thump thump thump* of the bombs. And so it was official: the Japanese in the Philippines were catching it from old Halsey and the U.S. Navy.

I want to pause here to give credit to the Navy. They did as much in the war in the Pacific as did the Army or the Marines or foreign forces or anyone else. It was Navy guns that softened up countless Japanese entrenchments prior to invasion, and it was the Navy that provided artillery and aerial and logistical support—not to mention cover from attack by the Japanese Navy—once forces had gone ashore at Iwo Jima and Okinawa. It was the Navy that carried and distributed supplies and equipment and ammunition. It was the Navy that transported the USAAF planes where they needed to be. It was Navy submarines that hunted and hounded Japanese transport, isolating the battlefield, cutting the Japanese off from the Philippines just as they'd done to us several years prior. Without the Navy doing the jobs only they could do, and doing them as well as they could be done, the outcome in the Pacific would likely have been very different.

By now it was October or November, 1944, and we got word that we were moving yet again. I guess this wasn't much of a surprise, given everything. We weren't told where we were going, maybe because the Japanese themselves didn't yet know. We were just loaded onto trucks again and brought back to Manila, to Bilibid Prison. And not much happened there. There were no work details, just confinement, more like we were felons. But there were no cells inside the main wall that held us all in, just a complex of open buildings. One night around nine o'clock we heard something heavy hit the ground outside of our barracks with a thump. We'd been warned not to leave the building after dark, but we did anyway, quite regularly, and so some of us scampered outside to check what had happened. We sneaked along the side of the barracks and what should we find except a Japanese guard, dead as a doornail, lying flat face-down on the ground. And we didn't want to be blamed for this somehow, so we sent a guy over to the guard at the main gate to tell him what we'd found. So a group of soldiers comes over to see what's happened. They take a look at the body, take a look around, and then pick the dead guy up and carry him away.

The next day we learned how he'd been killed. He was up on the wall, walking his area of responsibility, when he realized he had to take a leak, something he'd probably done a hundred times before. Well this time, he made the mistake of dropping trough directly above a 440-kilovolt high tension electrical wire. This was surely a bit more of a zap than you'd get crossing a carpet and putting your hand on a doorknob. Blew him clear off the wall. Remarkable, all the ways one can die in a war, most of them not at all what you would expect.

Chapter 8

MAYHEM ON THE MARUS

Our stay at Bilibid was ultimately a short one. On December 14th, 1944, we were hauled out of the barracks, put into formation, and marched through the city once more, down to pier #1. We arrived at 8 o'clock in the morning, and it was bedlam. Thousands and thousands of people evacuating, boarding ships, waiting for ships, jostling one another, pushing and yelling incomprehensively. There was the distinct feeling that the rules normally governing people's behavior were about to give way. For the first time, I understood how desperate the Japanese situation in the Philippines had become—including, particularly, the thousands of Japanese women and children who had materialized at the pier.

What were all these women and children doing in a war zone, you wonder? Well, that was all part of the Prosperity Sphere malarkey they'd sold their own people. The soldiers had been told that when Japan had extended its reach throughout the Pacific, they would be able to stay in the countries where they'd fought, given ten acres of land to farm and money to build a house. And many of them had believed this, and brought or started families once the Philippines had been conquered. Now, a few scant years later, their Sphere was collapsing and they themselves scrambling to get out before it all came down around them.

Across the harbor, it was a similar scene to the one I'd noted before, only worse: ships in various states of wreckage, limping in from the South China Sea, many of them sinking or capsizing before they could make it dockside or to a mooring. In short, Manila Bay was a graveyard for ships of all sizes and descriptions, so clogged with wrecks that if you wanted to sail in or out you had to slalom around the derelicts. Halsey's ships were running up and down the islands blasting the hell out of Japanese shipping, and here were the results. At this point, they had no Navy left to speak of, almost all their capital ships having been sent to the bottom of the ocean, and their merchant marine had been reduced to a fraction of its normal size. They didn't even have the capacity to evacuate their own people, so again I wondered why they were bothering with us. Someday I might hear or read about it, someone with access to Japanese records will come out and give the reason or reasons why American POWs were transported around at so much expense and trouble, eating up supplies and taking up precious space on ships, when the Japanese had so little left with which to do anything. Then and now, though, I can't think of a single reason why it made sense to do anything except leave us behind.

The only ones who did get left behind were the lame and the sick, i.e. those who had no value as laborers. I wish I'd been lame or sick enough to get left, especially given what was to follow for me; those prisoners were sent back to a camp in Luzon and only a couple of months later were rescued by a fast-assault battalion that tore through Luzon and killed the Japanese that remained.

But my fate would be different. Along with the other so-called healthy prisoners, including my dear friend and ally Jay Mercer, I was sent down the pier and told to sit and wait while the ship loaded Japanese passengers. Fortunately for us the place where they parked us had cover and a water spigot, so we were protected from the sun, at least, while we waited. The ship we were to board was named *Oryoku Maru*, "maru" again meaning "steam ship" in Japanese. We watched as roughly six hundred Japanese merchant mariners boarded her up, four separate gangplanks. These men were obviously crews from other boats that had been sunk, likely transports of some kind. I would learn later than dozens of these transport ships were shuttling prisoners, or at least attempting to shuttle prisoners, back to the Japanese homeland now that the Allied forces were taking the upper hand in the Philippines. There were no Navy or Japanese Marines it seemed among these crews—they were civilian boat crews, caught in a hellish situation for which they likely had no preparation and of which they likely had little understanding. Like everyone at that point—Japanese, Filipino, American, military or civilian—they probably just wanted to call the whole thing off and go home.

Following the merchant mariners, maybe a thousand Japanese women and children boarded. This was slow-going, the women hauling bags, suitcases, babies and smaller children, all the way up to A-deck, which loomed high above us—the *Oryoku Maru* having been a large and very nice tourist ship before the war, 700 feet long, occasionally even coming to port on the west coast of the United States.

And then finally, after waiting all morning, around noon we got to board. The exact number was 1,619 American prisoners aboard. We went up to the main deck via the gangplanks, then were separated by branch; the Navy men went to hold #4, which was the smallest, the ground and air crews went to holds #1 and #2 on the foredeck, and when those were full the remainder ended up in #3, aft of the superstructure. This took about an hour. The guards gave some of us a punch to the stomach or nose on the way into the hold, just for kicks. Mind you, at 90 pounds a full wind-up punch to the stomach organs can really have a terrible effect on a prisoner, especially one trying to prepare mentally and physically for bad times ahead.

The *Oryoku Maru* may have been a luxury ship at one point, but no longer: the holds were hot, clammy, smelly, and cramped, with bunks eight deep the only furniture, and those taking up every available inch from floor to bulkhead. The only ventilation came from the hatches above, and though the air exchange was grossly inadequate we were still lucky to have it; if the hatches had been closed we would have suffocated in twenty minutes, or certainly within an hour.

When you're sitting in the hold of a ship you can hear everything—the slosh of waves against the hull, the machinery of the engine room chugging away, the propeller turning in the water. The sounds reverberate off the walls, floors, and ceilings like an orchestra of sorts. We finally set off from the pier and I could hear very clearly a tug pushing against the bow, metal grinding on metal, and then the propellers turned over fast and we were under our own power, headed west toward Corregidor. Because the bay was so full of wrecks and other obstacles we had to cut a course so erratic and circuitous that it was sundown before we reached Corregidor, less than twenty miles from the pier.

The hold of a ship is not, of course, designed with passengers in mind. That means, among other things, that we had no latrines, no water, no plumbing at all. We weren't allowed up to the deck, and so the only choice we had was to designate one corner of the hold as an area for urinating and defecating. Imagine that. Just an open corner of the hold, filling fast with human waste. It didn't take long, in the stifling air, for this to become intolerable, and men began yelling up at the hatch for water, buckets, anything. Soon it fell to a Major Montgomery, who was senior among us, to deal with the matter somehow. This is customary in the Army; in the absence of an appointed commander, the senior officer must assume command. He has no choice. And among Majors, they would just compare their serial numbers and date of promotion to Majority, and whoever had achieved the rank first would be the officer in charge. In retrospect, it was impressive that we adhered to such formality. You'd think the strength and health of a man might trump rank at some point as situations deteriorated, but that was never the case. We stuck to the script our military had written.

So Montgomery complained, in an official capacity, to the Japanese guards about the lack of sanitation and having to go in the corner like animals. And he was promised buckets. Half an hour later here came the buckets, lowered on ropes into the hold, and then it was a matter of emptying the buckets when they became full—but not too full. Because getting up that rope ladder, on a moving ship, was a bit of risky business even with two hands. With only one hand, and the other carrying a bucket of you know what, it was near impossible. Would have been hilarious, really, if not for how miserable we all were.

Now the people on the bucket detail, taking our waste topside and dumping it overboard, were able to see Corregidor as we passed by near dark, and they reported that it was now just a barren, battered hulk of an island. Topside all the barracks, the beautiful, almost artful concrete-stucco barracks, had been reduced to gravel. Every last bit of vegetation was gone, the magnificent Hickory trees just shattered, nothing left but splintery stumps.

From the mouth of Manila Bay, the ship very soon took a noticeable turn, and there were enough pilots in the hold with elementary knowledge of celestial navigation, and those still going topside with buckets picked out a few constellations, and before too long enough information had been gathered and processed to say with confidence that we were sailing north along the west coast of Luzon. Where we were ultimately headed, though, was anyone's guess.

We were given no food and no water. We'd each boarded with a single canteen and, in rare cases, two, but those were gone quickly enough. And our misery was compounded during the day, as the sun came up. The heat was overpowering, the metal decks above absorbing and concentrating it, the sun shining directly down through the hold and beating against the hull above the water line, and many human beings in a closed space, each creating his own heat to add to the rest. It had to have been 120 or 130 degrees in there, and again, no water. But eventually the sun went down again, and the relief was so simple and pure as the heat dissipated and we even became a bit cool, though we certainly had no need of blankets. It was a strange, if not terrifying, situation to be shivering and sick in the hold while able to hear the children and civilians above also whimpering. Below and above deck things were not looking optimistic. It was not lost on anyone on ship that the gunners were poised to defend the Japanese civilians on deck.

But there were things that happened that night, as men became desperate and even crazed with thirst, that truly frightened me, and frighten me still even to recall. We'd had no food, of course, since our morning ration of rice the day before, and none of us carried any food because the Japanese either hadn't thought or hadn't cared to give us any before boarding. But that hardly mattered; what mattered that night was the fact that no water came down through the hatch. Men were lying all over the deck of the hold, splayed, prostrate from the heat, sick and weak with hunger, moaning, crying, doing terrible things. Mercer and I had our backs to the anchor chain locker in the bow of the ship and as we looked forward through the moonlight coming down through the hatch—we saw a man pee in a bottle and drink it. That's how desperate he was. Drank his own urine and promptly retched and vomited all over the deck, likely making his situation even worse than it had been, in terms of dehydration. Another fella took a glass water container, smashed it against a steel stanchion support beam, and used the cut glass to slash his own lips so he could suck at the blood. Just for the moisture in his mouth, he cut his own lips wide open. Imagine it. Just insanity in that hold, sickening madness, no hope of ever getting water because our cries thus far had gone unheeded, and there had been plenty, and plenty loud. And so despair was what descended on us, the despair of those who have been truly forsaken. Water was all that mattered—not even survival, exactly, but simply *water*. If someone had promised there would be water waiting for us if we died we would have to a man gladly killed ourselves if we could.

Mercer and I had a little bit of water left between the two of us. I had half a canteen or so, and his canteen was now empty. And in the meantime, it was clear that anyone, at any time, could become desperate enough to hit us over the head—or worse—if they knew we had water. It would have been understandable. Unforgiveable, but understandable. The demands of the body, the effect it has on the mind when the body is truly thirsty—it drives you to madness. That's all there is to it—utter madness. I saw it that night, and once you see it there's no way to mistake it for anything but what it is.

So Mercer and I decided we had enough water to get us through to the next day, and hopefully by then the Japanese would come to their senses—or remember we were down here—and actually get some water down to us. In the meantime, we had to protect our water, and ourselves, through the rest of the night. We agreed that under no circumstances could the two of us sleep at the same time. So we devised a system by which one of us would always be awake. Mercer sat on the deck with his back against the steel bulkhead, and I sat between his legs with my back to his chest. In this way, Mercer could take a nap while I kept watch. When I got too drowsy and didn't feel like I could stay awake any longer, I'd give Mercer an elbow and we'd change positions. Then I'd nap while Mercer kept his eyes peeled for silhouettes moving nearby, shadows intent on stealing our water. And in this way, swapping back and forth, we made it to daybreak without losing our heads or our water. I would estimate a good four dozen men were dead by sunrise, with no means to separate the living from the dead in the hold.

At first light you could see the men who had died overnight. There was no place to put them, so we left them where they lay. Around 8 o'clock, who should come to the hatch but our old friend Wada. Montgomery yelled up at him that men were dying down here for want of some water. Wada yelled something in response, and I heard Montgomery reply to never mind the food, it's not hunger that's killing us, it's thirst. Maybe he was daft, but it seemed like Wada was actually trying to be helpful. Not too much later, by the way, when the Japanese surrender was finalized and war trials commenced, Montgomery would testify against Wada, and Wada would get thirty years in the bastille. He got out after about twenty.

Now, though, in the hold, Wada got the message finally, and he said "Wait wait," and disappeared again. Before too long he came back, and we could hear other footsteps on the deck above us, too, and soon they were letting down these buckets full of water. It was like Wada was God, answering our most fervent prayers. And Montgomery, to his great credit, was able to organize things so it somehow did not become an ugly free-for-all, which you would have expected given the circumstances—just a mad rush and every man for himself, spilling half the water instead of drinking it. But that was the funny thing about captivity, and I saw it over and over again—when you expected people to be at their worst, often they ended up being their best. Like back in DAPECOL, when everyone knew they didn't have to worry about anyone (except the Japanese) stealing from them. The same thing happened now. Montgomery and a few of the other senior officers organized things very quickly, arranging for the men who had no water to go first, and the rest, those who still had a little, waited very honorably while Montgomery and the others tried to revive those who'd run out. Christ, even give Wada some credit—he did in fact cause a steady flow of water to come down into the hold, though the fact that there was evidently plenty of water on board, and the fact that they were willing to give plenty to us, raised the question of why we'd had to wait 36 hours before anyone thought to actually do so. But such was life as a POW, especially as things got more and more grim for the Japanese, and in any event within a couple of hours we were all full to bursting with water and feeling a lot better suddenly about our prospects.

That optimism didn't last long, naturally. Around 11:30 that morning Wada came back and poked his head in the hatch and said, "America, we are going to have anti-aircraft practice. The noises are very loud, so plug your ears or you will go deaf." When we'd boarded we'd seen, on the deck immediately above us between holds #1 and #2, a pair of three-inch anti-aircraft guns had been mounted. They were set on platforms that allowed the gunners space to load ammunition and maneuver the guns. And Wada, for whatever reason, was lying to us about the "practice" part. Probably because of that strange Japanese pride, not wanting to admit how bad things had gotten, particularly to us. The truth was they'd gotten word of a massive flight of American bombers and fighters headed their way, passing over Manila. It turned out our ship was part of a very large convoy, an attempt to get as many Japanese nationals, dependents, soldiers and mariners aboard the last few ships that remained and back to Japan. We of course had no idea that the plan was to take us all the way to the home island. But in any event, such a large convoy presented an obvious and tempting target for the Navy.

Around midday—this is the best time for an air raid, the sun at its apex in the sky, defenders having to peer straight up into the blinding sun—all hell broke loose. The three-inch guns on the deck started blasting away, but soon enough we could hear other things that indicated this was hardly target practice. The whistle of bombs falling, for one thing. The yawning roar of torpedo planes as they pitched over into their dives and lined up on a target. The chatter of wing-mounted .50-caliber machine guns. The woosh of air-to-surface rockets. The convoy was under heavy attack, and we were in the midst of it ourselves, and helpless. I peered through the hatch and with the sun off to one side I could see the sky filled with American planes, diving and swirling and firing everything they had, and then the guns on the deck would roar in response. Occasionally we could hear but not see these massive explosions, and the groan of ships going down in the water around us. It was a symphony of noise without melody, just plain noise. At times one noise would rise above the din, which was continuous and terrible, and it became evident that there were not less than 75 or 100 aircraft in the sky above us, just ripping this convoy to shreds. There were two raids, each about twenty minutes long. And talk about tension—we spent the whole time just waiting for a bomb to hit us on the head any second. We could hear the Japanese above decks screaming, women and children. Some men panicked and tried to climb the ladder out of the hold, but the guards fired at the hatch and drove them back. We were stuck and couldn't even see the entirety of the battle, though there was no doubt, from everything we heard and felt, that it was a devastating scene.

The *Oryoku Maru* had been hit multiple times, and was listing to starboard and sinking aft at the same time. The propellers were turning very slowly. Wherever they'd been planning to take us, we obviously weren't going to make it there, and so the ship turned into Subic Bay at the northwest corner of the Bataan Peninsula, near the town of Olongapo. By now it was evident the ship was no longer seaworthy at all, and we limped into the bay, drifted into shallow water, and became stuck in the mud.

By this time we had a violent list, maybe 15 degrees, the ship taking on massive amounts of water somewhere that threw everything off-balance, such that if one went a short distance down in the hold, you could no longer stand up. You had to crouch just to walk, the list was so bad. The way the wind was blowing now we could tell the ship was on fire. We could smell the burning paint. And this added further urgency to our situation; if the ship was burning we needed to get out, but looking at the angle of the rope ladder it became clear that if the ship listed much more the ladder would become useless and there would be no way out. But there was nothing you could do. You weren't going anywhere. Any attempts to climb out would be met with rifle fire. All you could do was hope to God above that somehow you'd get out of this alive. We stayed in the hold that night and the following morning, Wada came to the hatch again. Men called for water—we were all pretty desperate for water again by now—but Wada ignored this. He said, "In a short time you will hear a pistol shot across the hatch. When that happens, you can come out of the hold." And then Wada was gone once more.

You would have expected Montgomery to say "Alright men" and make plans for what to do when that shot came. But he cleverly stayed silent. Half an hour later, when the gun was heard, Montgomery pulled himself up three or four rungs on the ladder, elevating himself so he could be seen and heard. The rest of us were silent—why talk? And Montgomery called out to us, "There are sixteen bays in this hold, four, four, four, and four. Someone give me a number, one through sixteen." And someone called out the number 12, and Montgomery said "alright then, we will evacuate one bay at a time, beginning with 12 and proceeding clockwise," and we all listened to his orders and followed them. There was no massive crush to go up the ladder, everyone waited their turn. If a man was dead, Montgomery told us, we had to leave him, let him lie in peace. If a fella was sickly and needed help up the ladder, the men in his bay would assist him going up. And that was the way it went. Again, the worst of times, but we did what we could to conduct ourselves as men.

It took a long time to get out of that hold—over an hour before I personally was above deck And once there, sure enough we could see the ship was on fire in several places, a thick column of black smoke rising up from the stern, smaller streams of smoke elsewhere. By now, it was more urgent for me to find water than to get off the ship, so I ran aft, scrambling past the anti-aircraft guns, clutching at the railing as my feet repeatedly went out from underneath me on the slick, tilted deck. I ended up with one foot on the deck itself and one foot on the side of what would have been the first-class staterooms back when the ship was still a luxury liner. I was looking for a galley or at least some stairs that might lead to one, or even a latrine, anyplace where I might find some water. As I went past the staterooms and looked in, each one held probably twenty Japanese women and kids, all dead as doornails. Blood everywhere, the bodies twisted up and flung about. They'd been peppered by the dive bombers, you see. They'd machine-gunned the hell out of the ship and hundreds of people on the A and B decks had been slaughtered by the strafing of the dive bombers back and forth. It turned out that being in the hold had been a blessing—the thick steel plate of the deck was sufficient to cause .50-cal bullets to ricochet off, keeping us safe from the murderous dive bombers. Scarred the metal, but didn't penetrate. But the women and kids up here had no chance.

And I realized this was why we hadn't been allowed to come up until now—the Japanese had been busy moving their live and wounded passengers off the ship all night, and hadn't wanted us to get in the way and confuse things further. What a horrific and helpless feeling for the civilians to be sitting ducks under the American bombers. At this point, we were the only living people left on the boat by the time we came abovedeck.

I managed to find a set a stairs and go down one deck. At this point I'm not worried about the fires, and I'm not worried that the ship is going to sink. I've got only one thing on my mind, one thing that I care about, and that's finding a glass of water. I scrambled back and forth on the B deck, found nothing, went back to the stairwell and went down again, and it was here, on C deck, that I found a kitchen. I went to the sink and prayed as I turned the tap—and my prayers were answered. I drank and drank until I couldn't drink any more without throwing up, and then I filled my canteen and went back up to A deck as quickly as I could, looking for Mercer, no idea where he's gotten off to or what he's doing. Before long I found him and poured some of my water into his empty canteen, and he had a good drink. And now, with our most immediate and urgent need addressed, it was time to take a look at the state of things and decide what was next.

We could tell the ship was starting to list even more, which did not seem like a good sign. The fires still burning, though not seeming to reach a point where they were going to overwhelm the ship and force us off. There was not a single Japanese on board anymore, except the dead ones. We weren't that far from shore, but we also weren't exactly close—a mile and a half or two miles. Subic Bay is quite shallow, and the Japanese skipper, when he decided to beach the ship to keep it from sinking, I'm sure didn't get as close to land as he thought he would before he hit mud and the engines quit.

So now we had to figure a way, in our weakened state, to make it across the bay without drowning. A lot of GIs, thinking they had to abandon the ship immediately because it was going to sink, had jumped into the water the moment we came out of the hold. And now most of them were drowning. In those days, you didn't have to be able to swim to sign up for the Army, and a lot of these kids from the middle of the country, Missouri and Iowa and Oklahoma, they'd never been in the water in their lives. They didn't even know how to begin to swim. So when they jumped into twenty or thirty feet of water, if they came up at all—some of them didn't—they didn't stay up for long.

Mercer and I were not that hasty. We discovered that the platforms around the anti-aircraft guns had been shattered by strafing, and we pulled some serviceable 2x4s out of there and lashed them together with some GI flotation belts we found lying around. The deck was littered with all kinds of personal belongings—trousers, shoes, canteens, knapsacks, musette bags, everything. We gathered various items, took a pair of pants and tied off the legs and stuffed them with other clothes, canteens, a mess kit and a nice leather pouch. I took a peek inside the pouch and by God if there wasn't some tobacco in it and, of all things, a straight razor. I was overjoyed. There were even a few matches in there. I knew they'd get wet when we went in the water, and it occurred to me that an empty canteen would likely keep them dry. So I found a canteen, tipped it upside down—bone dry, of course—and I put the matches in there and closed it up tight and shoved the canteen into the float bag I'd made from the pair of pants.

And I realize it probably sounds odd, us being so quick to grab things that had belonged to others, but I assure you that the men who'd owned these things prior were not going to miss them. And besides, Mercer and I were escaping, and we'd need whatever we could find to survive. This was our chance. We were going to prepare ourselves as well as we possibly could.

Once we were ready we went over to the slanted side of the boat. There was no way to jump from the other side, if you did try to jump from the deck you'd have hit the barnacles that had been exposed, get all sliced up and never make it. So we went to the other side and tied everything to the raft we'd made from the 2x4s and flotation belts. We threw the raft over and waited a moment, to make sure that it floated. It did. And so Mercer and I jumped, thirty or forty feet down to the water, fought our way back up to the surface, caught up with our raft, and started kicking our way toward shore.

As I said, we had every hope at that time of escaping. We were not aware of any Japanese in the area, and there was no sign of any of the Japanese who'd been on the ship with us; they'd disappeared entirely. We knew now, with our raft, that we could get ashore. This was the end. We were getting the hell out of here, finally.

First, we had to navigate our way to land, and the water was choked with men swimming and thrashing and trying to survive. And then, here and there, we would see a different kind of thrashing, and a man would scream and the water would turn red, and those were, of course, the sharks. All this activity, all these bodies in the water, there was no way they wouldn't come around looking to find something to eat. But there was no point in worrying about it. You just try to survive. You try to live. And so you head shoreward, come what may. And that was challenge enough, let me assure you. Because even though the winds weren't up there was still the current and the tide to contend with. You might start out from the ship headed for point A shoreward, but before too long, and without you even noticing, in a very short distance you're not heading toward point A any longer, you're moving in a different direction entirely. It was baffling and exhausting but Mercer and I corrected again and again, and we avoided the sharks somehow, and after a while the land was drawing unmistakably closer, and then we were ashore. We gathered our soaked belongings and abandoned our little raft, and who was there to meet us, but the Japanese. Oh, we were so upset. We really thought we were free. But it was out of the frying pan and into the fire, a contingent of Japanese Marines still occupied Olongapo and we walked right into their arms. They were not happy to see us, and they expressed their displeasure by slapping and kicking and generally brutalizing all of us who came ashore. At this point in the ordeal most of us were more than fifty percent below our normal weights so it was new levels of pain to take a beating in that weakened state, particularly after jumping off a freighter and swimming a long distance through the sharks and drowning men. All the Japanese military men on land could see was this ship burning and sinking out in the water, and I don't know if they thought we somehow were responsible for the state of the ship, but they treated us as though they did. Maybe they just wanted some Americans to be mad at, in which case we would do as well as any others. There's no resetting bones, say a broken rib or wrist in these circumstances, and that meant prolonging pain and fixes when these men beat us.

They brought us to, of all places, a tennis court. We were locked inside the fence; fortunately there was a water spigot in there—Americans had built the tennis court and they always put a spigot or fountain in, thank God. Once men stopped coming ashore and the number of us at the tennis court stabilized, I counted around four hundred men. And boy were those four hundred in a dreadful state in the blazing heat. Most were naked, speechless, keeled over into some unnatural position trying to regroup, to stay alive just a bit longer.

So of the 4,500 or so people who'd boarded the *Oryoku Maru* at pier #1, few or none of the women and children survived on the A deck, and the same for the mariners on the B deck. Very few or none of the crew survived. As for us, of the 1,619 military personnel who departed Manila, the survivors were right here, less than one quarter of us. The others had gone any number of different ways. First, they died of thirst and illness. A few were murdered by Americans who plain lost their minds or saw an opportunity to take a man's canteen. I'm sure there were others, too, who found a way to commit suicide in that hold. I'm not sure how, perhaps a blade across a neck or wrists. Then, when the American planes attacked the second time, in addition to smaller-scale casualties here and there, hold #4 had caught a bomb. This was not a heavy-duty 500 or 1,000-pounder, because that likely would have sent the whole ship to the bottom in a matter of minutes, and besides, carrier-based planes didn't carry bombs that large, generally. But it was big enough that it went through the plating and took out the entirety of hold #4, where the 400 or so Navy personnel had gone. Not a single man survived. Maybe the bomb was phosphorous, incendiary; maybe that's where the fire came from. In any event, it did the job. And then, even after surviving everything else, a good number of men died in the water one way or another, drowning, sharks, take your pick. The net result was that nearly 400 of us at the tennis court were the last survivors. And we'd been captured yet again. The only bright spot worth noting, apart from the water spigot and not being dead, was the bombers who laid the *Oryoku Maru* to rest. It was nice to not be on ship when it was dealt its fatal blow, and it was even nicer to watch it sink. There was something about that big bastard sinking that lifted our spirits.

The Japanese did bring us some rice, too, a big heavy bag of rice, raw to go with our water spigot to wash it down. And it was great. You'd take out your GI mess kit, put in a ration of rice and some water, and let it soften up for fifteen or twenty minutes, served cold. It was the first food I'd had since the morning we'd left Manila.

It went on for a couple of days like that. Nothing happening at all. Stuck in the tennis court. Raw rice, add water, wait, eat. Urinate more or less wherever; we didn't have to defecate much because we hadn't been eating, but if you had to go you just picked a corner. After the sun went down, cover up as best you could in the cool, damp night. The temperature swung mightily from day to night, and back to day. It was a real test of acclimation. Those with stomach issues and unforgiving open wounds were going mad in the hot sun as it got hotter and hotter.

Then, after two days, they rounded us up, loaded us onto trucks, and drove us through the Zambales Mountains, 4,000 feet of elevation, back across the San Fernando River and back into San Fernando itself, where I ended up in jail again at the bastille, the same county prison I'd been in on the march three years before. The whole thing was starting to feel like a joke, or like Purgatory in the old mythologies—I moved from one place to another to yet another and back again, but I never really went anywhere; I should have by rights been dead a dozen times but never actually died; I was always a captive no matter what I did or what happened. Now here I was back at the county jail. I felt a little like an escapee who'd been hunted down and chucked back in the slammer. I never lost hope, but I did wonder, after all this time, if my captivity would ever actually come to an end.

We stayed in San Fernando for a week or so. It smelled terrible. Some men died, though we were fed and given water. Then we were taken once again to the train assembly yard, to be loaded onto the dreaded boxcars once more, the forty-and-eights, we called them. That was an expression from the first world war, from how the French cavalry loaded their trains: forty men and eight horses to a car. So off we rumbled in the forty-and-eights, northward this time, and ended up in Tuguegarao, a city on Lingayen Gulf. It was the 24th of December. The next day, Christmas, my third straight as a POW, we boarded a freighter ship, from which the Japanese were offloading horses and artillery. Apparently they were trying to reinforce Luzon, still bringing in supplies and troops with the idea of putting up a stand against MacArthur, who by this time, unbeknownst to us, had already taken the southern portion of Luzon and was gathering his forces for the march north toward Manila, the final push in his vow to return. The Japanese, though it would have appeared largely hopeless to any competent, objective military mind, had every intention of defending Manila. Now remember what I said much earlier in this story about conservation of forces—even when you have plenty to spare you don't want to waste them on lost causes, unless it's a delaying tactic to buy time elsewhere. And the Japanese did not have plenty of anything at this point, and certainly no troops or supplies to spare. But they were on the horns of a dilemma that couldn't really be solved: to fight the Americans here meant likely wasting resources in a futile effort, but it also meant more time that they could go on pretending the fight would never reach their shores. And their desire to keep pretending that was the case was strong enough to inspire a fierce defense of Manila.

Christmas Day that year, by the way, coincided with a Japanese holiday I can't recall the name or origin of, something to do with some important historical event. And it happened that in honor of that celebration, we were each given a big rice ball. They're made with rice that's not allowed to steam too long, so it stays sticky, and then they roll it up the size of a softball. God, it was marvelous! Once we'd had our celebratory rice balls, we were put aboard little lighters, 30- or 40-foot boats that took us out to the freighter not far offshore. Lingayen Gulf is a very deep body of water, such that a ship can put its bow about 100 feet from shore at low tide, or even closer at high tide, and then when the tide recedes you just sit there and offload. It's very convenient. You don't need to bother building piers when you have a harbor like that, just barge the troops and equipment right off the ship.

I mentioned they were offloading horses when we arrived; that meant we had a job to do immediately upon boarding the ship—clean up all the horseshit down in the holds. It was filthy, as you'd imagine, with that many horses in that small a space for that length of time. But as with all the other work we were given, you did what you had to do. Out of the holds came the manure and into the holds went all of us Americans, joined by some others who'd come from Manila. The ship was an old tramp steamer with two holds, fore and aft, and that's where we stayed. I was in hold #1, forward. We took off late that afternoon, eight ships in a small convoy, accompanied by a single Japanese destroyer. Those of us who'd been on the *Oryoku Maru* were just waiting to hear bombs and torpedo planes and machine guns any minute, but it didn't happen; I don't know if that was a blessing or not. We did hear, at nightfall, a massive rumble off in the distance.

Apparently an American submarine, lying in ambush off the China Sea, had plowed a couple torpedoes into one of the ships in the convoy, and that was all she wrote for those fellas. And by the next morning we found that we were alone, crawling up the west coast of Luzon, north of Lingayen. If we came to the mouth of a river the ship would turn in toward the mouth, to stay as close to the shore as possible. It being daytime, we were inching along, no more than three or four knots, trying to stay out of sight and keeping the ship on track to make a dash across the China Sea to Formosa in the darkness, thereby avoiding the submarine nests.

We once again pieced all this together by what we were able to see in the execution of our duties on bucket detail. *Shobin*, by the way, is urine in Japanese, and *dybin* is feces; we brought the *dybin* buckets topside and tossed them overboard, and occasionally, when one of our fellas succumbed to the usual causes of death, exhaustion, sickness of some kind, the accumulations of bad nutrition and stress and injury, we would take the body up and throw that over, too. We were pretty much on our own out to sea and just kept plugging along. It was a very unpleasant ride, as unpleasant as the boxcars but in a different way. The ship was not very big, half the size of the *Oryoku Maru*, a typical freighter of maybe 350 feet length. After two days the *dybin* detail sighted land and noted that the ocean was a deep brown, so we surmised we were off the coast of China, probably near the mouth of the Yangtze River, all that brown churn in the water silt from the river, even eight or ten miles out to sea. When we sailed closer to land we confirmed that was the case. We turned north again, up the Chinese coast, and then, at a point due west of Formosa (present-day Taiwan), we turned east. With some crude calculations we determined this was where the ship was headed; Formosa had been under Japanese control since well before the war and thus presented an established and comparatively safe rest stop.

Finally we arrived at Takao, on the southwest corner of Formosa. We didn't plan to stay long; our purpose in being there was merely to await the assembly of a handful of other ships, as well as some Japanese Navy vessels to escort us further north. But that never happened. Because the next day a flight of U.S. planes came in over the harbor in a large formation and performed a technique called "area bombing"—planes in the formation come in at the same altitude, and at a signal from the bombardier in the lead plane, all drop their bomb loads simultaneously. This particular flight was comprised of B-17s out of southern China. By now, three years into the war, American factories were churning out planes by the thousands, along with ships and tanks and all other materiel of war, amounts that no one could keep up with, especially not the Japanese. What was more, the situation in Europe was such that the allies, and America in particular, were able by now to route more and more of the war production to the Pacific theatre. There was no place the Japanese couldn't be reached by this point.

This particular flight of B-17s caught several Japanese ships at Takao Harbor, and we were on one of them. And as we know the B-17 does not drip little pebbles of stone. They drop large bombs, the kind that do significant damage to its recipient. Here I was, on another prisoner ship under Allied fire if you can believe that. Our ship was hit on the forward deck, and we had to abandon that thing in a hurry. This time the Japanese let us out right away. Fortunately the hold was not deep, maybe twelve or fifteen feet, a shallow draft freighter, and there were steel ladders on either side of the hold so we were able to scramble out of there on the double. The bloody thing was going down in a hurry and we barely had time to jump. I took my bags full of belongings and just went overboard. It wasn't much of a jump. We were all bobbing around the bay, floating on our backs, me trying to keep moving and stay afloat with these two heavy musette bags dragging in the water. They got soaked before too long and started pulling me down.

And then a bunch of small craft came zipping into the harbor, fishing boats mostly, and began plucking people out of the water. I was picked up by this squat fishing vessel, very low at the center of the water line, a little tub. I was dragged aboard and this Japanese fisherman gave me a kick in the behind and screamed at me, pointing to the aft end of the boat, so I went back there and sat down quietly and minded my own business. I did not see a good opportunity or clear upside to put him in the water and take the boat, unfortunately for me. Perhaps at this stage of the game, it was more about survival than looking for escape or a dangerous yet heroic action on a boat to flee to safety. We churned around the harbor some more, picking up survivors. Some boats were on fire, several including our own had been sunk.

Once the chaos had ended and all the survivors had been scooped from the water, we were moved to yet another ship, this one untouched by the bombing raid. This was a freighter as well, but larger than the one I'd just jumped from. A couple days later we set sail with a small convoy. At one point I came up on deck to empty a *dybin* bucket and saw off our starboard side a Japanese destroyer escort. The way such an escort worked was, the destroyer went out ahead and used its sonar to scan the water for subs. If it found one, another ship would scurry out and go after the sub with depth charges, freeing up the destroyer to continue its search, and in this way the entire convoy was protected from attack by submarine. It didn't always work, but on this trip it did—or else we just got lucky and sailed through the rare patch of Pacific water not teeming with American subs.

We sailed up the west coast of Formosa for several days, and arrived in Japan, on the southern island of Kyushu, sometime mid-January. Now understand, we've come quite a ways north by this time. We'd been in the sub-tropics of the Philippines for years. Formosa is three or four hundred miles north of the Philippines, and then from there it's another two hundred or so miles to Kyushu. Every day we sailed north in January it had gotten cooler, and when we arrived in Japan it was winter. And the contrast in weather had a surprisingly devastating effect on us. We were wearing tatters, we were sickly and ill-fed, skinny, just not in any way equal to that cold weather. Defenseless against it, really.

And accordingly, during the trip to Japan, the cold had set in fully and men started developing pneumonia, a cruel twist after suffering so terribly for so many years with diseases of the tropics, dysentery and malaria and the like. It wasn't long before some of them started dying. You'd wake up in the morning and see someone who appeared to have died overnight, and you'd yell out and whoever was on the burial detail would come and pull the body out of bed. And this will sound ugly, but if the man had any clothes that were of use whatsoever, he would be stripped. It was just too cold, and the Japanese did not provide us any clothing other than what we'd come with. There was no room, in such a circumstance, for sentimentality. The man was dead and no longer needed his clothes. There were living men who needed them quite badly—particularly if they wanted to go on living.

Burials were at sea, of course—there was no way or reason to keep the bodies on the ship. I took my turn on the burial detail, same as everyone else, and one time it happened that I had the job of casting Father Vanderheiden, one of the priests at DAPECOL, into the ocean. We gave this process as much formality and ceremony as we could, but it was of necessity a mostly practical affair. A Japanese crewman would find a piece of scrap metal, and using that and some rope, we would lash three or four or five or six cadavers together, however many we had, and tie the piece of metal to them like an anchor. Someone would say a word, a bit of scripture maybe, and then we'd throw the metal overboard and it would drag the bodies into the water and down. And that was how it went on our final passage to Japan.

In Kyushu we were marched off the ship in Japan and put into formation. Shivering now in the cold, near-freezing temperatures having traveled north this long distance, we walked a very short distance to this unheated warehouse, where we were met by what appeared to be female Japanese members of some kind of auxiliary, an organization similar, I suppose, to the Red Cross. And they were waiting for us with, of all things, box lunches. Which seemed great—at first. We were famished, of course, and even though it was Japanese food and most of it unfamiliar, it was also plentiful and some of it at least quite tasty. Fish, rice, vegetables. The problem, in large part, was the vegetables—there was little or no refrigeration in Japan in those days, and so the vegetables were preserved in brine, like a pickle. But that hardly stopped us from eating, and in no time at all guys were puking up all over the place from this terribly salted food. For the last three years, when we'd eaten at all it had been the most bland food, vegetables mostly, boiled and unsalted, and plain rice, sometimes with the faintest trace of salt sprinkled in it when we were lucky. Now—my goodness, that food seemed so rich, and the irony was that even when the Japanese tried to take better care of us, it backfired. For some of the guys it was a real mess, and a few even died from all the retching and vomiting. Their bodies were just too weak to take it. One hell of a way to go, really, after all we'd survived to that point.

We stayed in the same building overnight, and it turned out to be a very nice place—well-kept and clean other than the vomiting incident, seemed more like an assembly hall of some kind rather than a warehouse. We stayed there overnight and the next morning were marched to the rail yards, where we boarded a train and traveled a short three hours west to a Japanese prison camp right on the shores of the inland sea. This was in a town called Fukuoka. The camp itself was small compared to others we'd stayed in. There were no work details—which again raised the question of why we'd been brought here, why the Japanese had gone through so much trouble, and continued to use resources (however meager and insufficient), to keep us in captivity. I've read big-picture analysis claiming they needed slave labor to keep their empire running, but all I can tell you is if that was the case, they were not making use of us at all. We never left the camp, never did any work.

The buildings in the camp were built very low to the ground, as a defense against the harsh island winters, of course, such that when you left a hut you had to descend only three steps to the ground. They reminded me a lot of a mushroom cellar—damp, cold, a little pot-bellied stove in the center of the main room, enough to give off a little warmth. We were issued several blankets each, heavy cotton instead of wool, but they were quite warm. The camp had no bathing facilities, and certainly no running water, and especially given the shape we were in the ocean was far too cold for washing, unless you wanted to more or less guarantee yourself a case of pneumonia. There was no way of heating water, either, and so no way for any of us to bathe. And in no time, all of us were crawling with lice. A common pastime was a fella who had the strength to get out of his little sack of blankets would go outside and pick the lice off his body and out of his clothes; they gathered, mostly, for whatever reason, in the waist of our pants. This went on for a few months, until the Japanese finally relented and brought in a large bin-like container, intended for cargo of some kind, about twenty-five feet long, ten feet wide, and five feet deep. It served as a pool, a communal bath. We filled the container with water and on Fridays we'd stack piles of wood underneath and set them ablaze, and by Saturday the entire pool would be heated up and we could wash. With so many men only bathing once a week, the water got scummy pretty fast, but at least it was warm, and far better than the lice-infested alternative.

The days went by with agonizing slowness. No work, no distractions, certainly no entertainment, nothing to keep your mind occupied. This boredom was, in its way, far worse than any of the work we'd been made to do over the years; at least when you had a job it made the time pass. I was still somewhat committed to keep my mind churning but that became difficult with idle hands. I like to work even if it's under the boot of a Japanese prison guard—I could, apparently, survive them. Occasionally the air raid sirens would go off, usually at night, when darkness shrouded the bombers' flight paths, and we would be rousted out of bed and hustled into air raid shelters. These were crude and very dangerous hollows in the ground, no internal framing to reinforce the walls and ceilings, damp and crumbly from being so near the water. We probably would have been better off left in our huts; one bomb anywhere near any of the so-called shelters and they would collapse, smothering everyone inside. But we'd stay in them, sometimes for a couple hours, until the all-clear came and we went back to the huts.

As I mentioned, the camp was not very large, maybe the length of three or four city blocks, the width of two. There was no indication of what it had been used for before it became a prison camp. Maybe it had been worker housing of some kind, or maybe it had even been purpose-built for holding prisoners. That would have explained the utter lack of even the most basic facilities, now that I think about it. There was a section at the far end of the enclosure that housed about 100 British prisoners. These men had been here since the fall of Singapore, which seemed like several lifetimes ago at this point. They were a queer lot.

After more than three years of captivity in this place, it must have been like solitary confinement—no work, no travel, no contact with anyone or anything outside this postage-stamp-sized prison. I think if I'd spent that much time in Fukuoka I probably would have turned into an odd duck myself. But in any case, despite how small the place was, these men were not very communicative. Maybe being British, and mostly officers, members of the higher class, they just didn't deign to speak with us. Maybe they were ashamed of having been prisoners for so long. But we had no rapport, no real communication back and forth. They stayed in their quiet hell, and we stayed in ours. It was reported at this time, we were now losing quite a few of the men who had survived the *Oryoku Maru* sinking. You'll recall about 400 men made it off that ship alive, and now only about 200 to 300 of that group were still alive with a chance to get home. As the snow and cold whisked through the camps, it was a white-knuckle, low-odds proposition to get ourselves to warmer weather with hearts still beating. Another fifty or more of the *Oryoku Maru* survivors would not make it through the next couple months. It was simply too damn cold and we were too damn weak, pneumonia being our new, very formidable foe.

And then in the spring, on April 28th, we were informed that the following day, the Emperor's birthday, we were going to leave the camp. We were given rice balls in honor of the Emperor's birth, and while we happily ate the rice, in no way did we honor Hirohito. I'm not sure how we could have even if we'd wanted to, which we did not. The next morning we were marched two miles to the boat docks and boarded a large ocean-going ferry, the kind of boat that might run back and forth between Hyannis and Nantucket. A very modern, clean ship, to our surprise. The weather was pleasant, and we made a day-crossing of the Sea of Japan, landing in the southeast corner of Korea at Pusan. We were placed in a building at the docks and left there overnight. The next morning, early, the air-raid sirens went off. No one came for us, and there was nothing to do but sit there as the bombers came and blew the hell out of the whole area. Somehow, the building we were in did not get hit. That afternoon, when we were gathered into formation to leave Pusan, we saw that the ferry we'd come over on was sunk right at the dock, the portion of the hull and superstructure still above the water smoldering darkly. Imagine that, somehow skirting being bombed and sunk on a boat again—still, I doubt anyone was considering themselves lucky. We marched about a mile to yet another railway depot, and there we were in for the surprise of our lives. The train we boarded was an actual coach—a proper passenger train, with seats and bathrooms—and the railway itself was the same wide-track style we were familiar with in the United States, rather than the cramped narrow-gauge trains we'd been riding for years elsewhere in the Pacific. Coal-burning locomotives, but otherwise quite modern.

The car was practically luxurious and we were fed like human beings with plenty of room to breathe and regroup, although all the shades were drawn to keep us from seeing anything about the areas we passed through, and we'd been told, firmly and repeatedly, not to attempt to see out. But it was easy enough to tell our general route: first south and west, generally following the southern coast of Korea, then turning north and again following the shore until we reached Inchon. The Japanese called the city Jinsen, and if you recall I mentioned at some point that the Japanese had occupied Korea for a long time in one way or another, beginning in the 1870s. They'd assassinated the Korean queen, and through various wars with Russia and China increased their influence in the country until they forced out the Korean emperor and turned Korea into a Japanese colony more than thirty years before. None of this is to say the Koreans liked or supported the Japanese. To me, the Koreans seemed largely submissive, but that didn't mean there was a friendship or association of any kind between the Japanese and the Koreans, as there had been between us and the Filipinos.

When we arrived at Inchon, the first thing I noticed on deboarding the train was how still and quiet everything was. Eerie, is the word, especially after all the movement and violence of the past few months. We walked from the rail yard into the port, among numerous large warehouses, but there was no activity at all nearby. No other people, none of the bustle you'd expect at a major transportation hub in a city. Just us and these hulking, silent storage buildings. We'd find out later that, in the event of an invasion of Japan proper, as part of their defensive strategy the Japanese had every intention of falling back to Korea and Manchuria, places they'd occupied for decades and felt they had good control over and an infrastructure that served them. So these warehouses were loaded with war supplies, weaponry and ammunition, food, fuel, etc. Everything they would need to mount a defense. And there we were, in this strange, deserted place, and we were marched into two single-level barracks-style buildings with no floors. Down the center of each building was a dirt walkway, and on either side of the walkway were narrow bunk areas, elevated maybe two feet off the ground, covered in bamboo matting, and this was where we would sleep. No beds or even cots—the Japanese themselves don't use beds or cots, they just roll out their woven sleeping mats with a hard little pillow. It's what they're accustomed to, and it's what we got—it wasn't as though we were being denied some luxury they indulged in.

We were fortunate enough, in Inchon, to have work details again. Three long years into imprisonment at this juncture and many of us were still oddly pleased to have work to do. We were organized into ward groups and, within each group, divided further into work crews, some of which left the compound and some of which did not. If you had a job that required leaving the compound, you had to get out early, with what was called a bull cart, a very cumbersome, wooden-wheeled wagon pulled by a Brahma steer, five or six miles down the road to a factory that manufactured workers' uniforms. The uniforms were crude, some quilted, some not, all summer-weight clothing, all in olive green. Our job with the bull cart was to pick up piles of these uniforms, bundles of pants and jackets, and transport them all the way back to the compound, then back to the factory, and so on. Meanwhile, those who weren't healthy enough to do more strenuous jobs would work on the delivered clothes, cutting off all the loose threads, cutting buttonholes, bordering the buttonholes, then sewing buttons onto both the pants and jackets.

The other detail at Inchon was more like the jobs we'd had in the Philippines, which is to say agricultural. We worked in vegetable gardens near the barracks, planting and tending daikon and potatoes and that kind of stuff. Being on the farming detail meant you had to deal with human waste regularly, because that was the principal fertilizer. This was still very common is the Orient at the time, though I think there's a movement away from it now, if you'll pardon the pun, and into the chemical fertilizers we use here. We had to take the honey buckets, as they're ironically called, out into town and call at every house just like we were delivering eggs or the newspaper. Except instead of delivering we were picking up. We'd go in with our dip-pails and dump out the waste buckets in each home and when we'd made all the rounds we'd truck the waste back out to the fields for spreading. An unpleasant task under any circumstances, made worse by the fact that we didn't have any of the equipment you'd want for such a job, gloves and rubber boots and things of that nature.

After a month or so Mercer and I swapped off the garden detail and moved to working on clothes. In no time at all we became expert at buttonholes and buttons. It paid, so to speak, to get good at your job, because it was all piece work. A certain number of trousers and jackets were delivered every day, and we each had a quota to fill and once that quota was taken care of, you were done for the day. It was tedious work, mind-numbing in its repetitiveness, tearing loose threads and sewing buttons, but what could you do? When your choices are between that and carrying buckets of shit, that's really no choice at all.

One day it dawned on me that, in the leather pouch I'd found on the deck of the *Oryoku Maru,* in addition to the tobacco and matches and straight-edge razor, there was also a darning needle, three inches long, tough like a leatherworker's needle, with an eye big enough to drive a car through. It was beautiful. So I got to thinking about that needle and suddenly I had what seemed like a brilliant idea: instead of having to punch this small needle through the pants and jackets over and over to sew on the buttons, in and out and around, again and again, I could take that big leatherworker's needle, thread it three times, and only have to go through the cloth once, through the button loop, back through the cloth, then tie it off in the back. Mercer and I could be done in no time. We didn't let on that we'd devised a scheme for finishing our work in a fraction of the time, we just sort of casually wrapped up every day around 1, when the others still had most of the afternoon to go. Some of the other guys were astonished at our speed and skill, and we just let them go on being astonished, never told them what we were doing or how. We were almost famous, even among guys in the other parts of the building, for how fast we were with the buttons.

And then one day this officious-looking Japanese shows up, in plain clothes but with a typical military cap on, hands clasped behind his back, horn-rimmed glasses. He comes into the building and walks up the center aisle, gazing around with this little grin, and then he approaches someone at their station and peers down at them, watching as they work. He's conducting an inspection of the quality of work everyone's doing and we had a problem on our hands now. On this day Mercer happened to have the big needle with the three strands of thread in it, and there was no way to switch it out without being noticed. He was caught. And when the inspector saw what Mercer was doing he flew into an absolute rage. He kicked Mercer to the floor and gave him an unholy beating, mauling him quite badly. I felt bad, because it easily could have been me instead of Mercer; I just happened to be doing the buttonholes that day, and there was no way to cheat on the buttonholes because three strands of thread would have been too coarse and too heavy. So Mercer was sore for a couple of weeks and we lost that beautiful needle, had to go back to the same slow process everyone else in the tailor shop was using. And I never quite understood it, because the work we did with the big needle was as good, if not better, than the other technique. The Japanese should have been happy we'd found a more efficient way to do the same work.

They should have given everyone a big needle. Instead, they gave Mercer a beating.

Of course even though they fed us three times a day there was still never enough to eat, especially with the war going so badly for the Japanese and all resources, including food, at a premium. But one of the advantages of being on the garden detail was you could take the seed potatoes and seed daikon and, if you were careful not to be noticed, eat it right on the job. Now understand, they were not good to eat—neither the flavor nor the texture was appealing at all, and from experience you knew that when it came time to tend to your needs later you would pay a price. I remember a fella from Alabama or Mississippi, a southerner anyway, once said to us, "You know, back home on the farm, not even the pigs would eat potatoes." But we did. After more than three years of constant hunger, there was almost nothing you wouldn't eat, and nothing you wouldn't suffer through, to make yourself feel full.

Eventually the summer came along, and at least we weren't cold anymore. There were, however, a few deaths, as always, from one thing or another. It was never far away. But life was fairly casual and easy, very little contact with the Japanese, in fact. We just did our jobs and ate our rations and slept on our mats and that was it, day after day. In the mornings we'd line up for daily roll call, and in addition to sounding off we'd get our daily dose of Japanese propaganda in clumsy English from the Japanese interpreter. *Shigoto, shigoto, shigoto,* that was all, you'd think they were communists the way they harped on work and all its benefits, *good for you, healthy, stay alive.* The war would be over soon (they'd been promising us this since the beginning; one started to wonder what "soon" meant in the Japanese mind), we'd all be big friends, the same nonsense as always. But the central message was always: more work, more production, people are very hard workers but you Americans are not, you have to learn to work harder and work happier, so on and so forth. We'd all heard the script too many times to count, so we pretended to listen and then got on with it and did our jobs. Things continued as they seemingly always had, each day a carbon copy of the one that preceded it.

But then, toward the end of July and the beginning of August, things began happening that seemed to augur a real change, an end game, perhaps—did we dare believe it?—the conclusion of this terrible purgatory that had been our lives for going on four years. Even in the absence of newspapers and radios, even with an utter lack of real information from the outside world about what was happening in the war, it was quite apparent that something momentous was developing.

For example, one night a guard we knew well came into the barracks, quite drunk, carrying his rifle, muttering darkly about some sad circumstance or another. He knew a smattering of English, which he'd picked up from us. And we knew some Japanese, of course, having been their captives for so long, and needing to learn at least some of the language just to survive. So between us we were able to put together, through broken sentences and pantomime, a sense of what had him so drunk and upset. What it came down to was one phrase he said repeatedly: *senso pitai. Senso* meant "war" and *pitai* meant "finished and over." To probe him for further information was pointless because he was full of sake, but just understanding the import of those two words was enough. This wasn't canned propaganda about the war being over soon; this was unfiltered truth about the fact that the die was cast, Japan had lost, or was at least very far down the road toward losing. It had to be true, because the Japanese, with their pride, would never make such a thing up; they wouldn't even admit, especially to us, when the Philippines fell to the Americans, or Singapore. And we had intimations of how the war was going—at Fukuoka, for example, there had been a steady stream of troops and tanks and artillery coming in on the trains, night and day. The Japanese wouldn't have been bringing in such massive amounts of men and materiel except in anticipation of an assault. And so while this news was exciting, it also caused a kind of anxiety. We'd all survived so much; could our luck hold out a little bit longer, until it was truly over and we could finally go home?

One phrase that all the Japanese knew by now was *baymeju ku. Bay* is their pronunciation of our letter "B." *Meju* means "twenty" and *ku* means "nine." B-29. The bombers had become a scourge and a terror for the Japanese, flying at altitudes too high for anti-aircraft fire and free from worry about Japanese fighters, which had been all but eliminated from the skies by now. It was common for a flight of fifty or one hundred B-29s to come in and blast entire cities with firebombs, and because of the diminished Japanese air defenses, the bombers could sometimes come in as low as 5,000 feet, making their payloads all the more accurate and deadly. Can you imagine a hundred B-29s with four massive engines roaring away, coming at you at low altitude? You'd think the ocean was about to inundate. A terrifying thing, to be the target of such a force. Years later, when I was at the Pentagon, I had a colleague named Dean Fling, a colonel who'd commanded a flight of B-29s out of Okinawa (which, at the time I'm writing about, had been taken, though the Japanese would never admit that to us). He told me stories of flying low-level firebombing runs over Osaka and Tokyo and other population centers, coming in unchallenged and the staggering devastation they wrought. Why the Japanese didn't throw in the sponge, I'll never understand. Their Navy was demolished. Their air power was gone. Their merchant marine had been wiped off the oceans. They had no industrial capacity to replace any of it, and they were broke anyway. New Guinea, New Britain, Guadalcanal, Iwo Jima, the Philippines, Okinawa, Singapore had all been taken from them. They'd withdrawn almost entirely to the home islands, and MacArthur's next step was to invade Formosa, though Fat Man and Little Boy ended things before he had the chance. And in fact, the overall strategic plan for the Pacific did call for an invasion of mainland Japan. That plan involved the Navy feigning an attack on Tokyo, a false landing north of the capitol, while at the same time the real invasion would get underway on Kyushu, the southern island I had been incarcerated on before coming to Korea. The American estimates of casualties in such an invasion was half a million troops killed and wounded. Thanks goodness it never had to be launched. It would have been an order of magnitude larger than the invasion of Europe had been, and in addition to the estimated American casualties, the bombing of Japanese population centers alone, conducted to keep their heads down and immobilize their forces for the purposes of the landing, would have been hell on earth. As bad as the destruction in Japan ended up being, and as terrible as the atomic attacks were, a full-scale invasion would have been far worse.

At Inchon, further indications that the war was coming to a close: there was a Japanese warrant officer responsible for bringing us food two or three times a week, and on one occasion he came in looking forlorn, but also oddly relieved. And you could tell he wanted to say what was on his mind. Perhaps this change—the sudden gabbiness of our captors, their eagerness to spill now that the jig was truly up—was more than anything what convinced us something truly momentous was afoot. We asked what news, and he answered somewhat indirectly, saying it looked like America and Nippon would get together to talk very soon. A few days later he came in with the next food delivery and told us there had been two tremendous explosions in Japan. Through gestures and Japanese words he was able to convey to us how extraordinarily large these explosions had been. The upshot was that the Japanese themselves didn't quite understand what had happened, but somehow single bombs, dropped from single planes, had completely destroyed two Japanese cities. The Americans had a terrible new weapon, he said, and it wasn't until a month later, when it was all over, that we learned for ourselves that these were atomic weapons, dropped on the cities of Hiroshima and Nagasaki.

It's my belief, incidentally, that the bombing of those two cities was not decisive in the war. I'm making a fine distinction here, but one that's still significant. The *outcome* of the war, by the time the *Enola Gay* dropped the first nuclear bomb ever used in anger, was not in doubt. Japan was going to lose. The Germans had already folded three months before, and the collective resources and firepower of the three major Allies, any one of which by itself was more than Japan could muster at this point, was being brought to bear. There is no universe in which Japan would have been able to fight to even a stalemate, let alone a victory. It was over; the only question remaining was how much time, and how much death and suffering, would be necessary for Japan's defeat to be formalized. In this way, terrible as they were and are, the advent of nuclear weapons, at least in that moment in history, can be seen as a strange kind of blessing.

By now, at Inchon, the fiction of Japanese superiority in all matters had come completely unraveled. Our guards were no longer trying to pretend all was well. They were uptight and frightened and muttering darkly to themselves right in front of us. Gone were the days of constant Japanese radio broadcasts about this and that great victory, the conquest of this island that was welcomed by its inhabitants, the bounty of oil and sugar and other raw materials pouring into Japan's economy. That was all over. Word had gotten around and morale was low, a fact that was evident every moment of every day. B-29s thundered through nightly. The war was being brought to their doorstep, and I think they began to finally question the unquestionable philosophy of Bushido, that absolute fealty to the Emperor and obedience in all matters. They started to wonder, why have I spent the last four years risking my life, away from my family and friends, getting shot at and suffering all manner of diseases and privation, for nothing? And I think they realized that Bushido was not the natural law they'd been taught to think of it as, but really just something that came out of the barrel of a gun. So their attitudes changed, and quickly. Just the fact that they'd been silent for three and half years—you wouldn't be human if you weren't looking for an opportunity to speak and act how you really felt, instead of continuing to play the role of perfect imperial soldier. They were, to a man, full of fear, and fear loosened their tongues and their minds. In an odd way, it made them more human—and humane—to us than they had been the entire rest of the war. Funny how a sudden, ice-cold dose of humility will do that very thing.

Chapter 9

FATHER'S ARMS

From here on out, by the way, I have no reliable memory of dates. Events occurred very quickly and I didn't keep a diary, owing to the fact that I had nothing to keep a diary with—no writing utensils, no paper, nothing. You'll have to excuse my inability to cite events on a day-to-day basis, but please know that my intention is to relate the sequence of events as accurately as possible.

In early August, let's say, all work details suddenly stopped, just like that, without explanation. One day the interpreter told us simply, "You're not going out today," meaning to the factory or the farm area, and in that moment we had all done our last bit of labor for the Empire of Japan. We were confined to the small area of the compound with nothing to do. Mind you, in August it can be very hot in Korea, gnats and bugs buzzing around constantly. And we're stuck in a strange mental space where we're simultaneously bored out of our skulls, but also elated at the prospect of being freed for good any day now. And in a way, captivity was easier to take when you couldn't see any end to it. Then it was just the same day over and over, no difference at all, no hope for anything. Now, on the cusp of freedom, each minute stretched out like chewing gum. It was wonderful, and it was also unbearable.

After a while we just got to climbing up on the roof of the barracks and sunning ourselves in a moment of irony after spending years cursing the oppressive sun, for lack of anything better to do. And it was on the roof one day, with half a dozen other fellas, that we saw to our astonishment, out over the bay, this monstrous plane heading straight toward us at low altitude, maybe 1,500 feet. My first reaction was to jump off the roof, looking for a place to hide. I thought, God almighty, we've come this far, and just when it looks like we're at the end, the whole thing is over, now here comes this plane aiming right for us. What trauma went through my body! As bad as things had been at times over the previous years, I'd never felt the same rush of fear and despair I felt in that moment—I think it was to do, ultimately, with the fact that I'd allowed myself to believe for the first time that I would be going home. And now that belief was being shattered by the appearance of this bomber. It crossed the shoreline, almost overhead now, and I thought this was it, and as it passed overhead we saw the insignia with the two flags, the same insignia on the airplanes that had bombed the Japanese when we'd returned to Cabanatuan in 1944. The plane continued inland on an eastern path for two or three minutes, then made a slow turn to the left, 180 degrees, came back over the camp and went back out to sea. Now the bomber started to climb, rising to 2,000, then 3,000 feet, and as he rose he made another turn, this time to the right, toward us once more. And now I thought Sweet Jesus, this is it; he's lining up for a bombing run and we are well and truly done for now.

And here he came, straight at us once more, and sure enough we can see, as he approached over the water, the bomb bay doors opening in the plane's belly. It's just this long, black maw. If you've ever stood at the end of a commercial runway and listened to, say, a DC-6 take off with 150 passengers on board, you know the ear-shattering effect it has, all that power just roaring away. This B-29 was rattling the whole town the same way, shaking everything with the vibrations of its four monster engines. And as I look up into the black maw of the bomb bay, the plane noses forward ever so slightly and I see objects begin to drop from the bay, falling through the air straight at us, and all I can do is lie down on the ground and cover my head with my hands and pray to the Lord that I somehow survive this. Under different circumstances I likely would have noticed there was no way these things were bombs, but with that plane appearing out of nowhere and roaring at you doing 200 miles per hour, you didn't have time to even really react, let alone think through what you were seeing and what was happening. But the objects were not bombs, of course. They were oil drums, welded together in pairs so they were six or seven feet tall. They had parachutes attached, but most of these parachutes didn't work. I found out some months later that this plane had originated in Okinawa, that there'd been reconnaissance flights for days trying to locate prison camps, and ours had been found and this plane dispatched to drop food, clothing, and other supplies. That's what was in the barrels. Four hundred pounds of supplies and gear per two-barrel container. Rations, cigarettes, clean uniforms, infantry boots, hats, jackets, pants, coats, you'd think they were getting us ready for a Saturday morning parade review, all the great stuff they dropped for us. Machinists or engineers or someone, in their haste to improvise a way to fit oil barrels into the racks of a bomb bay, made them so that their parachutes mostly didn't deploy. The parachutes were color-coded, the same way they would be for paratroopers dropping into combat—orange, red, blue, white, and so on. Red, I think, meant the container held signal equipment; blue marked ammunition; white something else, and so on. The idea being that when paratroopers hit the ground they could immediately seek out the container that held what they needed to perform their job—radiomen, technician, medic, etc. In this way, any confusion was eliminated at a moment when speed was essential, and supplies could be sorted in minimal time so troops could advance and fight.

All of this involving the B-29 took maybe fifteen minutes, from the time he first appeared over the water to the moment he pulled up into the blue after dropping his wares and vanished. Once he was gone, we of course ran to examine the drums, and discovered it was Christmas in August. The drums on which the chutes didn't open were, of course, smashed on the ground, but we were still able to salvage plenty of their contents. And there were more than enough clothes to finally get rid of all the rags we'd been wearing for God knew how long—there was probably enough to dress all our guards, too, and the state of their uniforms were such that some of them could have used a new outfit. We even found a barrel full of soap; oh how glorious it was, after years without, to have a bar of soap in your hands.

By this time there were only about 175 of us at the camp. Those of us who survived the sinking of the *Oryoku Maru* had been separated at Pusan, told to split into two lines, take your pick, and I fell into one of the lines at random and ended up in Inchon. The other half went God knew where. And 25 or so of our group had died one way or another in the interim. So, 175 men received enough uniforms and boots to outfit a battalion. Just piles of boots everywhere, who knows what became of them, and frankly, who cared, the absurd bounty was just one tiny speck of the massive warmaking machine that the United States had become, and no one was worrying about a few hundred pairs of boots. Also, the amount of Spam in the barrels was, in a word, staggering. We ate like pigs. It was a celebration—now we knew the war was over, some kind of agreement or understanding had to have been reached between the U.S. and Japan in order for that single plane to have come in loaded with nothing but food and clothes. It was not, of course, fired upon. The entire mess was over. Our captivity was over. And to celebrate, we ate until we could not eat anymore.

In the meantime, the warrant officer responsible for bringing us food came and sort of meekly asked if we wanted rice. Overnight he'd gone from master to servant, and it was both strange and glorious. By way of explanation—though we'd reached our own conclusions and no longer needed it—he told us, *Nippon-America time to get together, let's have truce, both sides get along and things be very happy and it all be over.* He saved face, of course, by using the word *truce* instead of the word *surrender.* Bring the rice, we told him. Because his sudden change of orientation toward us was all we needed to know preliminary terms of surrender had been agreed upon by the Japanese. All that remained was the formality to come on the deck of the battleship *Missouri* in Tokyo Harbor, the Japanese in their top hats and finery, surrendering to—who else—Douglas MacArthur.

On the afternoon of the next day, another B-29 came in over the camp, so low it felt like it would shake us right into the ground. In fact, the plane was close enough to the ground that we could read the name on the fuselage: *Slick Dick.* We had a good laugh, and when we saw that we said it can only be Americans, it was hard to imagine anyone else would name a plane something like that. Certainly not the British. And just as with the first plane, Slick Dick dropped barrels instead of bombs, but this time one of them might as well have been a bomb: a barrel loaded with matches and cigarettes crashed into one of our barracks and set it right on fire. Well, how do you like that? We rushed to the kitchen and put water in every kind of vessel we could find, pots and pans, running back and forth and trying to, if not put the fire out altogether, at least confine it and keep the entire barracks from burning down. Eventually the Japanese brought in a wagon of water and a pumper and extinguished the blaze, but not before the building had been basically destroyed. What a mess.

Now half of us didn't have a place to stay. We still had full bellies, though, and fresh clothes and plenty of cigarettes from another barrel that hadn't caught fire. But the officer in charge, a Marine lieutenant colonel named Hortzman, called a meeting to discuss how we would keep from being killed by our own planes before someone finally came and got us out of there once and for all.

Hortzman knew a bunch of us had been pilots, and he asked if anyone had experience with laying out panels on the ground to form messages for aircraft flying overhead. I hadn't ever laid out panels, but being in the observation squadron I'd had plenty of experience reading panel messages, and I knew how big they were and how they were constructed. So I stepped forward.

The way things turned out, maybe I should have kept my mouth shut.

But the decision was made to take all the parachutes attached to the barrels and cut them into panels, then use the panels to form big letters, maybe ten feet long and a few feet wide. We got to work, cutting and shaping panels, laying them out on the ground and securing them so they'd stay put. In the end we had a sign in the open rear area of our enclosure that someone with 300 vision could see from altitude. It read "DO NOT DROP HERE." Seemed clear enough.

From the bottom of this message, we made a fifty-foot arrow pointing away from the compound and toward the beach. And then on the beach, some of us took white parachutes and made a massive circle, a target 75 feet in diameter, and staked it to the sand. The target was accompanied by another message: "DROP HERE."

In the meantime, at the moment anyone saw or heard an airplane approaching, they were to alert the kitchen, where someone would bang an alarm meant originally to call everyone to chow. The alarm was actually a beautifully fashioned piece of railroad track, fabricated into a large circle, and it made a clear, deep sound like a bell. The plan was to ring the alarm three times, and this would bring everyone quickly to the gates of the compound, where we would get into formation and depart the area in an orderly, controlled way.

The next day, sure enough another plane comes in. The alarm sounds, everyone gathers up and leaves the compound as the plane approaches. We move to a safe spot away from both the compound and the drop zone that's been set up and clearly marked. The bomber comes in over the water, approaches the shore...and proceeds to drop its barrels right over the camp again.

How could this be? Was the pilot blind? Did he not even bother looking down before opening his bomb bay and dropping the barrels exactly where we'd marked not to drop them again?

So by this time, of course, I'm looking like quite an ass. Everyone thinking, I'm sure, that they trusted Rafferty to do this the way it's supposed to be done, he claimed to know, and it all went to hell. But before too long we were able to figure out what had happened. A lieutenant named John Wright had, for some reason, gotten confused and decided on his own to go to the area in the compound marked "DO NOT DROP HERE" and remove the word "NOT." So when the plane had come in, the pilot and copilot looked down and what did they see? "DO DROP HERE." Unbelievable.

And once more, the compound just got plastered. In fact, a barrel with an inoperative chute hit a Japanese guard right at the gate, and that was the end of him. Another man, an artillery captain among our number, lost a leg when a barrel hit near him and shattered, the metal just as damaging as shrapnel from a bomb. I suppose we should have been grateful nothing else caught on fire, but it was awful, this close to being freed, to have such a thing happen—especially after we'd prepared carefully to prevent it.

Incidentally, despite his inexplicable blunder, John Wright went on to a long career, was even promoted to Lieutenant General in the 1960s and became chief of the U.S. Army Plans Headquarters. Go figure.

A small blessing: after that, there were no more flyovers by B-29s. Apparently someone at headquarters in Okinawa, or somewhere anyway, had figured that three days of supplies for such a small number of men was sufficient. And thank God. Any more help like that and it's possible none of us would have survived.

And I don't want to make it sound as if we weren't grateful. All of us had full bellies, were comfortable in our new clothes, and had more cigarettes than we had time to smoke. We all smoked cigarettes in those days and it was real treat to get our drags on some nice tobacco. We were even gaining strength in a few short days, putting on a little weight, which would have seemed only a week before like an impossibility. Major Montgomery, who'd been the officer in charge of our hold on the *Oryoku Maru*, and here served as camp adjutant, went to our Japanese interpreter and tried to reason that given the clear end of hostilities, not only should the Japanese disarm themselves (this was always a basic condition of a surrender), but we now former prisoners should be allowed to come and go as and where we pleased. The disarming was a non-starter—that would have involved a considerable loss of face, which you know by now the Japanese would not allow. I also imagine they weren't eager to be defenseless among the Koreans, who as I mentioned had no affection for their occupiers. But we were allowed freedom of movement, on the condition that we not travel in groups smaller than five or six and that we promise not to cause any trouble, blah blah blah.

After that, it wasn't long before we decided to go into town and see what was happening. And we did that, just walking sort of moonily along the streets of Inchon, nowhere in particular to go. There was no doubt that we weren't the only people for whom things were about to change dramatically. You could sense it in the Koreans, too. They were very polite, pleasant, smiling at us as we moved about town. But there was the language barrier, and beyond that a lot of the Koreans we encountered had probably never even seen white men before, and certainly not white men so gaunt and drawn from extended captivity. We probably looked to them like we were from outer space. But we were in a great mood nevertheless. We were free! And in the city there were no Japanese whatsoever. The only Japanese in this world were the soldiers at the compound.

After a full day of traipsing around Inchon, Mercer and I went back to camp and had an idea to take some of the surplus shoes, go downtown to the markets and see if we could trade them for eggs and fruit. Here we were with all these gorgeous infantry boots, great thick grippy soles and uppers that went halfway to your knee, they were like works of art, really. And then there were the Koreans, walking around in their wooden clogs, they hadn't seen footwear like these infantry boots ever, and they never would again. That would seem to make the boots a good item for bartering.

So we took a duffel bag and stuffed it full of boots, and the next day we set off for the markets. Before we even got there we saw, coming in the other direction, an old Korean man in his little black aerated hat made of straw. He's leading an old steer on a rope. As we approach each other we stop, and I take out a pair of boots and sort of wave them at the old man, and oh did his eyes light up. Just like that, we had our first customer. We agreed on a price of fifteen pairs of boots for the steer, which looked like a rhinoceros but we didn't care, we'd butcher that thing and get fresh meat. The trade was finalized, and here we were with this old animal with a ring through its nose. We broke a little branch from a tree to use as a switch, you know, the kind of stick herdsmen use to guide their animals, and off we went back to the compound.

The arrival of the steer caused a big stir, of course. We paraded him back to the rear area where we'd put the "DO NOT DROP HERE" sign that became "DO DROP HERE." Old Alsbrook, he of Austin, Texas, fancied himself an expert on all things cattle-related, and he drove a stake in the ground at about a 45-degree angle and said, "I'll show you how to slaughter an animal." He went off somewhere for tools and in the meantime a couple of guys put the steer's tether around the stake and began yanking on it, and before long the animal's nose was right on the ground with its front legs splayed wide, and he was grunting and groaning, this poor old dog.

In the meantime, Alsbrook returned from the kitchen with of all things a rail splitter, an axe-like implement for splitting logs. He came over to where the guys had the bull pinned to the ground, and he was flexing his muscles and making a big show, all 105 pounds of him, going to demonstrate the proper Texas way of doing in a steer. He hoisted the rail splitter and put the head of the mallet on top of the animal's head. "Now just watch this," Alsbrook said, and he reared back with all his might and whacked him, and all the bull did was wiggle its ears, as though brushing off a fly.

Of course, we all had a good laugh at that. But Alsbrook still had something to prove. He lifted the rail splitter again, brought it down—

same result. No way he was hurting that animal, let alone killing it. So we started ribbing him, of course: "Maybe this just isn't where your talent lies, Jim, maybe let someone else have a go at it." And in the meantime, someone else had gone to the kitchen and came back with a simple knife. He reached under the animal's chin and gave it one big, long stroke. Within a minute, the animal fell. Work smarter, not harder, I suppose, though Alsbrook likely did not take the lesson.

So we butchered the beast on the spot into hunks of meat, took it up to the kitchen, into the pots it went. We cooked it for two or three hours, and who was tasting it I don't know, but when it came off the stove the first time it was tough as a Russian boot. So we cooked it some more. And some more. And after many, many hours what we ended up with was a mushy, stringy, greasy meat dish of some kind. But it was fresh, that's what mattered, and we ate it with great glee.

Many other things happened, but I'm not quite sure they're worth the telling; more of the same, I suppose. Suffice it to say we were and remained ecstatically happy. We were suddenly free, and that was a glory in and of itself, but even better was the anticipation that in a few days someone would come for us and, shortly thereafter, we would be back in the United States, the war over. Against both the odds and common sense we had survived, and now we could go back to our lives.

Three or four days after we traded for the steer, a robust, strong, extraordinary man arrived alone at the gates of the compound. He was an American lieutenant colonel, and he'd been driving through Korea by himself in a Jeep. He asked to see the American commander at the camp, and he told us he'd flown into Seoul, which was about fifty miles away, on a transport plane. Having heard there was a prison camp at Inchon, he'd gotten in his Jeep and driven here to find out if there were any Japanese who we felt had been particularly cruel to us. American forces weren't far behind him; they hoped to have us out of here in two or three days, but in the meantime it was important they find out how we'd been treated and if any of our captors had behaved in ways that were out of line. And the only person we all could agree had been cruel to us was, strangely enough, the Japanese doctor. He was an army captain, an abusive monster, which I'll never understand how that coincides with the fact of being a physician. In the American military, doctors are strictly non-combatants, but in the Japanese military, they are armed like anyone else, and have many of the same duties. So this doctor often, for example, would be responsible for overseeing our morning roll call. And if you couldn't sound off in Japanese the way he wanted, *ichi, ni, san, shi, go,* and so on, if you were too slow or God forbid made a mistake, he would take his baton and paste you in the side of the head with it. There was no real reason for him to do this, other than that he enjoyed inflicting pain for its own sake; it didn't make us behave differently or better, and it didn't teach us anything. It wasn't corrective, it was purely punitive. And if a fella saw it coming and tried to cover up and protect himself, the doctor would kick him directly in the face. So we turned this Japanese doctor in to the lieutenant colonel, and I imagine that one day not too long after he was made to answer at the tribunals for the way he treated us.

After about an hour the lieutenant colonel roared off again, by himself, presumably back to Seoul. It still impresses me that he was willing to travel through that country alone and basically defenseless—anyone could have taken a shot at him, he could have been killed at any time, surrender or no surrender.

As we'd been told, sure enough, three days later across the bay came this massive grouping of ships. We could see what were obviously transports, many of them, dropping anchor five miles or so off shore. They deployed barges, and into the barges went troops. So this was to be, not surprisingly, treated as a combat landing. The troops were 7th Division, primary units and reinforcements at once, so around 20-22 thousand men. When we saw those barges coming in waves of six or seven abreast, my God, we got excited. Suddenly—for the first time, I realized, standing there—it was real. We were going home. They drew closer and we saw the soldiers were in full battle gear, intending to make an amphibious assault right on the beaches of Inchon. And when these steel boats hit the sand, carrying fifty or sixty troops per, the front end would drop down into a ramp with a tremendous splash, and the men would rush out and through the water and take up positions on the beach. There were barges with machine guns, barges with small artillery pieces. A full-scale invasion force. And they must have had Inchon mapped out completely, because all these men and units moved like they knew exactly where they were going, had been assigned to very particular places and responsibilities.

For some reason, in our excitement, we decided to take off toward downtown, about a fifteen or twenty-minute walk. Maybe we just wanted to be around other people, to feel what this felt like to everyone. When we got there we started talking to some of these troops. They were very communicative. They were ready for a fight. And our friend Jim Walsh, part of our very close group, said to one lieutenant leading a platoon, "Hey, what's all the excitement for? We've been here for months, we've got this town all covered. I assure you, everything is under control." And the lieutenant was aghast, didn't know what to think. He just looked behind him at some of the men in his unit, maybe hoping they would protect him from these kooks from outer space.

The next day, it was really and truly over.

We were rounded up, our names and ranks and serial numbers recorded, and then we departed the compound. We were allowed to take a modest amount of personal belongings with us, though most didn't have much to speak of at this point, other than the clothes on their backs. We headed to the docks, where we boarded a light amphibious craft and made our way out into the bay. How glorious it was, the sun shining brightly and the seas calm, being on the water, finally, in a boat we didn't need to worry would be bombed or shot to hell. Having room to stretch out instead of being packed together so tight some of us suffocated. Having a full stomach and knowing that if we needed a bathroom, one was available and we wouldn't need to use a bucket, or the floor. Truly glorious, all these little things I would never take for granted ever again.

Among the transports in the bay was a hospital ship. I don't know what I was expecting, but when we came aboard there was little excitement. None at all, in fact. Nobody welcomed us aboard, no one put their arms around us and praised our bravery or any of that. We were being processed, is the way to explain it. The whole thing was very clinical, everyone just checking boxes and making sure their job was done. Once again we gave our names, ranks, serial numbers, and branch of service for the record. We were asked a few questions about how we felt, but no physical examinations—at least, I didn't get one.

The next day we were moved off the hospital ship and onto a large American freighter, bound for Manila through the Sea of Japan. We thought the least they could do was fly us out of there, all of us feeling like we'd been on enough freighters to last us the rest of our lives. But I guess we just didn't have the airplanes at the time, or else, and this seems pretty likely, there were so many POWs being scooped up and processed they couldn't treat them all to a first-class flight home. That was just the reality. So, the freighter it was. We were told to stay away from the bow of the ship at all times, because the Japanese had mined the hell out of the waters we'd be sailing through and we could hit one at any time. It seemed there would be no end to things that might explode at any moment, though we kept hoping.

The run to Manila took about four days. I was sleeping regularly and well by now, feeling very good. But it was lonely at sea. I don't know if I was just so accustomed to being in close quarters for so long, but there was something uncomfortable about having my own space, somehow. In any case, we watched some movies on board, had a few drinks and a few laughs, and arrived in Manila on or about August 25, 1945. Hot as blazes in the Philippines that time of year—I'd forgotten, in fact, how hot it could get. I was sent to Camp McKinley, the old Army post east of the city, which had been converted into what they called a "Repo Depot." Basically meaning that soldiers, sailors, and airmen who were out of commission for whatever reason—wounds, illness, etc. The idea was to rehab at a place like this until you were well enough to be reassigned to another unit, at which point you'd go off to whatever your new assignment was. We only stayed for a few days, me and Mercer, owing to the fact that somehow there wasn't anything seriously wrong with us that food and rest hadn't already mostly cured. We went into the city, bumming rides along the way from GIs and others, to see some old friends. Neighbors from our shared apartment, the Baretto girls, and of course Louis Durosa, our old Filipino roommate who had thankfully survived the war.

We learned something frightful, from other friends, about Louis' sister, and what had happened to her toward the end of the Japanese occupation. Louis himself was around 25 and his sister was 29, maybe 30, with magnificent black sparkling eyes and beautiful hair, extraordinarily attractive. Well, she was the one who owned an abaca factory, the so-called Manila hemp from which they made all kinds of products: bags, lamp shades, rope and twine, netting, and something the reader is probably familiar with, rattan furniture. The plant grows in the jungle as a kind of vine, hundreds of feet long, winding its way through trees and underbrush. Incidentally, we were surrounded by it at DAPECOL; it's part of what makes the jungle so impenetrable. So abaca is harvested by tracing a vine back to its roots, which are then cut out of the ground, or rather excavated—it's not an easy process, similar to pulling out a small tree stump. The root is hitched to a pair of buffalo and they haul the entire vine out of the jungle—again, hundreds of feet, one solid unbroken vine about an inch thick that makes its way along the ground, snakes up one side of a massive tree and down the other, and so on. Getting it out of there is not easy. But once it's freed you can use it for just about anything, turn it into cloth, etc. Rattan furniture is made by heating the vine and bending it to the shape you want while it's still hot; when it cools it hardens that way, in the form of a chair leg, say, or the arm of a love seat. It's a very versatile, utilitarian material.

Anyway, Louis and his sister were in the abaca business, and she ran the factory where they made all manner of furniture: settee benches, chairs of course, tables, and so on. It was a big operation for the Philippines; they employed maybe 75 people. Now before the war, Louis' sister (who I won't name although I probably could now, given that she's no longer among us) was the girlfriend of a married man named Soriano, a member of the, without question, leading family of Manila. There was hardly a Filipino industry that the Sorianos didn't have a hand in. They owned breweries and plantations, vast holdings of land, shipping operations, rice milling and rice export, sugar refining and sugar export, lumber, and on and on. And it was an open secret that this Soriano fella had set Louis' sister up in business. He was the reason she owned this rattan factory. Louis was pretty closed-mouthed about it, for which I didn't blame him, then or now. And when the war came, there were elements of each of the ruling class of Filipinos—the Spaniards, Chinese, and half-breed Filipinos—who cooperated with the Japanese. Cooperation in the sense that they kept things running at the orders of the Japanese, for fear of losing their wealth, or their heads. The Sorianos, by and large, were wealthy and influential enough to escape the country altogether; many of them ended up in the United States. But Louis' sister could not escape, and either would not or could not run to the hills like so many others of the upper crust. So she was, according to the friends who told me all this, cooperating quite heavily with the Japanese, had relationships, knew things about what they did, and probably, it turned out, knew more than was good for her.

And when MacArthur encircled Manila, swooping up from the south with one mass of forces and coming in from Lingayen Gulf with the other, the Japanese imposed a scorched-earth policy on the city, burning and looting and generally causing chaos and destruction. And among other things, anyone who had cooperated extensively with them was systematically murdered, to keep them from telling the Americans anything about what the Japanese had done during their time here, or where they might have hidden their plunder. And that included, of course, Louis' sister. It was just one more ugly aspect of a dreadful war, and we were sorry as hell to hear it.

And it wasn't for that reason but, while visiting all these old friends, we weren't really happy to be there, weren't really excited down deep. All we wanted to do was get back to the United States. That would be the true end of things.

We knew that SOP [standard operating procedure] at that point was for former POWs to be taken back to the United States by ship. That was at best a two-week run, more if we had to stop and wait in one place or another, which we almost certainly would. And we figured, the very least the Air Corps could do was take their own pilots home. So Mercer and I went down to Nichols Field and got an audience with some Major. We told him we were just a couple of beat-up old POWs who'd really like to get home as soon as humanly possible, did he think he had two seats on a transport somewhere for us? Now in those days, immediately following the war, we didn't even register on the list of priority passengers for air transportation. First was generals and admirals, naturally, followed by diplomats, attaches, that kind of thing, all manner of high-ranking State Department personnel. So far, with regard to me and Mercer, 0-for-2. Next priority would be government workers, then someone else who wasn't us, and so on, until you got down to the end of the list and saw that people like us weren't even on it at all. Not low-priority, but no-priority, our pain and suffering as POWs notwithstanding. So we're half-crying to this Major, thinking it's hopeless, and then he surprises us by saying, "Listen, I'll tell you what. We have some transports going out of here tomorrow. Come back then and I'll see if we can find you a couple of seats."

Well, Mercer and I were just about over the moon. We hustled back to McKinley and gathered up our stuff, such as it was. We'd been issued mosquito nets, some old wool blankets—even winter uniforms, for some reason. We just grabbed it, or most of it, anyway. I took the winter uniforms, three sets of khakis, underwear, threw it all into some duffel bags. And we went back to Nichols and just sort of hung around, waiting, hoping. Planes came and went. We waited some more. I'm not even sure what we were planning to do in the event the Major couldn't or wouldn't find us seats somewhere. But damned if he didn't do just that. A converted B-24, which was a lesser-known 4-engine bomber that to this day remains the most-produced aircraft in American military history. The mechanics somehow engineered it so there was heat in the bomb bay, and that's where Mercer and I sat as we hopscotched to Okinawa, Midway, and finally Hawaii.

It turned out—and we sort of knew this, but also didn't know for sure—that in our haste to find a seat on a plane we hadn't dotted all the i's and crossed all the t's on our movement paperwork. So technically Mercer and I were AWOL—absent without leave, a big no-no. We had proceeded to somewhere other than where we were stationed without orders or proper authorization, and that's pretty much the definition of AWOL. To this day, Mercer and I will lead into our phone calls with each other asking if the other had been caught yet and speaking from a prison phone.

We were only in Hawaii for a day, then managed to secure actual seats on a flight to Oakland, California. When we got to Oakland we decided to report to the hospital in San Francisco, at the Presidio Army Base. We stayed there two or three days, got checked over, physicals and the like, just waiting for instructions. We'd told staff at the hospital about being AWOL, so there was paperwork and wire messages going back and forth. In all seriousness, no action was ever taken against us, of course; the war was over and we'd been POWs for nearly four years and I think anyone who could have made an issue of it decided it would be easier for everyone—themselves included—to just let it go.

Next thing, I got on a DC-3, a twin-engine transport, carrying about 25 passengers, and off we went across the United States. We had to take a southern route, first south through L.A., then a kind of half-loop around the southern Rockies, because the DC-3 didn't have the power to get up over the mountains. After five days we landed at Mitchell Field, an air base in New York out on Long Island. Then I flew from there to the big SAC base in Springfield, Massachusetts. I was taken by ambulance (not sure why; protocol, I suppose, but I was fine) to Camp Bevens, took another physical and stayed a couple of days. The doctor asked me how I felt as he poked and prodded me for odd bumps and pains and such, and I told him I felt great. And he said, "Then why don't you come see me again in about a month," and I did that, several times. In the meantime, I got my back pay and allowance—even got flight pay, though I hadn't flown a plane in four years. It was kind of funny in the way these things can have little pockets of surprises that have you just shaking your head.

There had been communication from the military to my mother that I had returned safely, and I had sent her a couple posts to Brookline and to my sister's in Florida, but I had yet to see my family in the flesh. And for a long time at the onset of my captivity my mother and father only knew I was missing in action. Communication was often incomplete or inaccurate, a very difficult, painful reality for a worried mother of a US soldier fighting in a hot warzone. So that moment of walking through the screen door to the family home in Brookline was quite remarkable. I recall having to use the handrail for support coming up the two concrete steps external to the back door to the kitchen. I arrived a couple hours before they were expecting me so I walked in on them arranging the furniture just so and something smelled awfully nice on the stove—my favorite pot roast in gravy. I almost cried at that familiar smell, how beautiful it was. No one noticed me at first as I lingered in the doorway that connected the kitchen to the sitting room. I felt like I was outside the scene of my own motion picture if that makes any kind of sense. It was out-of-body, as they say. Everyone was there, all eight brothers and sisters. My father, Joe, was in his sharp overcoat he was gifted many birthdays ago from the family. I was honored to see everyone so well-dressed and preparing the house just for me. Mom lifted her head from shuffling and organizing magazines on the side table next to the large sofa, and her eyes went wide as they met mine.

"Oh, my Patrick!" she shouted and ran across the room to embrace me.

"I'm home, mother," I said, and that is really all I could muster for words.

My father's hug was certainly the longest one I had ever received from him. He wasn't the hugging type, nor was I, I suppose. In that moment, though, I felt so safe and loved in the arms of a father, not unlike a young boy might feel. That hug from old dad was the moment above all others thus far where I felt like I was truly home from war. From Clark Field to the march, from the prison camps to jumping off those ghastly ships, from the plane rides home to the hospitals on the bases, I was finally home. My last transport. And it was glorious.

That night over a glass of White Horse scotch with my father, it dawned on me that I did not feel a need or a want to share much about what I had experienced as a prisoner. Not yet, anyway. I told him as much, which he thankfully respected and said he understood. And this position I took that night wouldn't ever change, really. There's a certain "you had to be there" to telling the story of being a prisoner of war under somewhat indescribable conditions. For the most part, there are no words. Still, there are scenes I will never attempt to describe to anyone else. It's difficult to embody the context and senses that comes with it, and to do so with any kind of English vocabulary that could do the people and places real justice was so very difficult. So we held it in, I suppose. Then, of course, there's the odd feeling of guilt that many of us would have in having returned to our lives while so many—most—of our fellow prisoners did not return home. Countless men turned to dust on roadsides and prison yards, or sunken to the bottom of a sea, all with mothers and families who will never get the opportunity to know what exactly happened to their dear boy or to say goodbye. And that, for me, has been a heavy thought and maybe I just haven't felt deserving of telling our story.

I would regret to learn over the years that most of the other POWs continued to battle severe illness from the camps, the usual pains of malnourished teeth, bones that had been broken and not set properly, that type of thing. I don't have the statistics that a government body would have at their disposal, but I would be hard-pressed to think even half the fellas who made it home lasted beyond, say, 50 years old. It was too much trauma, too much abuse to go on much longer than that.

Of course, there was the mental aspect of this deal, that heavy luggage a young man carries home from war and has no good place to store it. So it lingers there in the back of his thoughts finding those precise, horrific times to jump out and give a nasty reminder of the captivity. For me it was a nighttime experience, and I understand that was common, when the lights go down in the home and it gets real quiet outside. A door would slam shut or a salty sea smell would make its way into my bedroom in Duxbury or Falmouth, and there I was, back on the march with seashells under my pained feet smelling the seas of the Pacific. Despite those startling memories that can shoot a man out of bed in search of his pistol in a sweaty panic, I can't say I've had thoughts of revenge or found myself with blood pumping harder when in the company of a Japanese or Asian man. There are reports, and I would hear the odd personal account, that many returning POWs did, in fact, harbor a great rage and revengeful mind in the presence of a man who looked in some way like a Japanese prison guard, which I suppose is understandable given that tortuous memory bank we have and how clear the Japanese were of their utter hatred of us as a lesser race and soldier. For me, I felt it best to savor what comes from our country's melting pot, that heterogeneous population in the United States, where an immigrant family like mine could come from Louth, Ireland while another family could come from a rough deal in Japan, and we could both come with our proverbial shovels to build up a life for ourselves. This country had been through two long, taxing worldwide conflicts in less than thirty years with millions of our young men dying to secure our freedoms, and I say they died to allow for all the races, creeds, and colors to get a seat at the table back home. No free lunch will be served on the table where I sit, mind you, but no, I harbor no ill-will to the Japanese. And the older I get, the more I dread the thought of a young man of any background dying in war. It's a dastardly business, though necessary at times.

Months after reuniting with my family, I went up to Syracuse to see Mercer, and it only made sense that I was visiting him when I met the woman who would become my wife, Dorothy Helen O'Neil. Mercer and I had been through so much, somehow both surviving and staying together through it all. And now here was Dorothy widowed with a young boy, Oscar, soon to be joined by our beloved girls, Regina, Helen, Patricia, and Joan, and another beautiful boy, Brian. That was my bunch, I called it. Who'd have thought, while in a prison camp, or aboard one of those horrid Japanese ships, that any of it would or could happen? God love her and the children.

To future generations that will come in my bloodline, I hope you all stay well and never have to get into uniform. But if the time comes, do go. Don't shirk. Do go.

EPILOGUE

Allow me to bring this narration to an end with some comments on General Douglas MacArthur. Obviously MacArthur was very capable, but it's important, I think, to understand that on Bataan, when so many of us were dying and our fortunes declined daily and it seemed not just hopeless but, at times, also pointless, esteem for MacArthur plummeted. Bear in mind, for example, that he was the one who ordered the cut in rations to two meals a day, while at the same time he had his wife and child with him on Corregidor—and we all knew they weren't rationing food. He and his family no doubt continued to eat well, while we slogged through the mud in the heat, bitten by a thousand mosquitos, ducking bullets and hoping the next mortar didn't have our name on it—and now we did it all while hungry to boot.

And then, in mid-March, MacArthur took off on the PT boat for Australia, his wife, child, and maid in tow. So by that time he was held by many in just utter contempt. "Dugout Doug" was the derogatory nickname that came into common use around that time, "Doug," of course, for "Douglas."

However, looking back over the span of his career, the truth is exactly the opposite of what that nickname suggests. In World War I, World War II, and continuing in Korea, he led from the front, exposing himself to the dangers of combat and disease on innumerable occasions. There was no soft living for him, hundreds of miles behind the front lines in some comfortable rear area, waited on by hordes of GIs and servants. MacArthur was the essence of bravery, which is the conviction in the rightness of what one is doing and how one does it—when you believe in how you conduct yourself, and to what purpose, fear recedes.

There's an anecdote from MacArthur's time as a junior officer in Mexico that, to me, illustrates this quality of his perfectly. This was in 1914, when Woodrow Wilson ordered the occupation by American forces of Veracruz. MacArthur made a decision on his own to try to find and secure locomotives with which to make use of, and control, the railways, which he considered essential to the success of the American incursion. He hired three Mexicans and rented a handcar, and they went off in search of the locomotives. On three separate occasions, they were attacked by men on horseback, and MacArthur himself shot seven of these attackers (and one of their horses), completed the mission he'd set for himself, and returned with the locomotives. In the attacks, four bullets had gone through his uniform, but somehow none of the bullets hit MacArthur. And now here's the part that's perfectly MacArthur: for his actions, he was recommended for the Medal of Honor, but ultimately the board responsible for deciding the award declined. They wrote, "to bestow the award recommended might encourage any other staff officer, under similar conditions, to ignore the local commander, possibly interfering with the latter's plans." Basically, they said MacArthur was brave and capable enough to justify granting the Medal of Honor, but his brashness and disregard for any authority other than his own prevented them from doing so. And damned if that wasn't him in a nutshell.

Fast-forward to Lingayen Gulf in 1945, MacArthur right there with the landing ships, peering through his binoculars as the men came ashore and engaged the Japanese. His vessel could have collided with a mine, or they could have been hit by a Japanese dive-bomb or kamikaze attack. But there he was. Which is to illustrate that, in addition to his personal bravery and competence, MacArthur also provided extraordinary leadership to his troops. His presence and visibility mattered a great deal in terms of morale and fighting spirit, and he knew that. Very few commanding generals in modern warfare would have done the same. Indeed, very few did.

He was also belligerent, arrogant, disobedient, and one could argue, at certain times, he approached being traitorous. If he believed it was better to do something other than what he was ordered to do, then he would ignore those orders. This was the case, for example, when he was ordered by Washington to land in the Philippines at Leyte but he decided to go into the southern islands instead. He believed—and was probably correct—that he could see the state of things on the ground much more clearly than civilians could from the other side of the world, and he acted accordingly.

It's staggering to consider, even in brief, everything MacArthur did and accomplished during his career. Graduated first in his class from West Point in 1903. Only three years later, served as military aide to Teddy Roosevelt. In 1913 he was appointed to the General Staff in Washington, and only a year later led his cowboy raid in Veracruz, Mexico. In 1917 he was promoted to Colonel at just 37 years of age. He was largely responsible for, and the first chief of staff of, the 42nd

Division, known as the "Rainbow Division," the first unit comprised of soldiers from many different states rather than just federalized National Guard divisions. His job was to coordinate the actions of all the members of the staff: supply, quartermaster, intelligence, operations, planning, personnel, and to represent the commanding general in all matters, so that the division could function as a cohesive unit. But he was hardly a pencil-pusher. When the division was sent to France in 1918, MacArthur led raids on German trenches and earned the first of seven Silver Stars. He was gassed twice, and wounded while leading a reconnaissance patrol in no-man's land between trench lines, ending up being the only person on that patrol to have survived. He was even mistaken for a German officer and taken prisoner briefly by men of the American 1st Division. By the end of the war he was a Brigadier General, the youngest man in American history to have achieved the rank.

In 1919 he became superintendent of West Point. True to form, he wanted to change how just about everything was done at the Academy. In short, he wanted to modernize the school, eliminate hazing and emphasize academics, in particular science and mathematics, and get rid of a lot of the old graybeard courses. He sought to expand the idea of military character to include bearing, leadership, efficiency, and athletic performance. He even allowed upper classmen to travel to attend West Point football games. This was, of course, offensive and alarming to old Army types, old West Point graduates, and he was undone and removed. However, it didn't finish him. A lesser person would be defamed and resign, but not MacArthur.

In fact, just a few years later he was promoted again, becoming the Army's youngest Major General. Shortly after, he served on the court-martial of Brigadier General Billy Mitchell, who had been trying to demonstrate to the military that, with the maturity of air power, the cavalry had been rendered a useless organization, a waste of resources. MacArthur was the youngest of thirteen judges, none of whom had aviation experience, and voted unsuccessfully to acquit Mitchell. I think the experience was an important one for MacArthur, affirming his instinct that the best officers sometimes defy those above them. In defense of Mitchell, he wrote: "…a senior officer should not be silenced for being at variance with his superiors in rank and with accepted doctrine." A pure MacArthur line if ever one was written.

By 1930, at only 50 years old, MacArthur was appointed Chief of Staff. Five years later, he became Field Marshal of the Philippine Army, and not too long after that, of course, came the war, and we've seen by now the masterful way in which he conducted himself throughout that conflict, delaying the Japanese conquest of the Philippines with little support for as long as possible, leapfrogging back through the south Pacific from 1942-1945 and coming up with the tremendous strategy of simply isolating massive Japanese garrisons and allowing them to wither, instead of fighting them at great cost in lives and resources. This culminated in his acceptance, on the deck of the *Missouri,* the Japanese surrender. He presided over the war trials and executions of key Japanese commanders, including Yamashita and Yuma, the general in charge of the Philippines who had allowed or even encouraged the cruelty and slaughter that went on there.

And then, in 1950, he became the United Nations Commander in Korea, beating back the North Koreans, through that genius landing at Inchon, when it seemed all but certain they would win the conflict. MacArthur's final act of defiance, the one that sent him into retirement, was very much in keeping with what I told you at the beginning of this book about strategy and tactics, about the purpose of a general: he does not take the field with anything in mind but victory. If he doesn't believe he can win, he doesn't go. And if he goes, he's not interested in a draw—he wants, and intends, to win. MacArthur wanted to bomb the bridges and get after the Chinese and pound them to pieces. But for purely geopolitical reasons, President Truman would not allow MacArthur to advance on the Chinese past the Yalu River. They fought over this publicly, and MacArthur was relieved of command and ordered back to the United States for the first time in 14 years, since 1937. He was invited to address a joint session of Congress, and during that magnificent speech he touched on every one of the true, basic, fundamental beliefs that MacArthur was given to honor: Patriotism. Liberty. Belief in God. Skill and courage in equal measure. And he ended that famous speech with a line from a famous army song, what he referred to as a "barracks ballad" from his time as a cadet at West Point: "Old soldiers never die; they just fade away."

He was a brave and heroic person. A genius as a general. I do respect him.

I'll end with what I consider, among all the things I've read of MacArthur's writing, to be the most important and perennial idea he ever set down on paper, one that applies far beyond the scope of military operations:

> *The history of failure in war can almost be summed up in two words:* Too late. *Too late in comprehending the deadly purpose of a potential enemy; too late in realizing the mortal danger; too late in preparedness; too late in uniting all possible forces for resistance; too late in standing with one's friends.*